THE ENCYCLOPEDIA OF THE
ANCIENT AMERICAS

THE ENCYCLOPEDIA OF THE ANCIENT AMERICAS

EXPLORE THE WONDERS OF THE AZTEC, MAYA, INCA,
NORTH AMERICAN INDIAN AND ARCTIC PEOPLES

JEN GREEN   FIONA MACDONALD   PHILIP STEELE   MICHAEL STOTTER

southwater

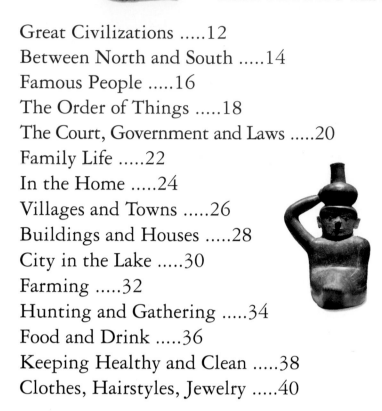

CONTENTS

Birth of Ancient American Cultures 6

THE AZTEC AND MAYA 10

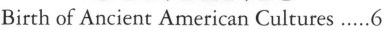

Great Civilizations 12
Between North and South 14
Famous People 16
The Order of Things 18
The Court, Government and Laws 20
Family Life 22
In the Home 24
Villages and Towns 26
Buildings and Houses 28
City in the Lake 30
Farming 32
Hunting and Gathering 34
Food and Drink 36
Keeping Healthy and Clean 38
Clothes, Hairstyles, Jewelry 40

Craftworkers 42
Merchants and Markets 44
Travel and Transport 46
Warriors and Weapons 48
Rival City-States 50
Aztec Conquests 52
Scholars and Scribes 54
Time, Sun and Stars 56
Gods and Goddesses 58
Temples and Sacrifices 60
Time for Celebration 62
Sports and Games 64
Myths, Legends and Omens 66
The Coming of the Spanish 68
Glossary 70

THE INCAS 72

Peoples of the Andes 74
The Great Empire 76
Makers of History 78
Lords of the Sun 80
The Inca State 82
Nobles and Peasants 84
On Land and Water 86
Master Masons 88
Town Dwellers 90
An Inca House 92
Inside the Home 94
Hunting and Fishing 96
Living on the Land 98
Food and Feasts 100
Textiles and Tunics 102

Jewels and Feathers 104
Everyday Crafts 106
Metals and Mining 108
Gods and Spirits 110
Temples and Sacrifices 112
Festivals and Rituals 114
Flutes, Drums and Dice 116
Medicine and Magic 118
Inca Knowledge 120
Married Life 122
Land of the Dead 124
Warriors and Weapons 126
Eclipse of the Sun 128
Glossary 130

THE NORTH AMERICAN INDIANS 132

The First Americans 134

Inhabiting a Vast Land 136

Brave and Bold 138

Nomadic Life 140

Travel and Transport 142

Tribal Society 144

Dress and Identity 146

Ornament and Decoration 148

Native American Homes 150

Family Life 152

Food and Farming 154

Hunting 156

The Mighty Bison 158

Language and Communication 160

Myths and Legends 162

Arts and Crafts 164

Games and Entertainment 166

Contact with Europeans 168

European Settlers 170

Horse Culture 172

Markets and Trade 174

Warriors and Warfare 176

War and Defeat 178

Beliefs and Customs 180

The Sweat Lodge and Other Rites 182

Sacred Dances 184

Death and Burial 186

North American Indians Today 188

Glossary 190

THE ARCTIC PEOPLES 192

An Ancient History 194

The Arctic World 196

Peoples of the North 198

A Frozen Land 200

Travelling with Reindeer 202

Settlements and Homes 204

Seasonal Camps 206

Home Comforts 208

Family Life 210

Arctic Children 212

Fun and Games 214

Over Ice and Snow 216

On the Water 218

Tools and Weapons 220

Going Hunting 222

Big Game Hunters 224

Hunting Magic 226

Food and Feasts 228

The Coming of Europeans 230

Trappers and Traders 232

Cold-Weather Clothing 234

Costumes and Ornaments 236

Arts and Crafts 238

Beliefs and Rituals 240

The Long Polar Night 242

Development of the Arctic 244

Learning and Change 246

The Arctic Today 248

Glossary 250

Index 252

Birth of Ancient American Cultures

The world of the native peoples and cultures of America covers the two vast continents known as North America and South America, as well as the narrow strip of land—called Central America—that connects them. The story of these lands spans a huge expanse of history—over 20,000 years—starting when Stone Age peoples first migrated into the Americas from northeast Asia. It ends with the events that followed the arrival of Europeans in the Americas, after the voyage of Christopher Columbus in 1492.

Throughout this period, many American peoples lived nomadic lives, moving from place to place depending on the seasons and the availability of food. They survived by hunting and fishing, and gathering nuts, roots and berries. The Arctic peoples, and the peoples of the Great Plains in North America, are both good examples of nomadic hunters and gatherers.

STONE SKULLS
Rows of human skulls, carved in stone, are used for decoration outside the Aztecs' Great Temple Pyramid in Tenochtitlan. Most Aztec temples also had skull-racks, where the heads of sacrificed captives were displayed to show the power of the Aztec Empire.

Other peoples discovered how to plant seeds to grow food. Many of them lived in small, settled communities or villages—for example, the Iroquoian and Algonquian groups of North America. Still other groups of native Americans established vast and impressive civilizations, based on organized farming, trade and military conquest. These included the city-states and empires of the Aztecs and Maya in Mesoamerica, and the Incas and their predecessors in South America.

PALENQUE
Lord Pacal, ruler of the Maya city of Palenque, was buried wearing this mask of green jade. Only the richest city-states could afford to bury their rulers with treasures like this.

Migrations to the Americas

The earliest peoples to set foot in the Americas were following the migrating herds of wild animals that they hunted. They came from the far northeast of Asia during the last great Ice Age. At this time, so much water was locked into icecaps that sea levels were much lower than they are today, creating a "land bridge" between Asia and America. As a result, these early hunters were able to travel across on dry land into what is present-day Alaska. Some people probably also came from Asia in

A HUNT GOES ON
The excitement of bison hunting is captured in this Blackfoot painting on a tepee lining. From the North American Indians' earliest days, tribes have hunted, fished and gathered their own food.

dug-out log boats, traveling along the coast. All of these early peoples used stone, bone and wooden tools, and dressed themselves in the skins and furs of the animals that they hunted. By about 12,000 years ago they had spread throughout the Americas, across present-day Canada and the United States, Mexico and all the countries of South America, right down to the southernmost tip of the continent.

The Influence of Environment

The environment in which people live affects how they organize and feed themselves. The huge variety of environments in the Americas, from deserts to rainforests, grassy plains to mountains, is reflected by the variety of cultures and lifestyles of its native peoples. Some ancient Americans, for example, became farmers, living in small villages. Others inhabited places rich in wild game, fish and plant foods. They were able to live in groups in villages, but instead of developing farming techniques they continued to live by hunting and gathering. Other peoples lived in hot, dry regions where food was scarce and difficult to grow. They had to concentrate most of their activities on getting enough to eat, and often lived in small groups, moving from place to place to forage for food.

HELPING IN THE FIELDS
This Inca boy has a sling and is attacking the flocks of birds that are robbing the corn fields in his village. Both boys and girls were expected to help with the farming and learn from their parents.

Early Experiments

In some regions, people began to experiment with controlling their environment. They learned to increase the amount of food they could grow by diverting the water from rivers into canals around their fields. In some very dry places, they learned to tap into water supplies deep underground. They increased the number of food animals they could keep by moving them around to different pastures in summer

WORN WITH PRIDE
Scalplocks of human hair hang down the front of this hide shirt. The Plains Indians made good use of their animals for food, clothing and tools.

SNOWSHOE DANCE
Winter was a hard time, food was
scarce and there were few animals to
hunt. The Snowshoe Dance was
performed by Woodlands Indians
to ask spirits for help to survive.

and winter. Wherever settled life developed in the Americas, real
growth began when people were able to increase the production
of food. This allowed larger groups of people to live in
permanent houses, and generation after generation to live in
the same place. At the same time, some members of the group
were able to devote time not to growing food, but to making
the many tools needed for farming and other tasks. These
objects were exchanged among their fellow villagers for food.
When it was discovered that baking clay in fire turned it
into a hard material, some people began to fashion pottery
containers for water and food. Still others built houses from mud-
bricks, or made clothes and ornaments.

Beliefs and Worship

Whatever lifestyles the peoples of the Americas followed, they all developed beliefs about the
world around them. These beliefs helped them to explain how the world began, what would

happen in the future, and what happened after a
person died. The world of the spirits was very
important and, as some men and women became
noted for their skills at interpreting signs in the
world around them, they became the spiritual leaders
of their communities.

In time, villages and towns became larger and
more numerous and trade began to develop between
them. Trading became yet another way of making a
living. As lifestyles became
more varied and complex, so
more organization was needed.
Powerful leaders began to take
charge of the distribution of extra food, and to make up rules about such matters as how the
products of farmers and craftspeople were to be shared, or about how people were to worship the gods.

A WARM HOME
An igloo near Thule in Greenland is lit up by the
glow of a stove. Such temporary shelters, made of
large blocks of tightly packed snow, kept the hunters
warm in even the harshest Arctic storms.

HUNTING TO SURVIVE
This harpoon point was carved from a
walrus tusk and used to hunt fish and sea
mammals. Even in ancient times, the people
of the Arctic were skilled craftspeople.

People like this became rulers, and often passed their power
and wealth on to their children. In some cases, for example in
the Inca and Aztec empires, rulers were believed to be
descended from the gods themselves.

GATEWAY OF THE SUN GOD
The great arch at Tiwanaku was the center of many religious activities. To the Inca people, the most important god was Inti, the golden Sun. As a descendant of the Sun, the Inca emperor was seen as a god.

Symbols of Power

To demonstrate a ruler's power, huge ceremonial centers were constructed and added to from one generation to the next. These buildings formed the centers of great cities, surrounded by the houses and workshops of the ordinary people. A group of selected people enforced the laws of these city-states.

MASSIVE FORTRESS
The massive fortress of Sacsahuaman was built on a hill, defended by a cliff and terraces. Like most South American cities, it was walled since siege warfare was common in the Inca Empire.

Sometimes there were disagreements between communities and, when disputes could not be settled with words, there was fighting between cities. Some peoples built up empires by conquering neighboring peoples, for example the Aztecs in Central America, and the Incas in South America.

The European Conquest

The civilizations of the Americas developed entirely independently from European cultures. Although the Vikings reached North America in the early 1000s, there was no direct contact between America and Europe until 1492, when the Italian sailor, Christopher Columbus, landed in the Bahamas. Columbus immediately began to claim land for his sponsors, the Spanish king and queen, and he was quickly followed by other European adventurers. To Europeans, the Americas became known as the "New World," while Europe, Africa and Asia was called the "Old World."

In some cases, the civilizations of the American peoples were conquered quickly by armed invasion. The Aztec, Maya and the mighty Inca empire of the Andean mountains were defeated by invading Spanish soldiers seeking gold and glory, and to spread the Christian faith. In other places the conquest, although no less violent, took several hundred years. The peoples of North America and of the Arctic were relentlessly driven from their homelands as European settlers moved across the continent. Nevertheless, today many of these native peoples continue to value and practice their traditional cultures and ways of life.

LEADING THE WAY
Sacawagea, a Shoshoni girl, guided two US captains from Mississippi to the Pacific coast in 1804. European settlers gradually moved west, and the US Government forced the Indians to leave their homelands.

AZTEC
AND MAYA

The story of Central America before the Spanish conquest is one of fine cities, astounding astronomical knowledge, ceremonial temple-pyramids and an appetite for human sacrifice. Trade flourished over long distances, and some rulers created empires by conquering neighbouring cities and towns.

FIONA MACDONALD

CONSULTANT:
CLARA BEZANILLA, THE MUSEUM OF MANKIND

Great Civilizations

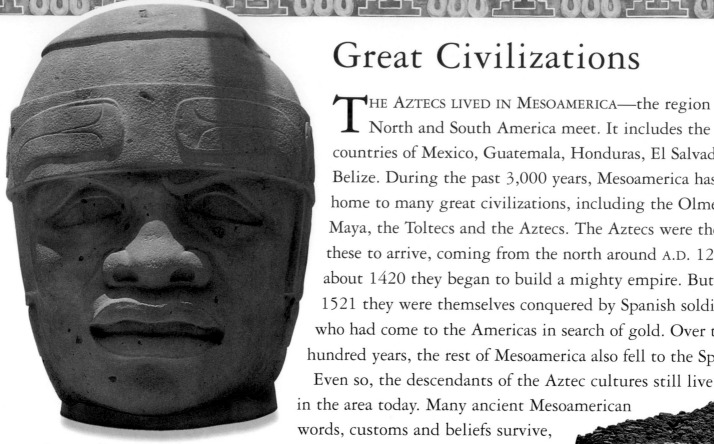

THE AZTECS LIVED IN MESOAMERICA—the region where North and South America meet. It includes the countries of Mexico, Guatemala, Honduras, El Salvador and Belize. During the past 3,000 years, Mesoamerica has been home to many great civilizations, including the Olmecs, the Maya, the Toltecs and the Aztecs. The Aztecs were the last of these to arrive, coming from the north around A.D. 1200. In about 1420 they began to build a mighty empire. But in 1521 they were themselves conquered by Spanish soldiers, who had come to the Americas in search of gold. Over the next hundred years, the rest of Mesoamerica also fell to the Spaniards.

Even so, the descendants of the Aztec cultures still live in the area today. Many ancient Mesoamerican words, customs and beliefs survive, as do beautiful hand-painted books, mysterious ruins and amazing treasures.

OLMEC POWER
This giant stone head was carved by the Olmecs, the earliest of many great civilizations that flourished in Mesoamerica. Like the Maya and Aztecs, the Olmecs were skilled stone workers and built great cities.

UNCOVERING THE PAST
This temple is in Belize. Remains of such great buildings give archaeologists important clues about the people who built them.

TIMELINE 5000 B.C. – A.D. 800

Many civilizations were powerful in Mesoamerica at different times. The Maya were most successful between A.D. 600-900. The Aztecs were at the height of their power from A.D. 1428–A.D. 1520.

5000 B.C. The Maya settle along the Pacific and Caribbean coasts of Mesoamerica.

2000 B.C. People begin to farm in Guatemala, Belize, southeast Mexico.

Olmec figure

2000 B.C. The beginning of the period known as the Preclassic era.

1200 B.C. Olmec people are powerful in Mesoamerica. They remain an important power until 400 B.C.

1000 B.C. Maya craftworkers begin to copy Olmec pottery and jade carvings.

900 B.C. Maya farmers design and use irrigation systems.

600 B.C. The Zapotec civilization begins to flourish at Monte Alban.

Maya codex

300 B.C. The Maya population starts to grow rapidly. Cities are built.

292 B.C. The first-known Maya writing is produced.

150 B.C. – A.D.500 The people living in the city of Teotihuacan grow powerful.

A.D. 250 The beginning of the greatest period of Maya power, known as the Classic Maya era. This lasts until A.D. 900.

mask from Teotihuacan

5000 B.C.   2000 B.C.   300 B.C.   A.D. 500

THE GREAT TEMPLE

The Maya built this pyramid at Chichen-Itza in southeastern Mexico around A.D. 1000. Historians believe that the Putun people may also have established themselves at Chichen-Itza. The pyramid was designed so that twice a year the sun casts a snake-shaped shadow down the steps. Buildings like this tell us about the religious beliefs of the Maya and also show what skillful builders they were. Maya and Aztec stone masons worked without the help of metal tools.

THE FACE OF A GOD

This mask represents the god Tezcatlipoca. It is made of pieces of semi-precious stone attached to a real human skull. Masks like this were worn during religious ceremonies, or displayed in temples as offerings to the gods.

MESSAGES IN CODE

These are Aztec picture-symbols for days, written in a folding book called a codex. Mesoamerican civilizations kept records of important people, places and events by picture-writing.

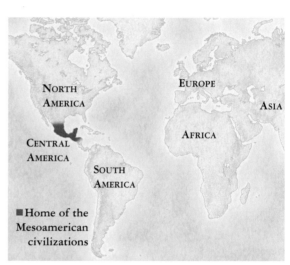

■ Home of the Mesoamerican civilizations

MESOAMERICA IN THE WORLD

For centuries, Mesoamerica was home to many different civilizations, but there were links between them, especially in terms of farming, technology and religious beliefs. Until A.D. 1500, these Mesoamerican civilizations had very little contact with the rest of the world.

A.D. 550 This is the time of the Maya's greatest artistic achievements. Fine temples and palaces in cities such as Kabah, Copan, Palenque, Uxmal and Tikal are built. These great regional city-states are ruled by lords who claim to be descended from the gods. This period of Maya success continues until A.D. 900.

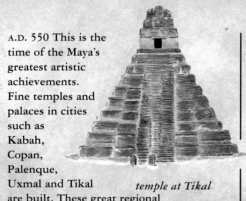

temple at Tikal

A.D. 615 The great Maya leader Lord Pacal rules in the city of Palenque.

A.D. 650 The city of Teotihuacan begins to decline. It is looted and burned by unknown invaders around A.D. 700.

A.D. 684 Lord Pacal's rule in Palenque ends. He is buried in a tomb within the Temple of the Inscriptions.

jade death mask of Lord Pacal

Bonampak mural

A.D. 790 Splendid Maya wall-paintings are created in the royal palace in the city of Bonampak.

A.D. 600   A.D. 700   A.D. 800

Between North and South

MESOAMERICA IS A LAND of contrasts. There are high, jagged mountains, harsh deserts and swampy lakes. In the north, volcanoes rumble. In the south, dense, steamy forests have constant rain for half the year. These features made travelling around difficult, and also restricted contact between the regions.

Mesoamerica was never ruled as a single, united country. For centuries it was divided into separate states, each based on a city that ruled the surrounding countryside. Different groups of people and their cities became rich and strong in turn, before their civilizations weakened and faded away.

Historians divide the Mesoamerican past into three main periods. In Preclassic times (2000 B.C.–A.D. 250), the Olmecs were most powerful. The Classic era (A.D. 250–900) saw the rise of the Maya and the people living in the city of Teotihuacan. During the Postclassic era (A.D. 900–1500), the Toltecs, followed by the Aztecs, controlled the strongest states.

Each civilization had its own language, laws, traditions and skills, but there were also many links between the separate states. They all built big cities and organized long-distance trade. They all practiced human sacrifice and worshipped the same family of gods. And, unlike all other ancient American people, they all measured time using their own holy calendar of 260 days.

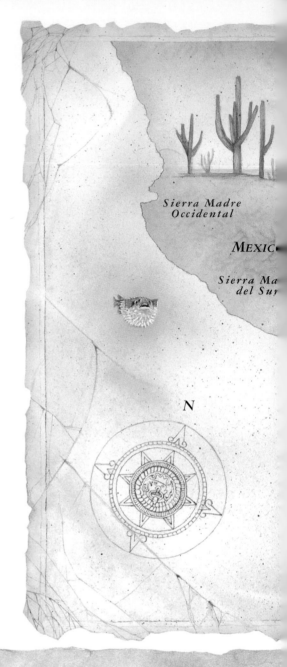

Sierra Madre Occidental

MEXIC

Sierra Ma del Su

N

TIMELINE A.D. 800–A.D. 1400

A.D. 800 The Maya palace-city of Palenque begins to decline.

A.D. 856 The Toltecs of northern Mexico begin to create the city-state of Tula.

Palenque

A.D. 900 Maya power begins to collapse. Many Mayan cities, temples and palaces are deserted and overgrown by the rainforest. This is the beginning of the period known as the Postclassic era. The era lasts until A.D. 1500.

A.D. 950 The city of Tula becomes the center of fast-growing Toltec power.

A.D. 986 According to legend, the Toltec god-king Quetzalcoatl leaves north Mexico for the Mayan lands of Yucatan.

Toltec warrior

A.D. 1000 The Mayan city of Chichen-Itza becomes powerful. Historians believe that the Maya may have been helped by Putun warriors from the Gulf coast of Mexico.

A.D. 1000 Toltec merchants do business along long-distance trade routes around the coast. They are helped by Mayan craftworkers. Long-distance trade has already been taking place in Mesoamerica for hundreds of years.

A.D. 1011–1063 The Mixtecs are ruled by the leader Eight Deer, in the area of Oaxaca. The Mixtecs are master goldsmiths.

A.D. 800   A.D. 900   A.D. 1000   A.D. 1100

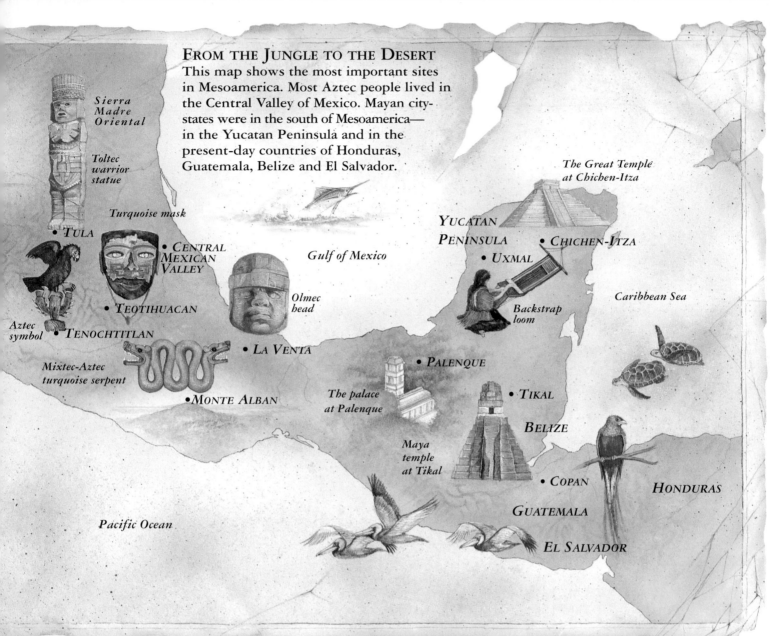

FROM THE JUNGLE TO THE DESERT

This map shows the most important sites in Mesoamerica. Most Aztec people lived in the Central Valley of Mexico. Mayan city-states were in the south of Mesoamerica—in the Yucatan Peninsula and in the present-day countries of Honduras, Guatemala, Belize and El Salvador.

Sierra Madre Oriental

Toltec warrior statue

Turquoise mask

• TULA

Aztec symbol

• CENTRAL MEXICAN VALLEY

• TEOTIHUACAN

• TENOCHTITLAN

Mixtec-Aztec turquoise serpent

• MONTE ALBAN

Gulf of Mexico

Olmec head

• LA VENTA

The palace at Palenque

• PALENQUE

Maya temple at Tikal

The Great Temple at Chichen-Itza

YUCATAN PENINSULA

• CHICHEN-ITZA

• UXMAL

Backstrap loom

Caribbean Sea

• TIKAL

BELIZE

• COPAN

GUATEMALA

HONDURAS

EL SALVADOR

Pacific Ocean

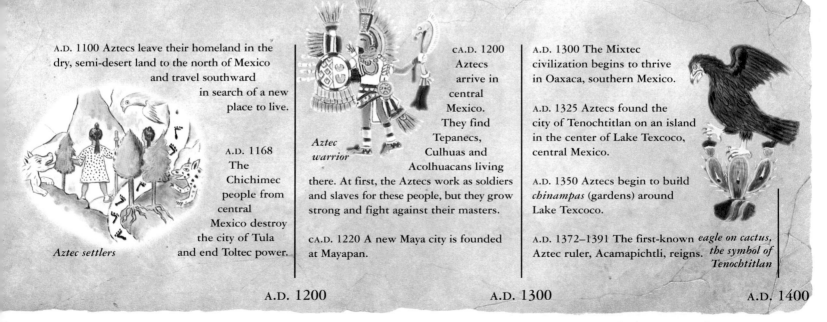

A.D. 1100 Aztecs leave their homeland in the dry, semi-desert land to the north of Mexico and travel southward in search of a new place to live.

A.D. 1168 The Chichimec people from central Mexico destroy the city of Tula and end Toltec power.

Aztec settlers

Aztec warrior

CA.D. 1200 Aztecs arrive in central Mexico. They find Tepanecs, Culhuas and Acolhuacans living there. At first, the Aztecs work as soldiers and slaves for these people, but they grow strong and fight against their masters.

CA.D. 1220 A new Maya city is founded at Mayapan.

A.D. 1300 The Mixtec civilization begins to thrive in Oaxaca, southern Mexico.

A.D. 1325 Aztecs found the city of Tenochtitlan on an island in the center of Lake Texcoco, central Mexico.

A.D. 1350 Aztecs begin to build *chinampas* (gardens) around Lake Texcoco.

A.D. 1372–1391 The first-known Aztec ruler, Acamapichtli, reigns.

eagle on cactus, the symbol of Tenochtitlan

A.D. 1200

A.D. 1300

A.D. 1400

Famous People

FAME IN Mayan and Aztec times usually came with power. We know the names of powerful Aztec and Mayan rulers, and sometimes of their wives. However, very few ordinary people's names have been discovered.

Rulers' names were written in a codex or carved on a monument to record success in battle or other great achievements. Scribes also compiled family histories, in which rulers often claimed to be descended from gods. This gave them extra religious power. Aztec and Mayan rulers made sure their names lived on by building huge palaces, amazing temples and tombs.

Some of the most famous Mesoamerican rulers lived at a time when their civilization was under threat from outsiders. Explorers from Europe have left us detailed accounts and descriptions of the rulers they met.

MAYAN RULER
This statue shows a ruler from the Mayan city of Kabah, in Mexico. Most Mayan statues were designed as symbols of power, rather than as lifelike portraits.

ROYAL TOMB
This pyramid-shaped temple was built to house the tomb of Lord Pacal. He ruled the Mayan city-state of Palenque from A.D. 615 to 684. Its walls are decorated with scenes from Pacal's life.

TIMELINE A.D. 1400–A.D. 1600

tribute items (taxes) collected by the Aztecs

A.D. 1400–A.D. 1425 The Aztec city of Tenochtitlan continues to thrive and grow.

A.D. 1415–1426 The Aztec leader Chimalpopoca reigns.

A.D. 1428 Aztecs defeat the Tepanecs and begin to conquer neighboring lands and collect tribute (taxes) from them.

A.D. 1428 Aztecs set up the Triple Alliance. This was an agreement with neighboring city-states Texcoco and Tlacopan that made them the strongest force in Mexico.

A.D. 1440 Moctezuma Ilhuicamina, the greatest Aztec ruler, begins his reign. He reigns until 1468.

A.D. 1441 The Mayan city of Mayapan is destroyed by civil war.

A.D. 1468 Aztec ruler Axayacatl reigns.

A.D. 1473 The Aztecs conquer the rich market city of Tlatelolco in central Mexico.

market traders in the market-city of Tlatelolco

A.D. 1400   A.D. 1425   A.D. 1450   A.D. 1475

GOLD SEEKER

Soldier and explorer Hernan Cortes (1485–1547) came from a poor but noble Spanish family. After Columbus' voyages, many Spanish adventurers traveled to Mesoamerica and the Caribbean hoping to make their fortunes. Cortes sailed to Cuba and then, in 1519, went on to explore Mexico. His example inspired many treasure seekers. One such man, Pizarro, went on to conquer the Incas of Peru.

BETWEEN TWO WORLDS

Malintzin (*far right above*) was from a Mesoamerican state hostile to the Aztecs. She was of vital help to the Spanish conquerors because she spoke the Aztec language and quickly learned Spanish. The Spanish called her Doña Marina.

THE LAST EMPEROR

Aztec emperor Moctezuma II (*above right*) ruled from 1502 to 1520. He was the last emperor to control the Aztec lands. Moctezuma II was a powerful warrior and a good administrator, but he was tormented by gloomy prophecies and visions of disaster. He was captured when Cortes and his soldiers invaded the capital city of Tenochtitlan in 1519. The following year he was stoned in a riot while trying to plead with his own people.

A.D. 1481–A.D. 1486 Aztec ruler Tizoc reigns.

A.D. 1486 Aztec ruler Ahuitzotl begins his reign.

A.D. 1487 The Aztecs' Great Temple in Tenochtitlan is finished. Twenty thousand captives are sacrificed at a special ceremony to consecrate it (make it holy).

A.D. 1492 The European explorer Christopher Columbus sails across the Atlantic Ocean to America.

Columbus lands

A.D. 1502 Columbus sails along the coast of Mesoamerica and meets Mayan people.

a comet appears in the sky

A.D. 1502–A.D. 1520 Moctezuma II reigns. During his reign, a comet appears in the sky. Aztec astronomers fear that this, and other strange signs, mean the end of the world.

A.D. 1519 Hernan Cortes, a Spanish soldier, arrives in Mexico. A year later, Cortes and his soldiers attack Tenochtitlan. Moctezuma II is killed.

A.D. 1521 The Spanish destroy Tenochtitlan.

A.D. 1525 Spain takes control of Aztec lands.

A.D. 1527 Mayan lands are invaded by the Spanish.

A.D. 1535 Mexico becomes a Spanish colony.

Spanish soldier

A.D. 1600 War and European diseases wipe out 10 million Aztecs, leaving fewer than a million, but the Aztec language and many customs live on. By A.D. 1600, between 75% and 90% of Mayan people are also dead, but Mayan skills, beliefs and traditions survive.

A.D. 1500   A.D. 1525   A.D. 1600

The Order of Things

MESOAMERICAN CITY-STATES were ruled by leaders with three separate tasks. They were army commanders, lawmakers and priests. Many rulers claimed to be descended from the gods. Rulers were almost always men. Mesoamerican women—especially among the Maya—had important religious duties but rarely took part in law-making or army life.

Mayan rulers were called *ahaw* (lord) or *mahk'ina* (great sun lord), and each city-state had its own royal family. The Aztec leader was called the *tlatoani* (speaker). Originally, he was elected from army commanders by the Aztec people. Later, he was chosen from the family of the previous ruler. He ruled all Aztec lands, helped by a deputy called *cihuacoatl* (snake woman), by nobles and by army commanders. Priests observed the stars, looking for signs about the future, and held religious ceremonies.

Rulers, priests and nobles made up a tiny part of society. Ordinary citizens were called *macehualtin*. Women looked after their families. Men were farmers, fishermen or craftworkers. There were also thousands of slaves, who were criminals, enemy captives or poor people who had given up their freedom in return for food and shelter.

OFFICIAL HELP
This Mayan clay figure shows a scribe at work. Well-trained officials, such as this scribe, helped Mesoamerican rulers by keeping careful records. Scribes also painted ceremonial pottery.

HONOR TO THE KING
Painted pottery vases like this were buried alongside powerful Mayan people. They show scenes from legends and royal palace life. Here, a lord presents tribute (taxes) to the king.

MAYAN NOBLEWOMAN
This terra-cotta figure of a Mayan noblewoman dates from between A.D. 600 and A.D. 900. She is richly attired and protecting her face with a parasol. Women did not usually hold official positions of responsibility in Mesoamerican lands. Instead, queens and other noblewomen influenced their husbands by offering tactful suggestions and wise advice. Whether she was rich or poor, a woman's main duty was to provide children for her husband and to support him in all aspects of his work.

THE RULING CLASS

A noble is shown getting ready for a ceremony in this Aztec codex picture. Aztec nobles played an important part in government. They were chosen by rulers to be judges, army commanders and officials. Nobles with government jobs paid no taxes and were given a free house to live in. Noblemen and women were born into ancient noble families, related to the rulers. It was, however, possible for an ordinary man to achieve higher rank if he fought very bravely in battle and captured four enemy soldiers alive.

WAR LEADER

This Mayan stone carving shows ruler Shield Jaguar (*below left*) getting ready to lead his army in A.D. 724. He is wearing a padded tunic and holding a knife in his right hand. His wife, Lady Xoc, is handing him his jaguar headdress. Mayan rulers also took part in religious ceremonies, where they offered drops of their blood to the gods to ask for their help.

MEN AT WORK

Here, Aztec farmers are harvesting ripe ears of corn. This painting comes from the Florentine Codex. This 12-volume manuscript was made by a Spanish friar. Codex pictures like this tell us a lot about ordinary peoples' everyday lives. Notice how simply the farmers are dressed compared to the more powerful people on these pages.

The Court, Government and Laws

THE REMAINS OF MANY splendid palaces survive in Mesoamerican lands. In the 1500s European explorers described the vast palace of the Aztec ruler Moctezuma II in Tenochtitlan. It had banquet rooms big enough to seat 3,000 guests, private apartments, a library, a schoolroom, kitchens, stores, an arsenal for weapons, separate women's quarters, spectacular gardens and a large zoo. Etiquette in the presence the emperor was very strict. Captains of the royal bodyguard had to approach Moctezuma barefoot, with downcast eyes, making low bows and murmuring, "Lord, my lord, my great lord." When they left, they had to walk backward, keeping their gaze away from his face.

Palaces were not just rulers' homes. They were also official government headquarters where rulers greeted ambassadors from neighboring city-states and talked with advisors.

Rulers also had the power to make strict laws. Each city-state had its own courts, where formidable judges had the power of life and death over people brought before them.

ROYAL RECORD
Mayan rulers set up carved stone pillars in their cities to record major events during their reigns. These pillars are called stelae. This one celebrates a Mayan ruler in Copan, Honduras.

THE SEAT OF POWER
This carved jade ornament shows a seated Mayan king. Although Aztec and Mayan leaders had the final responsibility for decisions, they also relied on judges, officials and scribes to help them rule.

MAKE A FEATHER FAN

You will need: pencil, thick cardboard, thin red cardboard, scissors, double-sided tape, green paper, feathers (real or paper), masking tape, colored felt, white glue and brush, paints, paintbrushes, bamboo cane, colored yarn, tape.

1 Draw two rings about ¾ in. in diameter and 3 in. wide on thick cardboard. Cut them out. Make another ring the same size from thin red cardboard, as above.

2 Cut lots of leaf shapes from green paper. Stick them around the edge of one thick cardboard ring using double-sided tape. Add some real or paper feathers.

3 Cut two circles about 4 ¾ in. in diameter from thin red card. Draw around something the right size, such as a roll of tape. These are for the center of the fan.

LOCKED UP

Here, a group of Aztec judges discusses how to punish two prisoners. You can see them cowering in a wooden cage. By modern standards, punishments were very severe. If ordinary citizens broke the law, they might be beaten or speared with cactus spines. For a second offense, they might be stoned to death.

THE RULE OF THE GODS

This stone carving shows a human face being swallowed by a magic serpent. Royal and government buildings were often decorated with carvings such as this. They signified the religious power of the ruler of a particular city.

FIT FOR A KING

This picture from an Aztec codex shows visitors to a ruler's palace. It was reported by Spanish explorers that over six hundred nobles came to the Aztec ruler's palace every day to attend council meetings, consult palace officials, ask favors of the ruler and make their views heard. The ruler would sit on a mat on the floor with his council, as was the Aztec tradition.

Aztec nobles and rulers cooled themselves with beautiful feather fans.

4 Paint a flower on one of the two smaller red circles and a butterfly on the other. Cut V-shapes from the felt and glue them to the large red ring.

5 Using tape, attach lengths of colored yarn to the back of one of the red circles, as shown. Place the red circle in the center of the ring with leaves.

6 Tape the lengths of yarn to the outer ring to look like spokes. Coat the ring with white glue and place the second ring on top, putting a cane in between.

7 Use double-sided tape to stick the second red circle face up in the center. Glue the red ring with felt V-shapes on top of the second thick cardboard ring.

Family Life

FAMILIES WERE very important in Mayan and Aztec times. By working together, family members provided themselves with food, jobs, companionship and a home. Each member of a family had special responsibilities. Men produced food or earned money to buy it. Women cared for babies and the home. From the age of about five or six, children were expected to do their share of the family's work by helping their parents. Because family life was so important, marriages were often arranged by a young couple's parents, or by a matchmaker. The role of matchmaker would be played by an old woman who knew both families well. Boys and girls got married when they were between 16 and 20 years old. The young couple usually lived in the boy's parents' home.

Aztec families belonged to local clan-groups, known as *calpulli*. Each *calpulli* chose its own leader, collected its own taxes and built its own temple. It offered help to needy families, and kept a close eye on how its own members behaved. If a member broke the law, the whole clan might be punished for that person's actions.

MOTHER AND SON
These Mayan clay figures may show a mother and her son. Boys from noble families went to school at about 15. They learned reading, writing, math, astronomy and religion.

SPICE
Hot, spicy chile peppers were an essential part of many Mayan and Aztec meals. In fact, the Aztecs said that if a meal lacked chiles, it was a fast, not a feast! Chiles were used in stews and in spicy sauces, and they were used in medicine, too. They were crushed and rubbed on aching muscles or mixed with salt to ease toothache.

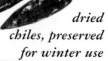

red, ripe chiles

dried chiles, preserved for winter use

unripe green chiles

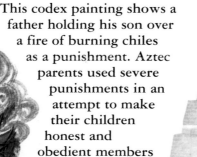

PAINFUL PUNISHMENT
This codex painting shows a father holding his son over a fire of burning chiles as a punishment. Aztec parents used severe punishments in an attempt to make their children honest and obedient members of society.

IXTILTON
This Aztec mask is made of a black volcanic stone called obsidian. It shows the god Ixtilton, helper of Huitzilopochtli, the Aztecs' special tribal god. Aztec legends told how Ixtilton could bring darkness and peaceful sleep to tired children.

HUSBAND AND WIFE
The bride and groom in this codex picture of an Aztec wedding have their clothes tied together. This shows that their lives are now joined. Aztec weddings were celebrated with presents and feasting. Guests carried bunches of flowers, and the bride wore special makeup with her cheeks painted yellow or red. During the ceremony, the bride and groom sat side by side on a mat in front of the fire.

GUARDIAN GODDESS
The goddess Tlazolteotl is shown in this codex picture. She was the goddess of lust and sin. Tlazolteotl was also said to watch over mothers and young children. Childbirth was the most dangerous time in a woman's life, and women who died in childbirth were honored like brave soldiers.

LEARNING FOR LIFE
A mother teaches her young daughter to cook in this picture from an Aztec codex. The girl is making tortillas (flat corn pancakes). You can see her grinding the corn in a *metate* (grinding stone) using a *mano* (stone used with the *metate*). Aztec mothers and fathers trained their children in all the skills they would need to survive in adult life. Children from the families of craftworkers learned their parents' special skills.

In the Home

MESOAMERICAN HOMES were not just safe places to eat and sleep. They were workplaces, too. There were no refrigerators or household appliances, so women had to work hard preparing food for the day's meals or for winter storage. Vegetables were cleaned and chopped with stone knives, as there were no metal ones. Beans and chiles were spread out in the sun to dry and corn kernels were ground into flour. Homes had to be kept clean as well. Firewood and water had to be fetched and clothes washed. Women and girls spent long hours spinning thread and weaving it into cloth, then sewing it into tunics and cloaks for the family. Some women wove cloth to sell or to give to the government as a tax payment. Homes were also where most sick or elderly people were cared for.

HEART OF THE HOME
Throughout Mesoamerica, the hearth fire was the heart of the home. This statue shows Xiuhtecuhtli, the Aztec god of fire. The top of his head is hollow, so a fire can be kindled there. The rays on his headdress represent flickering flames.

MAYAN POT
The Maya decorated ceremonial pottery with pictures of gods, kings and important people. This pot shows a corn merchant. Pottery used in the home for food and drink would be less ornate.

A BACKSTRAP LOOM
You will need: paintbrush, water-based paint, 2 pieces of thick dowel about 2 ft. long, string, scissors, thick cardboard, masking tape, colored yarn.

1 Paint the pieces of dowel brown. Leave them to dry. Tie string to each dowel and wind it around. Leave a length of string loose at each end.

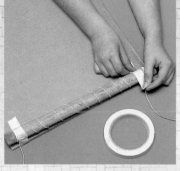

2 Cut a piece of thick cardboard about 27 in. x 40 in. This is a temporary base. Lightly tape the stringed dowels to it at the shorter sides with masking tape.

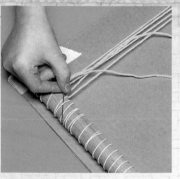

3 Now take your yellow yarn. Thread the yarn through the string loops and pull through to the other end, as shown. Try to keep the yellow yarn taut.

GLOWING COLORS

Many craftworkers worked at home. This painting by Diego Rivera shows craftworkers from the region of Tarascan dying hanks of yarn before they are woven into cloth. Mesoamerican dyes were made from fruits, flowers, shellfish and the cochineal beetles that lived on cactus plants. Only rich people were allowed to wear clothes made from brightly colored cloth. Poorer people wore natural colors.

A HELPING HAND

Aztec girls were expected to make themselves useful by helping their mothers at home. This Aztec codex picture shows a girl sweeping the floor with a bundle of twigs.

WEAVING

Threads spun from plant fibers were woven into cloth on backstrap looms. The finest fabric was made from silky cotton. Rough yucca and cactus fibers made a coarser cloth. Looms like this are still used in Mexico today.

To weave, take the loom off the cardboard. Tie the loose string around your waist. Attach the other end of the loom to a post or tree with the string. Lean back to keep the long warp threads evenly taut.

4 Cut a rectangle of thick cardboard (12 in. x 1 ½ in). Now cut a small rectangle of cardboard with one pointed end, as shown. Wind red yarn around it.

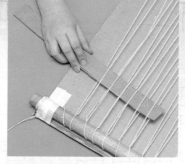

5 Now take your long cardboard rectangle. This is your shed rod. Carefully slide it through every second thread on your loom, as shown.

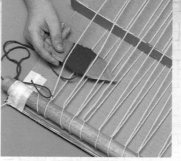

6 Turn your shed rod on its side. This will lift the threads up. Tie one end of your red yarn to the yellow wool. Feed the card of yarn through the lifted threads.

7 Lay the shed rod flat. Use the pointed end of your cardboard to pick up each of the first or alternate threads. Thread the yarn on the cardboard through these.

Villages and Towns

MOST PEOPLE in Mesoamerica lived in country villages. They made a living from the land, taking their produce to nearby market towns to sell. Villages and towns all had to obey the strongest city in the region. Usually they also had to pay a tribute (a tax of goods or labor) to it as well. Villages were small, often with fewer than fifty families, but the biggest cities were huge. Historians estimate that over 150,000 people lived in the city of Teotihuacan in A.D. 600. Cities, towns and villages were linked by roads cleared through the forest or by steep paths cut into mountain slopes.

The center of most Mesoamerican cities was dedicated to religion. The greatest temples stood there, close to a vast open space used for holy ceremonies, dances and processions. Other important buildings, such as royal palaces and ball-courts, stood close by. The homes and workshops of ordinary citizens were built outside the ceremonial area.

HIDDEN IN THE TREES
Today the remains of the great Maya city of Tikal are almost hidden by the rainforest. In Maya times, the trees would have been felled to make room for houses and fields. In around A.D. 800, about 50,000 people lived here.

DESERT FRUITS
Several kinds of cactus thrive in Mexico's dry, semi-desert regions. The prickly pear is a sweet, juicy fruit, but the maguey cactus was even more popular. Its sap was used as a sweetener and to make an alcoholic drink. Its fibers were made into clothing and baskets. Its spines were used as needles.

BIG CITY
The Mayan city of Copan in present-day Honduras covered an enormous area, perhaps 8 mi. long and 2 mi. wide. The religious center and the nearby Great Plaza are shown here. Both were rebuilt in splendid style on the orders of King Yax Pac around A.D. 750. The temples and royal palace are painted a glowing red—the color of life and power.

BIRDS OF A FEATHER

These little pictures are from an Aztec codex. They show just some of the many beautiful wild birds that lived in Mesoamerica. The Maya and the Aztecs hunted many of them for their brightly colored feathers. These feathers could then be used to make fans or shields.

quetzal

humming bird

toucan

parrot

parrot

MOUNTAINS AND CORN

On steep, cold mountain slopes, such as those of Popocatapetl, farmers grew hardy crops. *Chia* and *huautli* were both bushy plants with edible seeds. They were well suited to this environment. In sunny, fertile areas, corn was grown.

owl

crocodile

FROM DESERT TO RAINFOREST

The landscape of Mesoamerica is extremely varied. Many different creatures, from crocodiles to deer inhabit it. The Maya and the Aztecs hunted many of these animals for their meat or skins.

deer

butterfly

rabbit

snake

Buildings and Houses

PEOPLE LIVING in Mesoamerica used local materials for building. They had no wheeled transport, so carrying building materials long distances was quite difficult. Stone was the most expensive and longest-lasting building material. It was used for religious buildings, rulers' palaces and tombs.

The homes of ordinary people were built more quickly and easily of cheaper materials, such as sun-dried mud bricks, called adobe, or mud smeared over a framework of wooden poles. For strength, the walls might have stone foundations.

All Mesoamerican homes were very simply furnished. There were no chairs or tables, curtains or carpets—just some jars and baskets for storage and a few reed mats. Everyone, from rulers to slaves, sat and slept on mats on the floor. Most ordinary Aztec homes were L-shaped or built around a courtyard, with a separate bathroom for washing and a small shrine to the gods in the main room.

FAMILY HOME

This present-day Maya family home is built in traditional style, with red-painted mud-and-timber walls. It has one door and no windows. The floor is made of pounded earth. The roof, thatched with dried grass, is steeply sloped so the rain runs off it.

BURIED UNDERGROUND

Archaeologists have discovered these remains of houses at the Mayan city of Copan. The roofs, walls and doors have rotted away, but we can still see the stone foundations. The houses are small and tightly packed together.

MAKE A MAYAN HOUSE

You will need: thick cardboard, pencil, ruler, scissors, glue, masking tape, terra cotta plaster paste (or thin plaster colored with paint), water container, wide gummed paper tape, paintbrush, balsa wood strips, short lengths of straw.

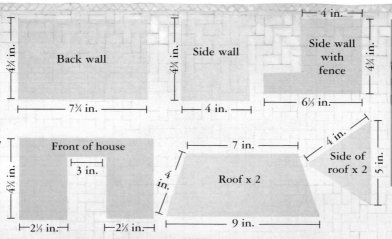

Back wall — 4¼ in. / 7¾ in.

Side wall — 4¼ in. / 4 in.

Side wall with fence — 4 in. / 4¼ in. / 6⅓ in.

Front of house — 4¼ in. / 3 in. / 2⅓ in. — 2⅓ in.

Roof x 2 — 7 in. / 4 in. / 9 in.

Side of roof x 2 — 4 in. / 5 in.

Draw the shapes of the roof and walls of the house onto thick cardboard, using the measurements shown. (Please note that the templates are not shown to scale.) Cut the pieces out.

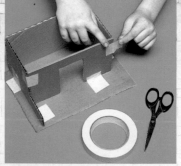

1 Cut out a rectangle 10 in. x 6 in. from thick cardboard for the base. Stick the house walls and base together with glue. Use masking tape for support.

STONEMASONS AT WORK

Mesoamerican masons constructed massive buildings using very simple equipment. Their wedges were made from wood, and their mallets and hammers were shaped from hard volcanic stone. Until around A.D. 900, metal tools were unknown. Fine details were added by polishing stonework with wet sand.

PLASTER

Big stone buildings, such as temples, were often covered with a kind of plaster called stucco. This was then painted with ornate designs. Plaster was made by burning limestone and mixing it with water and colored earth. By the 1400s, there was so much new building in Tenochtitlan that the surrounding lake became polluted with chemicals from the plaster making.

plaster

limestone

SKILLFUL STONEWORK

This carved stone panel from the Mayan city of Chichen-Itza is decorated with a pattern of crosses. It was used to provide a fine surface for thick walls made of rubble and rough stone. This wall decorates a palace building.

A Mayan house provided a cool shelter from the very hot Mexican sun, as well as keeping out rain.

2 Paint the walls and base with plaster paste. This will make them look like sun-dried mud. You could also decorate the doorway with balsa wood strips.

3 Put the house on one side to dry. Take your roof pieces and stick them together with glue. Use masking tape to support the roof, as shown.

4 Moisten the wide paper tape and use it to cover the joints between the roof pieces. There should be no gaps. Then cover the whole roof with glue.

5 Press lengths of straw into the glue on the roof. Work in layers, starting at the bottom. Overlap the layers. Attach the roof to the house using glue.

City in the Lake

THE AZTECS built their capital city, Tenochtitlan, on an island in the middle of Lake Texcoco in the Central Valley of Mexico. It was founded around A.D.1325 and soon grew into one of the largest cities in the world. Historians estimate that over 200,000 people lived there by 1500. As the center of Aztec government, the city saw traders, ambassadors, scribes and porters streaming in with huge loads of tribute (taxes) from all over Mesoamerica. Thousands of enemy soldiers captured in battle were also brought there to be sacrificed to the gods.

The city was divided into four districts—Flowery Place, Mosquito Fen, Herons' Home and, at the center, the Sacred Precinct. The four districts of the city were linked to one another, and to the mainland, by countless little canals and causeways of pounded earth. These causeways ran above the surface of the lake. Fresh drinking water from the nearby mountains was carried by a tall stone acqueduct.

EAGLE AND CACTUS

According to legend, the Aztecs chose the site for Tenochtitlan after they received a message from the god Huitzilopochtli. He told them to build their city where they saw an eagle sitting on a cactus, eating a snake. Priests and rulers told stories like this to give reasons for their past actions and make people accept their future plans.

GIVING THANKS

The Aztecs decorated many parts of their city with images of their special god, Huitzilopochtli. Here we can see a brazier decorated with Huitzilopochtli's image, among the ruins of the great temple of Tenochtitlan.

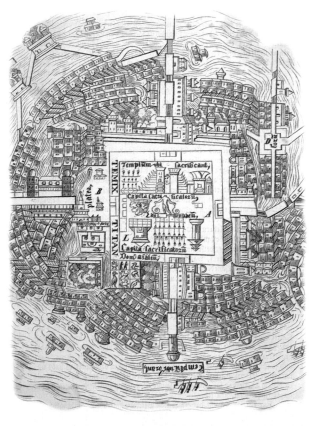

EYEWITNESS REPORTS

Today, Tenochtitlan is buried under modern Mexico City. However, we can gain some idea of what it was like from drawings like this one, made by a European artist in the 1500s. It shows how causeways and canals allowed easy movement around the city.

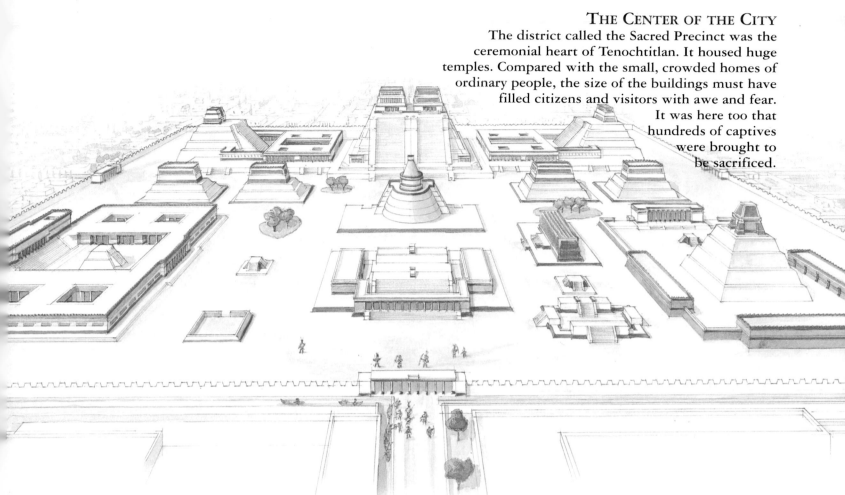

THE CENTER OF THE CITY

The district called the Sacred Precinct was the ceremonial heart of Tenochtitlan. It housed huge temples. Compared with the small, crowded homes of ordinary people, the size of the buildings must have filled citizens and visitors with awe and fear. It was here too that hundreds of captives were brought to be sacrificed.

STONE WORSHIPPERS

These stone statues of standard bearers were found among the ruins of the Great Temple. This temple stood in the center of Tenochtitlan. It had two tall pyramids, topped by shrines. These shrines were dedicated to Tlaloc, god of rain, and Huitzilopochtli, the Aztec's own special god of war. The remains of steps leading up to these shrines can be seen today. When the Spanish conquered the city, they pulled down the Great Temple and built a cathedral near the site.

THE LAKE OF THE MOON

This is the name the Aztecs gave to Lake Texcoco. This fanciful picture shows an 18th-century artist's idea of the Aztec ruler, Tenoch. This ruler founded the city of Tenochtitlan.

Farming

PEOPLE LIVING in different regions of Mesoamerica used various methods to cultivate their land. Farmers in the rainforests grew corn, beans and pumpkins in fields they cleared by slashing and burning. They cut down thick, tangled bushes and vines, leaving the tallest trees standing. Then they burned all the chopped-down bushes and planted seeds in the ashes. But the soil was only fertile for a few years. The fields were left to turn back into forest, and new ones were cleared. Mayan farmers also grew crops in raised fields. These were plots of land along the edge of rivers and streams, heaped with rich, fertile silt dug from the riverbed.

Aztec farmers planted corn wherever they could, on steep rocky hillsides and the flat valley floor. But they grew their biggest crops of fruit, flowers and vegetables in gardens called *chinampas*. These were reclaimed from the marshy shallows along the shores of Lake Texcoco and around the island city of Tenochtitlan.

CORN GOD
This stone statue shows Yum Caax (Lord of the Forest Bushes), the Mayan god of corn. It was found at Copan. All Mesoamerican people honored corn goddesses or gods, as the crop was so important.

DIGGING STICKS
Mesoamerican farmers had no tractors, horses or heavy plows to help them prepare their fields. Instead, a sharp-bladed wooden digging stick, called an *uictli*, was used for planting seeds and hoeing weeds. Some farmers in Mesoamerica today find digging sticks are more efficient than the kind of spade traditionally used in Europe.

FIELD WORK
This painting by Mexican artist Diego Rivera shows Aztecs using digging sticks to hoe fields of corn. You can see how dry the soil is. If the May rains failed, or frosts came early, a whole year's crop would be lost. Mesoamerican farmers made offerings to the rain god between March and October.

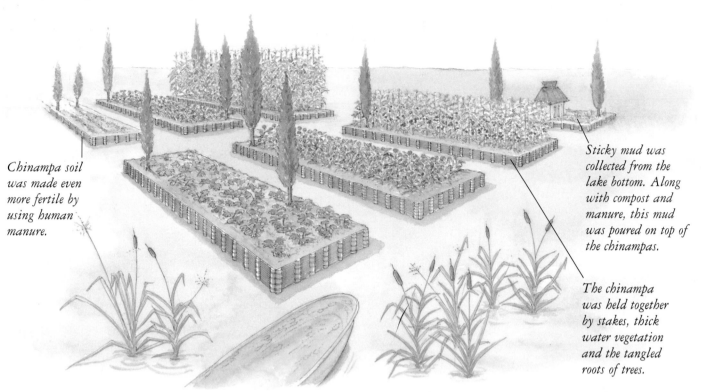

Chinampa soil was made even more fertile by using human manure.

Sticky mud was collected from the lake bottom. Along with compost and manure, this mud was poured on top of the chinampas.

The chinampa was held together by stakes, thick water vegetation and the tangled roots of trees.

FLOATING GARDENS

Chinampas were a sort of floating garden. They were made by sinking layers of twigs and branches under the surface of the lake and weighting them with stones. *Chinampas* were so productive that the government passed laws telling farmers when to sow seeds. This ensured there would be a steady supply of vegetables and flowers for sale in the market.

VEGETARIANS

Many ordinary Mesoamerican people survived on a largely vegetarian diet, based on corn and beans. This would be supplemented by other fresh fruits and vegetables in season. Meat and fish were expensive, luxury foods. Only rulers and nobles could afford to eat them every day.

beans

prickly pear

SLASH AND BURN

Mesoamerican farmers used a technique called slash and burn to clear land for farming. Crops grew very quickly in Mesoamerica's warm climate.

FOREST FRUITS

This Aztec codex painting shows men and women gathering cocoa pods from trees. Cocoa was so valuable that it was sent as tribute to Tenochtitlan.

Hunting and Gathering

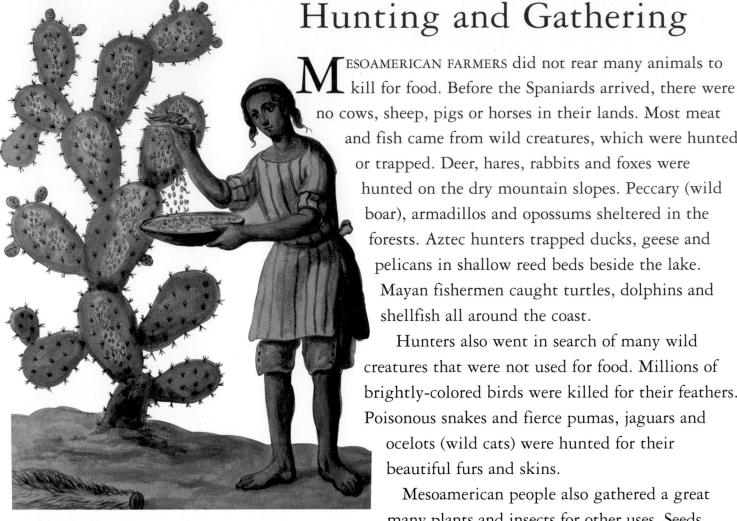

ESOAMERICAN FARMERS did not rear many animals to kill for food. Before the Spaniards arrived, there were no cows, sheep, pigs or horses in their lands. Most meat and fish came from wild creatures, which were hunted or trapped. Deer, hares, rabbits and foxes were hunted on the dry mountain slopes. Peccary (wild boar), armadillos and opossums sheltered in the forests. Aztec hunters trapped ducks, geese and pelicans in shallow reed beds beside the lake. Mayan fishermen caught turtles, dolphins and shellfish all around the coast.

Hunters also went in search of many wild creatures that were not used for food. Millions of brightly-colored birds were killed for their feathers. Poisonous snakes and fierce pumas, jaguars and ocelots (wild cats) were hunted for their beautiful furs and skins.

Mesoamerican people also gathered a great many plants and insects for other uses. Seeds, leaves, bark and flowers were used for medicine and to make paper, mats and baskets. Wild bees supplied honey, and locusts were eaten as snacks.

INSECT HARVEST
Mesoamerican people collected many kinds of insects for use in medicines, as dyes and as food. This codex picture shows cochineal beetles being gathered from a cactus. It took about 70,000 beetles to make two pounds of red dye.

HUNTERS
Mesoamerican men went hunting with bows and arrows, slings, clubs and spears. Hunters' bows were made of wood, and their arrows were tipped with obsidian, a sharp volcanic glass. Their clubs were made from lumps of rock lashed to wooden handles with rope or leather thongs. To make their spears fly further, they used an *atlatl*. This was a grooved piece of wood that acted like an extra-long arm to increase the power behind the throw.

CHOCOLATE TREE

This picture from an Aztec codex shows a cocoa tree and two Aztec gods. Cocoa pods could be gathered from cocoa trees all over Mesoamerica. Once ground, the cocoa beans were mixed with water to make chocolate. Chocolate was a highly prized drink and only nobles could afford to drink it. It was often sweetened with honey and flavored with vanilla. The Aztecs and Maya did not know how to make bars of solid chocolate, like those we enjoy today.

FAUNA

Wild creatures such as turtles, and rabbits were abundant in Mesoamerica. Rabbits were hunted for their fur. Turtles were a popular catch for many fishermen. Their shells could be used in crafts and their flesh could be eaten.

turtle *blacktail jackrabbit*

FEATHERS

Mesoamerican merchants bought feathers from hunters who lived in the rainforest. The picture above shows different kinds of feathers sorted and ready for sale.

SEA PRODUCE

This Mayan beaker is decorated with a picture of a god emerging from a shell. Beautiful seashells were highly prized in Mesoamerica and were often used in jewelry and craftwork. One species of shellfish was caught for its sticky slime. This slime was milked from the shellfish and then used to make a rich purple dye.

fisherman used sticks and paddles to drive fish into nets

flat-bottomed boats could sail across Mexico's shallow marshy lakes

RIVERS AND LAKES

In this Aztec codex picture, we can see a boy fishing. He is standing in a flat-bottomed boat, hollowed from a single log. This boy is using a bag-shaped net, woven from cactus fiber. Fish were also caught with hooks, lines and harpoons. Long nets, draped across canoes, were used to catch waterfowl.

Food and Drink

MESOAMERICAN PEOPLE usually had two meals a day. They ate their main meal around noon and a smaller snack in the evening. Ordinary peoples' food was plain and simple but very healthy—if they could get enough of it. When crops failed, there was famine. Everyday meals were based on corn, beans, vegetables and fruit. Peppers, tomatoes, pumpkins and avocado pears were popular vegetables, but the Aztecs also ate boiled cactus leaves (with the spines removed!). Gruel made from wild sage or amaranth seeds was also a favorite. Meat and fish were luxuries. Deer, rabbit, turkey and dog were cooked for feasts, along with frogs, lizards and turtles. The Aztecs also ate fish eggs and green algae from the lake.

USEFUL POTS
Mesoamerican people did not have metal cooking pots, so women cooked and served food in pottery bowls. Special pottery dishes were also used for specific jobs, such as cooking tortillas. The ones above were used for grating chiles and sweet bell peppers. They have rough-ridged bases.

CACTUS WINE
Sweet, sticky sap from the maguey cactus was collected in leather flasks, then left to ferment in open troughs. It quickly turned into a strong alcoholic wine, which the Aztecs called *pulque*. Aztec men and women were not usually allowed to drink much alcohol. On special festivals honoring the dead, *pulque* was served by women wine makers from huge pottery jars.

MAKE TORTILLAS
You will need: scales, 8oz corn flour, 1 tsp salt, 1¹⁄₂ oz butter, bowl, jug, ¹⁄₂ cup cold water, spoon, a little plain flour for kneading and flouring, rolling pin, pastry board, butter or oil for frying, frying pan.

1 Carefully weigh out the ingredients. If you cannot find corn flour, use plain flour instead. Aztec cooks had to grind their own flour.

2 Mix the flour and salt together in a bowl. Rub the butter into the mixture with your fingers until it looks like bread crumbs. Then pour in the water.

3 Use your hands to mix everything together until you have a loose ball of dough. Do not worry if there is still some dry mixture on the sides.

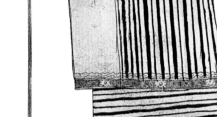

DOG FOOD
The Aztecs kept several breeds of small dog for eating.

TORTILLAS AND TAMALES
This painting shows women grinding corn kernels into flour on a flat stone. They then shaped balls of raw dough into pancakes (tortillas) and stuffed dumplings (tamales). Tortillas were cooked on a hot baking stone, while tamales were baked in a shallow dish.

CHOCOLATE
Mayan cooks dried and pounded cocoa pod seeds into a thick paste. This was then boiled with water. To make the mixture smooth and frothy, they poured it from one bowl to another, often from a great height.

NEW FOOD
In the years after the conquest of Mesoamerica, many vegetables were introduced to Europe, Asia and the Middle East. At first, gardeners found them difficult to grow, and cooks did not know how to prepare them. But today, many meals include tomatoes, peppers, chiles and avocado pears.

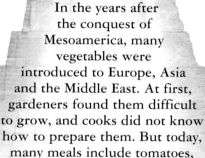

tomato   *avocado pear*

You could eat your tortillas with spicy bean stew and juicy tomatoes, just like the Aztecs did.

4 Knead the dough for at least 10 minutes until it is smooth. If the dough or your hands get too sticky, add a little plain flour to the bowl.

5 Transfer the dough out of the bowl to a floured pastry board. Divide it into egg-sized balls, using your hands or a knife. You should have about 12 balls.

6 Sprinkle the board and the rolling pin with a little plain flour to stop the dough from sticking. Then roll each ball of dough into a thin pancake shape.

7 Ask an adult to help you fry the tortillas, using a nonstick frying pan. Fry each tortilla for one minute per side. Use a little oil in the pan if you want to.

Keeping Healthy and Clean

MESOAMERICAN PEOPLE liked to keep themselves and their houses clean. They washed in river water, took baths and swept their rooms with brushes of twigs and leaves. However, despite their attempts to stay clean and healthy, illness was common. Diseases recorded in Aztec lands, for example, include dysentery, chest infections and skin complaints. Throughout Mesoamerica, children often died from infections or in accidents around the home. Women died in childbirth, and many men were killed in battle. People were considered old by the time they were 40. Aztec medicine was a mixture of herbalism, religion, magic and first aid. Aztec doctors gave out powerful herbal medicines and encouraged patients to say prayers and make offerings to the gods. Sometimes their cures worked, but often the patients died.

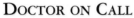

DOCTOR ON CALL
A woman and child are shown consulting a doctor in the local market in this picture by Diego Rivera. The Aztecs made medicines out of many different fruits and herbs, some of which could kill or seriously damage the patient.

FOREIGN BODIES
Spanish settlers brought deadly diseases, such as measles and smallpox, to Mesoamerica after the conquest. Because of this the population of central Mexico fell from around 12 million in 1519 to only one million in 1600.

BURNING REMEDY
This scene from an Aztec codex advises people how to deal with fleas on their body. Pine resin was applied to the affected area and set on fire. Patients could drink only cold water.

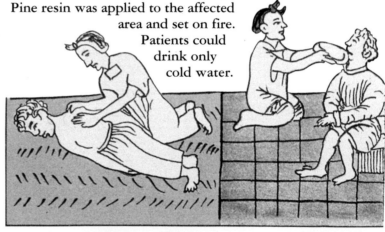

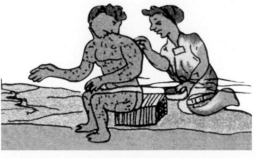

RASH MOMENT
A woman is shown treating an outbreak of sores on this man's skin. The patient would then drink and bathe in cactus sap.

HERBAL HEALTH

Many plants were cultivated or gathered for use in medicines. Their roots, seeds, leaves and resin could be used.

BROKEN SKULL

This man is suffering from a broken skull. The wound would be washed with urine to disinfect it.

DEADLY BITES

Many dangerous creatures lived in the deserts and rainforests of Mesoamerica. Bites from dangerous spiders and venomous snakes were common hazards. Herbal remedies, such as the roots of a tree called rabbit fern, were used to treat bites and stings.

BREAK A LEG

To cure broken limbs, the Aztecs would grind various roots into a powder. These were placed on the break. A splint would then be tied to the broken limb.

tarantula   *rattlesnake*

AFTER CARE

The man shown here is recovering from a broken leg. After 20 days, a poultice of lime and powdered cactus root would be applied to his leg. When the leg was strong, the patient was advised to take a hot bath.

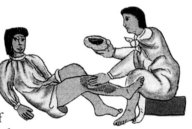

COUGH MIXTURE

A persistent cough could be cured by an infusion of *teouaxin* cooked with chile and salt.

BATHING ILLNESS AWAY

Steam baths like this were used for keeping clean. The Aztecs also used them to try to cure illness. They believed the baths would drive out the evil spirits that caused many diseases. Steam baths worked like a present-day sauna. Bathers sat in a small cabin, close to a fire, which heated large stones. When the stones were very hot, water was poured over them, creating clouds of steam.

Clothes, Hairstyles, Jewelry

AZTEC CLOTHES were very simple. Women wore a skirt and tunic, while men had a cloak and loincloth. But clothes still revealed a lot about the wearer. Strict laws described suitable clothing for different people. Ordinary families were meant to wear plain, knee-length clothes woven from rough *ixtle* (cactus fibre) and no jewelry. Nobles were allowed to wear longer-length clothes of fine white cotton, decorated with embroidery or woven patterns. They could also wear earrings, necklaces, labrets (lip-plugs) and bracelets of gold and precious stones. Mayan clothes were also simple—just strips of fabric wound around the body. Their ideas of beauty would be strange to us. They filed their teeth and encouraged their children to grow up cross-eyed. Mothers also bound their babies' heads to flatten them.

GLITTERING GOLD
This gold chest ornament is in the shape of a skeleton-faced god. It was made by Mixtec goldsmiths from southern Mexico. Jewelry was worn only by nobles. In Mesoamerica, both noblemen and women wore fine jewelry.

CEREMONIAL CLOTHES
Musicians and actors walk in procession in this picture. It is copied from a wall painting in a Mayan ruler's palace at Bonampak. The procession forms part of a celebration to honor the ruler's child. The men on the right are all wearing white cloth headdresses and wrap-around skirts, tied with sashes at the waist.

MAKE A BAT BROOCH
You will need: pencil, thin cardboard, scissors, black and gold paint, small paintbrush, paint container, palette, glue, glue brush, string, small safety pin, masking tape.

1 Draw the shape of your brooch in pencil on thin cardboard (2⅓ in. x 4 in.). This brooch is based on a gold Aztec pendant shaped like a vampire bat god.

2 Carefully cut out the finished shape with scissors. Aztec jewelry designs were very delicate and complicated. They often featured gods.

3 Use black paint to color in the eyes, mouth and hair of your bat, as shown above. It is best to use the paint fairly thickly.

CLOAK AND DAGGER

This Aztec warrior is wearing a long, brightly colored cloak and an elaborate feather headdress. Aztec cloaks were simple rectangles of cloth, fastened at the shoulder by a knot. There were strict rules governing their length. Only nobles or soldiers who had legs that had been badly scarred in battle could wear cloaks like this one, coming below the knee. Ordinary men had to wear short cloaks.

MEXICAN STYLE

A Huastec woman from Veracruz, on the north coast of Mexico, is shown in this statue. She is wearing a wide tunic and a long skirt. Her hair is tied up in a carefully-folded headdress, and she wears a necklace and disk-shaped earrings. Although different patterns were favored by the peoples of the various Mesoamerican cultures, the style of clothing was essentially very similar.

SKIRTS, TUNICS AND CLOAKS

A well-off Aztec couple sit by the fire, while their hostess cooks a meal. Both women are wearing long skirts. The bright embroidery of their tunics is a sign of high rank. Their long hair is braided and tied on top of their heads to make horns in a typical married woman's style. Girls and unmarried women wore their hair loose down their backs.

4 Cut teeth out of cardboard and glue in place. Use the glue to stick string on the bat's face, head and body. Coil the string into spirals for the hair. Let brooch dry.

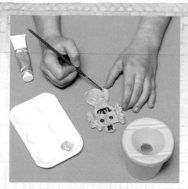

5 Carefully paint the brooch all over (except for the black areas) with gold paint. Let stand in a warm place for the paint to dry.

6 When the paint is dry, turn the brooch over and tape a safety pin on to the back with masking tape. Make sure it is secure.

You could wear your brooch on your chest, as the Aztecs did, or pin it on your sleeve.

Craftworkers

S PANISH EXPLORERS arriving in Mesoamerica were amazed at the wonderful objects they found there. They were different from anything they had seen in Europe. Pottery, jewelry, fabrics, mosaics, masks, knives and feather work were all made by skilled Mesoamerican craftworkers using simple, hand-powered tools. In big cities such as Tenochtitlan, Aztec craftworkers organized themselves into guilds. These made sure that all members worked to the highest standards and trained new workers. Many craft skills were passed from parents to children. Sometimes whole families worked as a team in workshops next to the family home.

MOSAIC MASK
This ritual mask is inlaid with a mosaic of turquoise. This valuable stone was brought back from mines in North America by Aztec traders.

Many Mesoamerican craft goods were decorated with beautiful patterns. Often, they had special religious meanings. Aztec warriors marched into battle carrying magic feathered shields. Jewelry was decorated with death's-head designs. Many Mayan rulers and nobles were buried with elaborately decorated pots.

LIVING JEWELS
Featherworkers wove or glued thousands of feathers together to make headdresses, cloaks, warriors' uniforms, shields and fans. Men drew the designs on stiffened cloth and made light wooden frames to support the finished item. Women cleaned and sorted the feathers.

MAKE A MOSAIC MASK

You will need: balloon, petroleum jelly, newspaper, papier-mâché mixture (1 part white glue to 3 parts water), bowl, paintbrush, scissors, palette of paints, container, self-drying clay, gummed paper tape, cardboard, plaster colored with paint.

1 Inflate a balloon to the size of your head. Cover with petroleum jelly. Soak strips of newspaper in papier-mâché mixture. Add five layers to the front of the balloon.

2 Once dry, pop the balloon. Draw a mask shape on to the papier-mâché and cut it out. Use clay to add eyes and a nose. Cover the edges with gummed paper tape. Let dry.

3 Mix white and blue paint to create three different shades. Paint one sheet of cardboard with each. When dry, cut them into little pieces.

WARRIOR DISH

This dish was made in the Mayan city of Tikal, (present-day Guatemala). It is painted with slip (a liquid clay colored with minerals) and shows the figure of a warrior. All Mesoamerican pots were shaped by hand—the potter's wheel was unknown.

WEAVINGS

Cloaks and blankets were sent as tribute (taxes) to the great city of Tenochtitlan, as well as being sold in markets.

MOLDING GOLD

This painting by Diego Rivera shows Aztec goldsmiths with molten gold. Most jewelry was made by melting gold-dust in a furnace, then pouring it into a mold.

TREASURES

Mesoamerican people treasured many beautiful semi-precious stones, such as turquoise, obsidian and rock-crystal. They paid high prices for corals, pearls and shells from the sea. But they valued jade, a hard, smooth, deep-green stone, most of all, because it symbolized eternal life.

turquoise   *obsidian*

Aztec craftworkers carefully cut semi-precious stones into tiny squares. Turquoise, jade, shell and obsidian were all used for this purpose. The craftworkers used these pieces to create beautiful mosaic masks like this.

4 Cover the mask (except the eyes and mouth) with plaster paste. Press the cardboard pieces into this, using glue to help any awkward ones stick.

5 Paint the eyes with black and white paint. Cut out teeth from white cardboard and carefully glue in position. Leave the mask in a warm place to dry.

6 Now coat the whole mask with a thin coat of white glue. This will seal the surface of the mask.

Merchants and Markets

THE MARKET PLACE was the heart of many Mesoamerican cities and towns. Traders, craftworkers and farmers met there to exchange their produce. Many market traders were women. They sold cloth or cooking pots, made by themselves or their families, and corn, fruit, flowers and vegetables grown by their husbands. In big cities, such as the trading center of Tlatelolco, government officials also sold exotic goods that had been sent to the Aztec rulers as tribute (taxes) by conquered city-states. After the Aztecs conquered Tlatelolco in 1473, it soon became the the greatest market in Mesoamerica. It was reported that almost 50,000 people came there on the busiest days.

Long-distance trade was carried out by merchants called *pochteca*. Gangs of porters carried their goods. The work was often dangerous, but the rewards were great.

MERCHANT GOD

Yacatecuhtli was the Aztec god of merchants and traders. In the codex picture above, he is shown standing in front of a crossroads marked with footprints. Behind him (*right*), is a tired porter with a load of birds on his back.

CORN MARKET

Mesoamerican farmers grew many different varieties of corn, with cobs that were pale cream, bright yellow, or even deep blue. Their wives took the corn to market, as selling was women's work. This modern wall-painting shows Aztec women buying and selling corn in the great market at Tlatelolco. At the market, judges sat in raised booths, keeping a lookout for thieves and cheats.

MAKE A MAYAN POT

You will need: self-drying clay, board, rolling pin, masking tape, water bowl, small bowl, petroleum jelly, modeling tool, white glue, glue brush, yellow and black paint, paintbrush, water container.

1 Roll out the clay until it is approximately ¼ in. thick. Cut out a base for the pot with a modelling tool. Use a roll of masking tape as a guide for size.

2 Roll out some long sausages of clay. Coil them around the base of the pot to build up the sides. Join and smooth the clay with water as you go.

3 Model a lip at the top of the pot. Let it dry. Cover a small bowl with petroleum jelly. Make a lid by rolling out some clay. Place the clay over the bowl.

JOURNEY'S END

This modern painting shows merchants and porters arriving at the market city of Tlatelolco. Such travelers made long journeys to bring back valuable goods, such as shells, jade and fig-bark paper. Young men joining the merchants' guild were warned about fatigue, pain and ambushes on their travels.

SKINS

Items such as puma, ocelot and jaguar skins could fetch a high price at market.

BARTER

Mesoamerican people did not have coins. They bought and sold by bartering, exchanging the goods they wanted to sell for other peoples' goods of equal value. Costly items such as gold-dust, quetzal feathers and cocoa beans were exchanged for goods they wanted to buy.

colorful feathers   *cocoa beans*

MARKET PRODUCE

In Mexico today, many markets are still held on the same sites as ancient ones. Many of the same types of foodstuffs are on sale there. In this modern photograph, we see tomatoes, avocados and vegetables that were also grown in Aztec times. Today, as in the past, most market traders and shoppers are women.

Mesoamerican potters made their pots by these coil or slab techniques. The potter's wheel was not used at all in Mesoamerica. The pots were sold at the local market.

4 Turn your pot upside down and place it over the rolled-out clay. Trim the excess clay with a modeling tool by cutting around the top of the pot.

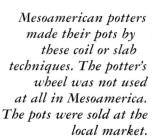

5 Use balls of clay to make a turtle to go on top of the lid. When both the lid and turtle are dry, use white glue to stick the turtle onto the center of the lid.

6 Roll three small balls of clay of exactly the same size for the pot's feet. When they are dry, glue them to the base of the pot. Make sure they are evenly spaced.

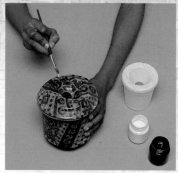

7 Paint the pot with Aztec designs in black and yellow. When you have finished, varnish the pot with a thin coat of white glue to make it shiny.

Travel and Transport

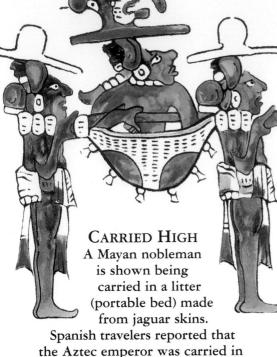

MESOAMERICAN PEOPLE knew about wheels, but they did not make wheeled transport of any kind. Carriages and carts would not have been suitable for journeys through dense rainforests or along steep, narrow mountain tracks. Many Mayan cities were also linked by raised causeways that would have been difficult for wheeled vehicles to travel along.

Most people traveled overland on foot, carrying goods on their backs. Mesoamerican porters carried heavy loads with the help of a *tumpline*. This was a broad band of cloth that went across their foreheads and under the bundles on their backs, leaving their arms free. Rulers and nobles were carried in beds, called litters.

On rivers and lakes, Mesoamericans used simple dug-out boats. At sea, Mayan sailors traveled in huge wooden canoes that were able to make voyages of many miles in rough seas.

CARRIED HIGH
A Mayan nobleman is shown being carried in a litter (portable bed) made from jaguar skins. Spanish travelers reported that the Aztec emperor was carried in the same way. Blankets were also spread in front of the emperor as he walked, to keep his feet from touching the ground.

MEN OR MONSTERS?
Until the Spaniards arrived with horses in 1519, there were no animals big and strong enough to ride in the Mesoamerican lands. There were horses in America in prehistoric times, but they died out around 10,000 B.C. When the Aztecs saw the Spanish riding, they thought they were monsters—half man, half beast.

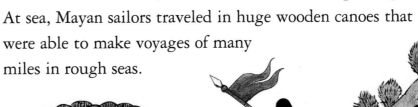

A WHEELED DOG

You will need: a board, self-drying clay, 4 lengths of thin dowel about 2 in. long and 2 lengths about 2¾ in. long, thick cardboard, scissors, water bowl, board, modeling tool, paintbrush, white glue, paint container, masking tape.

1 Roll a large piece of clay into a fat sausage to form the dog's body. Push the 2 in. pieces of dowel into the body to make the legs. Let dry.

2 Cover the dowel legs with clay, extending the clay ¾ in. beyond the end of the dowel. Make a hole at the end of each leg with a piece of dowel. Let dry.

3 Push the dowel through the holes in the legs to join them horizontally. Make the dog's head and ears from clay. Attach them to the body using water.

HARDWORKING PORTERS

This engraving from the 1900s shows Aztec slaves and commoners carrying loads for Spanish conquerors. Being a porter was very hard work. They were expected to cover up to 62 mi. per day, carrying about 55-66 lbs. on their backs. Like most Mesoamerican people, they traveled these long distances barefoot.

BY BOAT

Aztec soldiers and the citizens of Tenochtitlan used boats with flat bottoms to travel around the city. Boats like this were also used to carry fruits and vegetables to market. Dug-out canoes were popular, too. They were made from hollowed out tree trunks.

AZTEC WATERWAYS

The Aztecs paddled their canoes and flat-bottomed boats on Lake Texcoco. Today most of this lake has dried up. The lakeside *chinampas*, where they grew food and flowers, have almost disappeared. This photograph shows modern punts sailing along one of the last remaining Aztec waterways between the few *chinampas* that survive.

Toys like this dog are proof that the wheel was known in Mesoamerica. Wheeled vehicles were not suitable for rugged Mesoamerican land.

4 Cut four circles 1⅓ in. in diameter from cardboard to make wheels. Pierce a hole in the center of each. Make the holes big enough for the dowel to fit through.

5 Make four wheels from clay, the same size as the cardboard wheels. Glue the clay and cardboard wheels together. Make holes through the clay wheels and let dry.

6 Paint the dog's head, body, legs and wheels with Aztec patterns. When the paint is dry, give the dog a thin coat of white glue to act as a varnish.

7 Put the wheels on the ends of the dowels that pass through the dog's legs. Wrap strips of masking tape around the ends to stop the wheels from falling off.

Warriors and Weapons

AZTEC ARMIES were very large. All Aztec men learned how to fight and had to be ready to hurry off to battle when they heard the sound of the great war drum outside the ruler's palace in Tenochtitlan. Ordinary soldiers wore tunics and leg-guards of padded cotton that had been soaked in saltwater. This made it tough—strong enough to protect the wearer from many fierce blows. Aztec army commanders wore splendid uniforms decorated with gold, silver, feathers and fur.

Both the Maya and the Aztecs greatly admired bravery. Aztec armies were led by nobles who had won promotion for brave deeds in battle or for taking lots of captives.

It was a disgrace for an Aztec soldier to try to save his own skin. It was more honorable for him to be killed fighting, or to be sacrificed, than to survive.

Mayan soldiers went to war to win captives for sacrifice, but they also fought battles to control trade routes, to obtain tribute and to gain power. They wore a variety of garments, including sleeveless tunics, loincloths, fur garments and cotton armor.

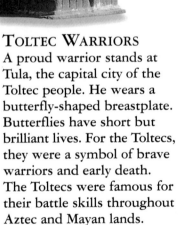

TOLTEC WARRIORS
A proud warrior stands at Tula, the capital city of the Toltec people. He wears a butterfly-shaped breastplate. Butterflies have short but brilliant lives. For the Toltecs, they were a symbol of brave warriors and early death. The Toltecs were famous for their battle skills throughout Aztec and Mayan lands.

HELD CAPTIVE
An Aztec warrior is shown capturing an enemy in battle in this codex picture. The warrior is dragging his captive along by the hair. Young Aztec men had to grow their hair long at the back and could only cut it when they had taken their first prisoner in battle.

AN EAGLE HELMET

You will need: ruler, thick cardboard, pencil, scissors, masking tape, stapler, self-drying clay, white glue, glue brush, gummed paper tape, paints, paintbrush, water container, ribbon, felt, green paper, Velcro.

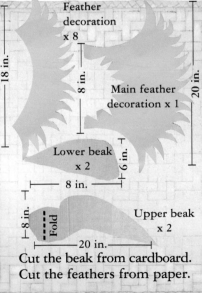

Feather decoration x 8

18 in.

8 in.

Main feather decoration x 1

20 in.

Lower beak x 2

6 in.

8 in.

8 in.

Fold

Upper beak x 2

20 in.

Cut the beak from cardboard. Cut the feathers from paper.

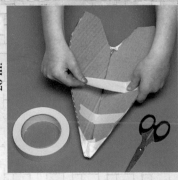

1 Make your helmet by joining the two parts of the upper beak with masking tape. Join the two parts of the lower beak in the same way, as shown.

2 Fold the two rounded ends of the upper beak toward each other and staple them together. Cover the staples and the seam with masking tape.

JAGUAR AND EAGLE KNIGHTS

Ocelotl, the jaguar, is shown in this picture from a codex.

Warriors had to prove their bravery in battle and capture lots of prisoners for sacrifice. Those who succeeded were invited to join special fighting brotherhoods of jaguar and eagle knights. They wore costumes made of real feathers and skins.

WARRIOR SPIRIT

This stone carving is from the Mayan city of Yaxchilan. In it, Lady Xoc, wife of ruler Shield Jaguar, kneels before a vision serpent. This serpent was made to appear by a special religious ritual. Mayan rulers made offerings of their own blood to their ancestor spirits and to the gods to ask for help in battle.

CLUBS AND SPEARS

Aztec soldiers face Spanish soldiers on horseback. They are armed with war clubs called *macuahuitl* and protected by wooden shields.

War clubs, made of wood and razor-sharp flakes of obsidian, could cut an enemy's head off with a single blow. The Spaniards are armed with metal swords and lances.

Fasten your eagle helmet by tying it under the chin. You can make wings from cardboard and attach them to your arms with ribbon. Now you are a brave eagle knight! Eagles were admired by the Aztecs as superb hunters who could move freely to the sun.

3 Make two eyes from self-drying clay and stick them on the upper beak with glue. Neaten the edges of the beak and eyes with gummed paper tape.

4 Decorate both parts of the beak with paint. If desired add pieces of ribbon, felt or paper, too. Remember that you want to look brave and fierce.

5 Ask an adult to curl the feathers by running a scissor blade along them. Glue the layers of feathers onto the main feather decoration. Trim to fit.

6 Use tape and glue to attach feathers to the inside of the upper beak. Tape ribbon from the upper beak to the lower one to join. Leave some ribbon loose to tie.

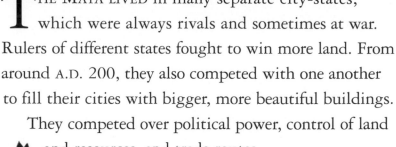

Rival City-States

THE MAYA LIVED in many separate city-states, which were always rivals and sometimes at war. Rulers of different states fought to win more land. From around A.D. 200, they also competed with one another to fill their cities with bigger, more beautiful buildings. They competed over political power, control of land and resources, and trade routes.

Between about A.D. 850 and A.D. 900, many Mayan cities became poorer, and their power collapsed. The great city centers were abandoned, and Mayan scribes and craftworkers no longer carved important dates on temples and tombs. The last date documented is A.D. 889. No one knows why this happened. Perhaps it was because of famine, bad weather or farmers over-using the land, or it may have been the result of war. However, Mayan civilization did not totally disappear. A few Mayan cities, in the far north and south of Mexico, continued to thrive.

Around A.D. 900, the Putun people from the Gulf coast moved into Mayan lands. In cities like Chichen-Itza, Putun ideas blended with Mayan traditions to create a new culture.

TIKAL
This figure was painted on a pottery vase from the city of Tikal. From about A.D. 600 to A.D. 900, Tikal was the greatest Mayan city-state. It was wealthy, busy and very big. About 75,000 people lived there, and its buildings covered an area of 39 square miles. Around A.D. 400, Tikal conquered the nearby Mayan state of Uaxactun. Trading and religious links were then developed with the powerful non-Mayan city of Teotihuacan.

CHICHEN-ITZA
Pilgrims came from miles around to throw jewelry and fine pottery into the Well of Sacrifice in the city of Chichen-Itza. These items were offerings to the god of rain. Human sacrifices were made here, too. Chichen-Itza was founded by the Maya around A.D. 800. Later, Mayan craftsmen built a massive new city center, with temples and ball-courts. Many of these new buildings were based on designs similar to those found in central Mexico. Some historians think this means that the city was conquered by the Putuns.

UXMAL

The city of Uxmal is in the dry Puuc region of Yucatan, Mexico. There are no rivers or streams in the area, so Mayan engineers designed and built huge underground tanks, called *chultun*, to store summer rainfall. People living in Uxmal relied on these water tanks for survival.

NAMES AND DATES

This stone slab was once placed above a doorway in the Mayan city of Yaxchilan. It is carved with glyphs, or picture-symbols, recording important names and dates. The city of Yaxchilan is famous for the fine quality stone carvings found there, especially on tall pillars and around doors.

PALENQUE

Lord Pacal, ruler of the Mayan city of Palenque, was buried wearing this mask of green jade. Only the richest city-states could afford to bury their rulers with treasures like this. Palenque was at its strongest between A.D. 600 and A.D. 800.

COPAN

This stela (tall stone pillar) is from Copan (in modern Honduras). Copan was the southern-most Mayan city. The front of the stela is carved with a larger-than-life portrait of 18 Rabbit (Waxaklahun ubah k'awil), the thirteenth ruler of the city. Archaeologists know much about Copan's past from the inscriptions carved in several monuments and buildings.

Aztec Conquests

TOTONAC TRIBUTE
Ambassadors from lands conquered by the Aztecs came to Tenochtitlan to deliver the tribute (taxes) demanded by their new rulers. This painting shows splendidly dressed representatives of the Totonac people meeting Aztec tax collectors. The Totonacs lived on the Gulf coast of Mexico, in Veracruz. Here they are shown offering tobacco, fruit and vanilla grown on their lands. They hated and feared the Aztecs.

W AR WAS ESSENTIAL to Aztec life. As newcomers in Mexico, the Aztecs had won their homeland by fighting against the people already living there. From then onward, they relied on war to bring more land, new cities and tribute (taxes) under their control. Without these riches won through war, the Aztec empire would have collapsed. Big cities such as Tenochtitlan needed steady supplies of tribute to feed their citizens. War was also a source of captives. The Aztecs believed that thousands of prisoners needed to be sacrificed each year.

Each new Aztec ruler had to start his reign with a battle. It was his duty to win fame and glory by conquering new territory and seizing enemy captives. During the 1400s, the Aztec empire grew rapidly, until the Aztecs ruled most of Mexico. This drive to conquer new territory was led by rulers Itzcoatl (1426–1440), Moctezuma Ilhuicamina (1440–1468) and Axayacatl (1468–1481). Conquered cities were often controlled by garrisons of Aztec soldiers and linked to the government in Tenochtitlan by large numbers of officials, such as tax collectors and scribes.

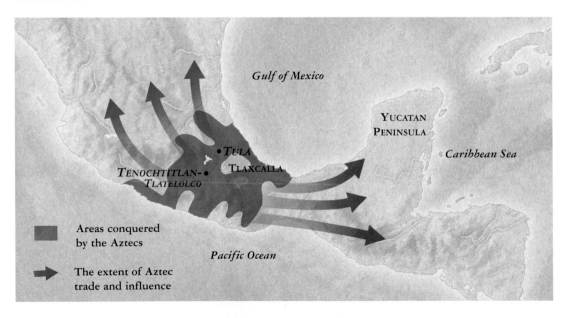

Gulf of Mexico

YUCATAN
PENINSULA

Caribbean Sea

Tula
TLAXCALLA

TENOCHTITLAN-
TLATELOLCO

Pacific Ocean

▬ Areas conquered
by the Aztecs

➤ The extent of Aztec
trade and influence

AZTEC LANDS
This map shows the area ruled by the Aztecs in 1519. Conquered cities were allowed to continue with their traditional way of life but had to pay tribute to Aztec officials. The Aztecs also put pressure on two weaker city states, Texcoco and Tlacopan, to join with them in a Triple Alliance. One nearby city-state, Tlaxcalla (see map), refused to make an alliance with the Aztecs and stayed fiercely independent.

CANNIBALS

One of the Aztecs' most important reasons for fighting was to capture prisoners for sacrifice. In this codex picture, we can see sacrificed bodies neatly chopped up. In some religious ceremonies, the Aztecs ate the arms and legs of sacrificed prisoners.

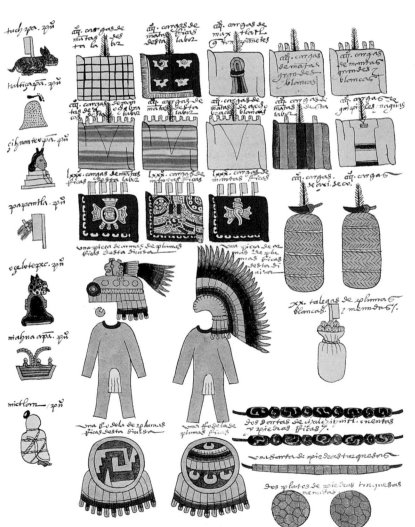

FROM HUMBLE BEGINNINGS

Aztec settlers are shown on their difficult trek through northern Mexico. The Aztecs built up their empire from humble beginnings in a short time. They first arrived in Mexico some time after A.D. 1200. By around 1400, they had become the strongest nation in central Mesoamerica. To maintain their position, they had to be ready for war. The Aztecs invented many legends to justify their success. They claimed to be descended from earlier peoples living in Mexico, and to be specially guided by the gods.

TRIBUTE LIST

The Aztecs received vast quantities of valuable goods as tribute (taxes) each year. Most of the tribute was sent to their capital city of Tenochtitlan. Aztec scribes there drew up very detailed lists of tribute received, like the one on the left. Among the goods shown are shields decorated with feathers, blankets, turquoise plates, bracelets and dried chile peppers.

Scholars and Scribes

THE MAYA were the first—and only—Native American people to invent a complete writing system. Maya picture-symbols and sound-symbols were written in books, carved on buildings, painted on pottery and inscribed on precious stones. Mayan scribes also developed an advanced number system, including a sign for zero, which Europeans at the time did not have.

Mayan writing used glyphs (pictures standing for words) and also picture-signs that stood for sounds. The sound-signs could be joined together, like the letters of our alphabet, to spell out words and to make complete sentences. The Aztecs used picture-writing too, but theirs was much simpler and less flexible.

Mayan and Aztec picture-symbols were very difficult to learn. Only specially trained scribes could write them and only priests or rich people could read them. They could spare time for study and afford to pay a good teacher.

MAYA READER
This Mayan statue shows a wealthy woman, seated cross-legged with a codex (folding book), on her lap. A Mayan or Aztec codex was made of long strips of fig-bark paper, folded like an accordian. The writing was read from top to bottom and left to right.

CITY EMBLEM
This is the emblem-glyph for the Mayan city-state of Copan. It is made up of four separate images, which together give a message meaning "the home of the rulers of the royal blood of Copan." At the bottom, you can see a bat, the special picture-sign for the city.

MAKE A CODEX

You will need: thin cardboard, ruler, pencil, scissors, white acrylic paint, eraser, large and small paintbrushes, water container, paints in red, yellow, blue and black, palette, tracing paper.

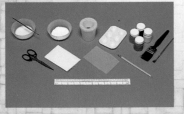

1 Draw a rectangle about 40 in. x 10 in. onto thin cardboard. Cut out the rectangle, Cover it evenly with white acrylic paint. Let it dry.

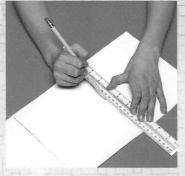

2 Using a pencil and ruler, lightly draw in four fold-lines 8 in. apart. This will divide the painted cardboard into five equal sections.

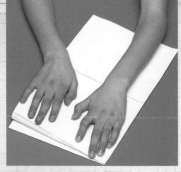

3 Carefully fold along the pencil lines to make a zig-zag book, as shown. Unfold the cardboard and rub out the pencil lines with an eraser.

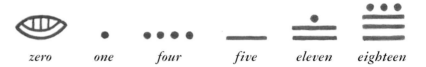

MAYAN CODEX

Mayan scribes wrote thousands of codices, but only four survive. All the rest were destroyed by Spanish missionaries. These pages from a Mayan codex show the activities of several different gods. The figure at the top painted black with a long nose is Ek Chuah, the god of merchants.

zero	one	four	five	eleven	eighteen

AZTEC ENCYLOPEDIA

These pictures of Aztec gods come from a book known as the Florentine Codex. This encyclopedia was compiled between 1547 and 1569 by Father Bernardino de Sahagun, a Spanish friar. He was fascinated by Aztec civilization and wanted to record it before it disappeared. This codex is the most complete written record of Aztec life we have.

MAYAN NUMBERS

The Mayan number system used only three signs – a dot for one, a bar for five, and the shell-symbol for zero. Other numbers were made by using a combination of those signs. When writing down large numbers, Mayan scribes put the different symbols on top of one another, rather than side by side as we do today.

If you went to school in Aztec or Mayan times, you would find out how to recognize hundreds of different picture-symbols. You would also be taught to link them together in your mind, like a series of clues, to find out what they meant.

4 Trace or copy Aztec or Mayan codex drawings from this book. Alternatively, make up your own, based on Mesoamerican examples.

5 Paint your tracings or drawings, using light, bright colors. Using the Mayan numbers on this page as a guide, add some numbers to your codex.

Time, Sun and Stars

Like all other Mesoamericans, the Maya and the Aztecs measured time using a calendar with a year of 260 days. This was used in Mexico as early as 500 B.C. and is probably based on human biology—260 days is about how long it takes a baby to develop before it is born. The calendar was divided into 13 cycles of 20 days each. Mesoamerican farmers used a different calendar, based on the movements of the sun, because sunlight and the seasons made their crops grow. This calendar had 360 days, divided into 18 months of 20 days, plus five extra days that were unlucky. Every 52 years, measured in our time, these two calendars ended on the same day. For five days before the end of the 52 years, people were anxious, because they feared the world might end. A third calendar, of 584 days, also existed for calculating festival days.

SUN STONE
This massive carving was made to display the Aztec view of creation. The Aztecs believed that the world had already been created and destroyed four times and that their Fifth World was also doomed.

STUDYING THE STARS
The Caracol was constructed as an observatory to study the sky. From there, Mayan astronomers could observe the planet Venus, which was important in the Mesoamericans' measurement of time.

MAKE A SUN STONE

You will need: scissors, thick cardboard, self-drying clay, modeling tool, board, rolling pin, masking tape, white glue, glue brush, water bowl, pencil, thin cardboard, water-based paints, paintbrush, water container.

1 Cut a circle about 10 in. in diameter from thick cardboard. Roll out the clay and cut out a matching circle. Place the clay circle on the cardboard one.

2 With a modeling tool, mark a small circle in the center of the clay circle. Use a roll of masking tape as a guide. Do not cut through the clay.

3 Carve the sun god's eyes, mouth, teeth and earrings. You can use the real Aztec sun stone, shown at the top left of this page, as a guide.

alligator

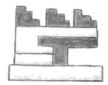
wind

house

lizard

serpent

death's head

deer

rabbit

NAMES OF DAYS

These pictures from an Aztec codex show the 20 names for days from the farmers' calendar. These symbols were combined with a number from one to 13 to give the date, such as Three Vulture. The days were named after familiar creatures or everyday things, such as the lizard or water. Each day also had its own god. Children were often named after the day on which they were born, a custom that still continues in some parts of Mexico up to the present day.

Water

dog

monkey

grass

Your finished sun stone will not be as big as the original Aztec one. That measures 13 feet across and is the largest Aztec sculpture discovered so far.

reed

jaguar

eagle

vulture

motion

flint knife

rain

flower

4 Roll out more clay and cut out some sun's rays, a tongue and eyebrows. Glue them to the clay circle. Smooth the edges with water and let dry.

5 Copy the 20 Aztec symbols (*above*) for days onto squares of thin cardboard. The cardboard squares should be no more than ¾ in. x ¾ in. Cut out. Paint brown.

6 Cover the clay circle with a thin coat of dark brown paint. Let it dry. Then add a thin coat of white paint to make the circle look like stone.

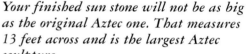
7 Glue the cardboard symbols evenly around the edge of the clay circle, as shown. Paint the sun stone with a thin layer of white glue to seal and varnish it.

Gods and Goddesses

RELIGION WAS a powerful force throughout Mesoamerica. It affected everything people did, from getting up in the morning to digging in their fields or obeying their ruler's laws. Everyone believed that the gods governed human life. People could not fight their decisions, but the gods could sometimes be persuaded to grant favors if they were offered gifts and sacrifices. The Aztecs and Maya believed in ancient nature gods such as the fire god, the god of corn and the god of rain, and worshipped them with splendid festivals and ceremonies. Mesoamerican people also honored the spirits of their dead rulers. The Aztecs had their own special tribal god, Huitzilopochtli, Lord of the Sun. He rewarded his followers with victories in war.

Religious ceremonies and sacrifices were led by temple priests. With long, matted hair, red-rimmed eyes and painted bodies splattered with blood, they were a terrifying sight.

GOD OF SPRING
Xipe Totec was the Aztec god of fertility. He protected the young shoots of corn. Each year, captives were skinned alive as a sacrifice to him. Priests dressed in their skins in religious ceremonies to remind everyone of the skin of young plants.

CHACMOOL FIGURE
This stone statue from the city of Chichen-Itza shows a Chacmool, or reclining figure. It is holding a stone slab on which offerings may have been made.

A STATUE OF A GOD

You will need: pencil, paper, self-drying clay, modeling tool, water bowl, petroleum jelly, cotton balls, plaster of Paris, terra cotta paint, small paintbrush.

1 Make a drawing of any Aztec god. Model it as a flat figure from self-drying clay. Keep it flat on the bottom. Let the clay figure dry.

2 Completely cover the surface of your model with petroleum jelly. Then smooth a layer of clay over the jelly, pressing it down gently into any grooves.

3 Spread more clay on top to make a strong rectangular block, at least 1 in. thick. This will become your mold. Let it dry thoroughly.

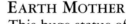

WATER AND RAIN

Tlaloc was the Aztec god of life-giving rain, "the god who makes things grow." Under different names, he was worshipped throughout Mesoamerica. Tlaloc was honored when he sent water to nourish the crops and feared when he sent deadly floods. In times of drought, the Aztecs sacrificed babies to Tlaloc. They believed the babies' tears would make rain fall.

SUN AND JAGUAR

This Mayan carving was part of a wall at Campeche in southeastern Mexico. It shows the sun god, whom the Maya called Kinich Ahau. The Maya believed that he disappeared into the underworld every night, at sunset. It was there that he turned into a fierce jaguar god. At the beginning of every new day, they believed that Kinich Ahau then returned to earth as the life-giving sun.

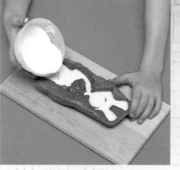

EARTH MOTHER

This huge statue of Coatlicue (Great Lady Serpent Skirt) stood in the Sacred Precinct at Tenochtitlan. She was the fearsome Aztec earthmother goddess. Coatlicue gave birth to the Aztecs' national god, Huitzilopochtli, the moon goddess, and the stars.

This model (right) is based on an Aztec statue. It shows a goddess holding two children. Figures of gods were often created from molds (left).

4 Carefully ease the little model out of the solid block, using the modeling tool. The petroleum jelly should ensure that it comes out cleanly.

5 Clean any loose bits of clay from the mold and smear petroleum jelly inside. Use a cotton ball to make sure the jelly is pushed into every part.

6 Mix up some plaster of Paris and pour it into the mold. Tap the mold gently to remove any air bubbles. Let the plaster dry for at least an hour.

7 Gently remove the plaster statue from the mold. Dust it with a brush, then paint it a terra-cotta color, so that it looks like an Aztec pottery figure.

Temples and Sacrifices

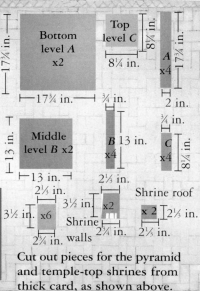

MESOAMERICAN PEOPLE believed that unless they made offerings of blood and human lives to the gods, the sun would die and the world would come to an end. Mayan rulers pricked themselves with cactus thorns and stingray spines, or drew spiked cords through their tongues, to draw blood. They pulled out captives' fingernails so the blood flowed or threw them into holy waterholes. Aztecs pricked their earlobes each morning and collected two drops of blood to give to the gods. They also went to war to capture prisoners. On special occasions, vast numbers of captives were needed for sacrifice. It was reported that 20,000 victims were sacrificed to celebrate the completion of the Great Temple at Tenochtitlan in 1487. It took four days to kill them all. Mesoamerican temples were tombs as well as places of sacrifice. Rulers and their wives were buried inside. Each ruler aimed to build a great temple as a memorial to his reign.

TEMPLE TOMB
Pyramid Temple 1 at Tikal was built in the A.D. 700s as a memorial to a Maya king. Nine stone platforms were built above the burial chamber to create a tall pyramid shape reaching up to the sky.

HOLY KNIFE
This sacrificial knife has a blade made from a semiprecious stone called chalcedony. It was made by Mixtecs from south Mexico. Mesoamerican priests used finely decorated knives of flint, obsidian and other hard stones to kill captives for sacrifice. These were trimmed to be as sharp as glass.

A PYRAMID TEMPLE

You will need: pencil, ruler, thick cardboard, scissors, white glue, glue brush, masking tape, thin strips of balsa wood, thin card, corrugated cardboard, water bowl, paintbrushes, paints.

Cut out pieces for the pyramid and temple-top shrines from thick card, as shown above.

Bottom level A x2 — 17¾ in. — 17¾ in.

Top level C — 8¼ in. — 8¼ in.

A x4 — 17¾ in. — 2 in. — ¾ in.

Middle level B x2 — 13 in. — 13 in.

B x4 — 13 in. — ¾ in.

C x4 — 8¼ in.

Shrine roof — 2⅓ in. — x2 — x 2 — 2⅓ in. — 2¾ in. — 2⅓ in.

3½ in. x6 — 3½ in. — 2⅓ in.

Shrine walls — 2¾ in.

1 Use white glue and masking tape to join the thick cardboard pieces to make three flat boxes (A, B and C). Leave the boxes until the glue is completely dry.

2 From the remaining pieces of cardboard, make the two temple-top shrines, as shown. You could add extra details with strips of balsa wood or thin cardboard.

SKULL SHRINE

Rows of human skulls, carved in stone, decorate this shrine outside the Aztecs' Great Temple in the center of Tenochtitlan. Most Aztec temples also had skull racks, where rows of real human heads were displayed. They were cut from the bodies of sacrificed captives.

PERFECTION
The ideal victim for human sacrifice was a fit and healthy young man.

RELIGIOUS GIFTS
Mesoamerican people also made offerings of food and flowers as gifts to the gods. Corn was a valuable gift because it was the Mesoamerican people's most important food. Bright orange marigolds were a sign of the Sun, on which every person's life depended.

corn

marigolds

HUMAN SACRIFICE
This Aztec codex painting shows captives being sacrificed. At the top, you can see a priest cutting open a captive's chest and removing the heart as an offering to the gods.

This model is based on the Great Temple that stood in the center of Tenochtitlan.

3 Glue the boxes, one on top of the next. Cut out pieces of cardboard the same size as each side of your boxes. They should be about ¾ in. wide. Stick down, as shown.

4 Cut out two strips of cardboard ¾ in. x 10¼ in. Glue them to a third piece of cardboard 5½ in. x 10¼ in. Glue corrugated cardboard 3¾ in. x 10¼ in. in position.

5 Stick the staircase to the front of the temple, as shown. Use a ruler to check that the staircase is an equal distance from either side of the temple.

6 Paint the whole temple a cream color to look like natural stone. Add details, such as carvings or wall paintings, using brightly colored paint.

Time for Celebration

Festivals, with music and dancing, were a very important part of Mesoamerican life. All big Aztec and Mayan cities had a huge open space in the center, where crowds gathered to sing and dance to honor the gods on festival days. Every twenty days, there were celebrations to mark the start of a new month. There were also festivals, with prayers and sacrifices, to mark important seasons of the farming year. In July and August, the Aztecs celebrated flowering trees and plants. In September, there were harvest festivals, and in October, festivals where hunters gave thanks for plentiful prey. For the Aztec rulers and their guests, feasts and entertainment were a regular event.

All of these special occasions involved music and song. Favorite instruments included rattles, whistles, ocarinas, flutes, bells and shells blown like trumpets. Aztec musicians also played a two-tone wooden drum, called a *teponaztli*, to provide a lively beat for dancing. Stringed instruments were unknown until after the Spanish conquest.

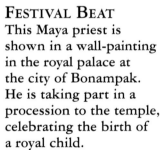

FESTIVAL BEAT
This Maya priest is shown in a wall-painting in the royal palace at the city of Bonampak. He is taking part in a procession to the temple, celebrating the birth of a royal child.

AN AZTEC ORCHESTRA
Musicians played conch shells, rattles and drums while crowds of worshippers sang and danced in the main square of Tenochtitlan.

AN AZTEC RATTLE

You will need: self-drying clay, modeling tool, plastic wrap, water bowl, dried melon seeds, bamboo cane, white and terra cotta paint, paintbrush, water container, feather, white glue, glue brush.

1 Make a solid model gourd from self-drying clay. You can copy the shape shown above. When it is dry, wrap the "gourd" completely in plastic wrap.

2 Cover the wrapped model gourd with an outer layer of self-drying clay about ¾ in. thick. Smooth the clay with water to give an even surface.

3 Let the outer layer of clay get hard but not completely solid. Cut it in half with the thin end of the modeling tool and remove the model gourd.

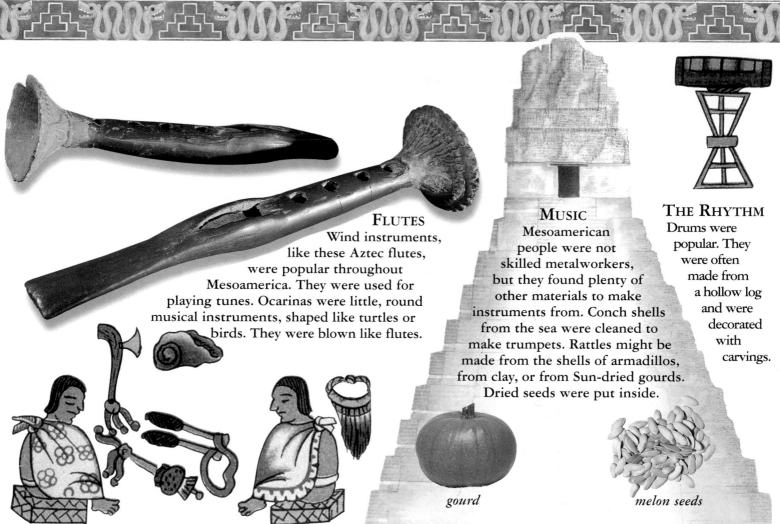

FLUTES
Wind instruments, like these Aztec flutes, were popular throughout Mesoamerica. They were used for playing tunes. Ocarinas were little, round musical instruments, shaped like turtles or birds. They were blown like flutes.

MUSIC
Mesoamerican people were not skilled metalworkers, but they found plenty of other materials to make instruments from. Conch shells from the sea were cleaned to make trumpets. Rattles might be made from the shells of armadillos, from clay, or from Sun-dried gourds. Dried seeds were put inside.

gourd

melon seeds

THE RHYTHM
Drums were popular. They were often made from a hollow log and were decorated with carvings.

INSTRUMENTS
This picture from a codex shows two Aztec musicians with some of the instruments they played: a conch shell trumpet, dried-gourd rattles, and flutes made from clay. Some of the instruments are decorated with tassels and bows.

JUMPING FOR JOY
These pictures from an Aztec codex show a rattle-player, a drummer and a juggler. Acrobats, jugglers and contortionists performed at many joyful festivals, such as harvest-time celebrations.

4 Cover the edge of one half of the hollow gourd with wet clay. Put dry seeds or beans inside and a cane through the middle. Press the halves together.

5 When it is dry, decorate the rattle with painted patterns, and push a feather in the top of the bamboo cane. Coat the rattle with white glue for a shiny finish.

Gourd-shaped rattles were very popular instruments in Mesoamerica. The seeds inside the dried gourds would provide the rattle sound. Codex pictures often show people carrying rattles in processions. The rattles were often decorated with feathers.

Sports and Games

MESOAMERICAN PEOPLE enjoyed sports and games after work and on festival days. Two favorite games were *tlachtli* or *ulama*, the famous Mesoamerican ball game, and *patolli*, a board game. The ball game was played in front of huge crowds, while *patolli* was a quieter game. Mesoamerican games were not just for fun. Both the ball game and *patolli* had religious meanings. In the first, the court symbolized the world, and the rubber ball stood for the sun as it made its daily journey across the sky. Players were meant to keep the ball moving in order to give energy to the sun. Losing teams were sometimes sacrificed as offerings to the sun god. In *patolli*, the movement of markers on the board represented the passing years.

PATOLLI
A group of Aztecs are shown here playing the game of *patolli*. It was played by moving dried beans or clay counters along a cross-shaped board with 52 squares. It could be very exciting. Players often bet on the results.

THE ACROBAT
This Olmec statue shows a very supple acrobat. Mesoamericans admired youth, fitness and beauty. Sports were fun, but they could also be good training for the demands of war. Being fit was considered attractive.

FLYING MEN
Volador was a ceremony performed on religious festival days. Four men, dressed as birds and attached to ropes, jumped off a high pole. As they spun around, falling toward the ground, they circled the pole 13 times each. That made 52 circuits—the length of the Mesoamerican holy calendar cycle.

PLAY PATOLLI

You will need: thick cardboard, pencil, ruler, black felt tip pen, paints, small paintbrush, water container, colored papers, scissors, dried beans, self-drying clay, white glue and glue brush.

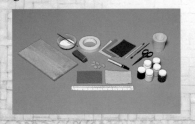

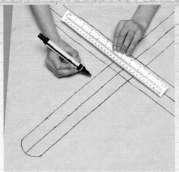

1 Measure a square of thick cardboard about 20 in. x 20 in. Using a felt tip pen and a ruler, draw three lines from corner to corner to make a cross-shape.

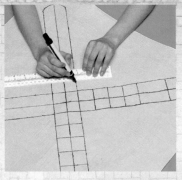

2 Draw seven pairs of spaces along each arm. The thirdspace in from the end should be a double space. Paint triangles in it.

3 Draw eight jaguar heads and eight marigold flowers on different colored paper. Cut them out. Paint the face of the sun god in the center.

TARGET RING

This stone ring comes from Chichen-Itza. Ball game players used only their hips and knees to hit a solid rubber ball through rings like this fixed high on the ball-court walls.

ALL DRESSED UP

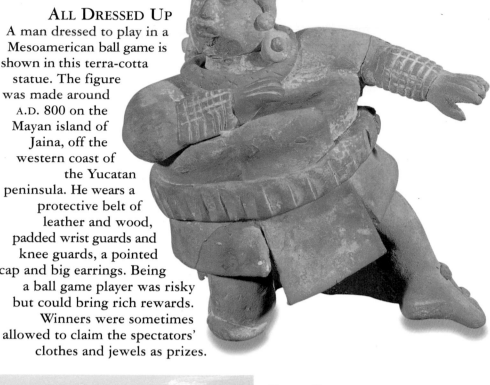

A man dressed to play in a Mesoamerican ball game is shown in this terra-cotta statue. The figure was made around A.D. 800 on the Mayan island of Jaina, off the western coast of the Yucatan peninsula. He wears a protective belt of leather and wood, padded wrist guards and knee guards, a pointed cap and big earrings. Being a ball game player was risky but could bring rich rewards. Winners were sometimes allowed to claim the spectators' clothes and jewels as prizes.

PLAY BALL

The ruins of a huge ball court can still be seen in the Maya city of Uxmal. The biggest courts were up to 65½ yards long and were built next to temples, in the centers of cities. People crowded inside the court to watch. Play was fast, furious and dangerous. Many players were injured as they clashed with opponents.

4 Stick the jaguars and marigolds randomly on the board. Paint a blue circle at the end of one arm, and a crown at the opposite end. Repeat in green.

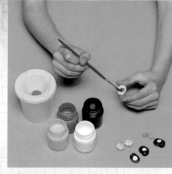

5 Paint five dried beans black with a white dot in the middle of one side. The beans will be thrown as dice. Make two markers. Paint one green and one blue.

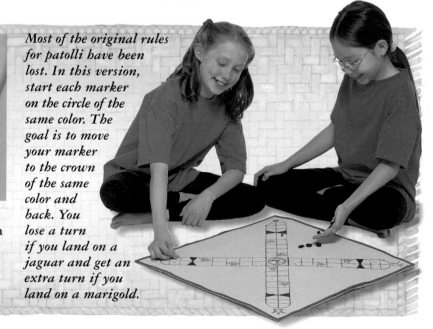

Most of the original rules for patolli have been lost. In this version, start each marker on the circle of the same color. The goal is to move your marker to the crown of the same color and back. You lose a turn if you land on a jaguar and get an extra turn if you land on a marigold.

Myths, Legends and Omens

THE AZTECS lived in constant fear that their world might come to an end. Ancient legends told that this had happened four times before. Each time, the world had been born again. Yet Aztec priests and astrologers did not believe that this would happen the next time. If the world ended a fifth time, it would be forever. The souls of all Aztec people would be banished to a dark, gloomy underworld. The Wind of Knives would cut the flesh from their bones, and living skeletons would feast and dance with the Lord of the Dead. Then the Aztecs would vanish forever when they reached Mictlan (hell).

The Maya told similar stories about the underworld—which they called Xibalba (the Place of Fright) in a great epic poem, the Popol Vuh. This poem featured two brothers called the Hero Twins.

Aztec legends also told that the end of the world would be heralded by strange signs. In A.D. 1519 these gloomy prophecies seemed to be coming true. Ruler Moctezuma II had weird, worrisome dreams. Astronomers also observed eclipses of the sun and a moving comet with a fiery tail.

FEATHERED SERPENT
Quetzalcoatl was an ancient god-king. His name meant feathered-serpent. He was worshipped by many Mesoamerican people, but especially by the Toltecs. They believed that he had sacrificed himself to help his people. A Toltec legend said that one day he would return, heralding the end of the world.

HEROS AND LEGENDS
This court is in Copan, Guatemala. The ball game featured in many Maya legends about the Hero Twins. They were skilled ball game players and also expert hunters with deadly blow guns.

CREATURES OF LEGEND

This Maya bowl is decorated with a picture of a spider monkey. Many different kinds of monkeys lived in the rainforests of Mesoamerica. Monkey-gods played an important part in Maya myths and legends. Because monkeys were quick and clever, the Maya believed that monkey-gods protected clever people, like scribes.

THE NEW FIRE CEREMONY

Every 52 years, the Aztecs believed that the world might come to an end. To stop this from happening, they held a special ceremony. People put out their fires and stayed indoors. At sunset, priests climbed to the top of a hill and waited for the planet Venus to appear in the sky. At the moment it appeared, a captive was sacrificed to the gods. His heart was ripped out and a fire lit in his chest. The priests then sent messengers all over the Aztec lands, carrying torches to relight the fires. People then believed the world was safe for another 52 years.

HEAVENLY MESSENGER

The ruler Moctezuma is shown here observing the brilliant comet that appeared in the Mexican sky in 1519. Aztec people carefully studied the stars for messages from the gods. They remembered the old Toltec legend that said that one day the god Quetzalcoatl would return and bring the world to an end.

AZTEC HERITAGE

Many Aztec and Mayan traditions still survive today. Millions of people speak Nahuatl (the Aztecs' language) or Mayan languages. Aztec and Mayan beliefs have mingled with Christian traditions to create new religious festivals. The most famous of these festivals is the Day of the Dead. Families bring presents of flowers and candies shaped like skulls to their ancestors' graves.

The Coming of the Spanish

IN 1493, the explorer Christopher Columbus arrived back in Spain from his pioneering voyage across the Atlantic Ocean. He told tales of an extraordinary "new world" full of gold. Excited by Columbus' stories, a group of Spanish soldiers sailed to Mexico in 1519, hoping to make their fortunes. They were led by a nobleman called Hernan Cortes. Together with the Aztecs' enemies, he led a march on Tenochtitlan. For the next two years, the Aztecs fought to stop Cortes and his soldiers from taking over their land. At first, they had some success, driving the Spaniards out of Tenochtitlan in May, 1520. Then, in 1521, Cortes attacked the city again, set fire to its buildings and killed around three-quarters of the population. In 1535, Mexico became a colony, ruled by officials sent from Spain.

A similar thing happened in Mayan lands, but more slowly. The Spanish first landed there in 1523. They did not conquer the last independent city-state, Tayasal, until 1697.

AGAINST THE AZTECS
This picture comes from *The History of the Indies*. It was written by Diego Duran, a Spanish friar who had sympathy for the Aztecs. Spanish soldiers and their allies from Tlaxcalla are seen fighting against the Aztecs. Although the Aztecs fought bravely, they had no chance of defeating Spanish soldiers mounted on horseback and armed with guns.

A SAD NIGHT
On May 6, 1520, Spanish soldiers massacred Aztecs gathered for a religious festival in Tenochtitlan. The citizens were outraged and attacked the Spaniards, many of whom died. During this night, the emperor Moctezuma II was stoned to death, probably by Aztecs who believed he had betrayed them. Cortes called this the *Noche Triste* (sad night).

THE END OF AZTEC POWER
This Aztec picture shows the surrender of Cuauhtemoc, the last Aztec king, to Cortes. After Moctezuma II died in 1520, the Aztecs were led by two of Moctezuma's descendants—Cuitlahuac, who ruled for only one year, and Cuauhtemoc. He was the last king and reigned until 1524.

RUNNING FOR THEIR LIVES

This illustration from a Spanish manuscript shows Aztec people fleeing from Spanish conquerors. You can see heavily-burdened porters carrying stocks of food and household goods across a river to safety. On the far bank, mothers and children, with a pet bird and dog, hide behind huge maguey cactus plants.

WORKING LIKE SLAVES

Spanish settlers in Mexico took over all the Aztec and Mayan fields and forced the people to work as farm laborers. They treated them cruelly, almost like slaves. This modern picture shows a Spanish overseer giving orders.

AFTER THE CONQUEST

Mexican artist Diego Rivera shows Mesoamerica after the Spanish conquest. Throughout the 1500s and 1600s, settlers from Spain arrived there. They drove out the local nobles and forced ordinary people to work for them. Spanish missionaries tried to replace local beliefs with European customs and Christianity. In Tenochtitlan, the Spaniards pulled down splendid Aztec palaces and temples to build churches and fine homes for themselves. You can see gangs of Aztec men working as laborers in the background of this picture.

Glossary

A

adobe Sun-dried mud bricks, used as a building material.

ahaw One of the special names the Maya gave to their rulers.

amaranth A bushy plant with edible seeds.

amate Paper made from fig tree bark.

ancestors Those from whom a person descended.

atlatl A spear-thrower, made of wood. It acted as an extension of the arm, so that the spears could be thrown with greater force.

Aztecs Mesoamerican people who lived in central Mexico. Their civilization existed between A.D. 1350 and A.D. 1520.

B

ball court The place where the Mesoamerican ball game was played. A large, open courtyard surrounded by rows of stone seats.

barter Exchanging goods for others of equal value.

C

calpulli An Aztec family or neighborhood group. The *calpulli* enforced law and order. It also arranged education, training and welfare benefits for its members.

causeway A roadway raised above the surrounding land or water.

cenote A holy waterhole, or natural well occurring in limestone areas. In some of them captives or other valuable possessions were sacrificed as offerings to the gods.

Chacmool A stone statue in the shape of a warrior or a rain god, carrying a dish in his arms. The dish was used to hold blood or hearts from human sacrifices. Chacmool statues have been found in many Mesoamerican lands.

chalcedony A bluish-white semiprecious stone.

chia A bushy plant with edible seeds.

chinampa An Aztec garden built on the fertile, reclaimed land on the lake shore.

chultun An underground tank for storing water.

cihuacoatl The Aztecs' name for their deputy leader.

clan A group of people related to one another through their ancestors or by marriage.

cochineal A red dye made from crushed beetles.

codex A folding book.

compost Rotting vegetation used to make the soil fertile.

conch shell The huge horn-shaped shell of a tropical sea creature. It was used as a musical instrument in Mesoamerican lands.

D

dugout canoe A type of canoe made by hollowing out a tree trunk.

G

garrison A band of soldiers living in a particular place.

glyph A picture-symbol used in the Mesoamerican system of writing.

H

herbalism Trying to heal people with medicines made of herbs.

Huastecs Mesoamerican people who lived on the gulf coast of Mexico. They were most powerful between around A.D. 500 and A.D. 1400.

huautli A bush with edible seeds.

human sacrifice Killing humans as an offering to the gods.

I

inscribed Letters or pictures carved on stone or another hard material.

J

jade A smooth, green stone. Jade was highly prized in Mesoamerica.

K

katun A Mayan measurement of time—72,000 days.

L

litter A portable bed on which Mesoamerican rulers were carried.

loom A piece of equipment used to weave cloth.

M

macehualtin The Aztec name for ordinary people.

mahk'ina One of the special names the Maya gave to their rulers.

maquahuitl An Aztec war-club.

Maya Mesoamerican people who lived in south-eastern Mexico, Guatemala and Belize. The Maya lands were conquered by the Spanish between AD1524 and AD1546.

Mixtecs Mesoamerican people who lived in southern Mexico.

mosaic Tiny pieces of stone, shell or glass used to decorate objects.

O

obsidian A black, glassy stone. It is produced when volcanoes erupt.

ocarina A musical instrument played by blowing into it.

overseer A supervisor or boss.

Olmecs A Mesoamerican people who lived in southern central Mexico. Their civilization existed between 1200BC and 400BC.

P

patolli A popular Aztec boardgame.

peccary A wild pig.

peninsula An area of land surrounded by sea on three sides, making it almost like an island.

plaza A big open space in the centre of a town or city.

pochteca Aztec merchants.

pulque An Aztec fermented drink.

Q

quetzal A rainforest bird with beautiful, long, green tail-feathers.

R

rock-crystal A transparent, semi-precious stone.

S

silt Fine grains of soil found at the bottom of rivers and lakes.

slash and burn A method of farming in the rainforest.

slip Clay mixed with water and minerals to form a liquid. It was used to decorate pottery.

stela A tall stone pillar.

sting-ray A fish with a long, poisonous spike in its tail.

stucco Plaster used to cover and decorate important stone buildings, such as temples.

T

tamales Dumplings made of corn with a meat or vegetable filling.

terracotta Baked clay.

tlachtli The Aztec name for the ballgame played throughout Mesoamerica.

tlatoani The Aztec name for their ruler.

Toltecs Mesoamerican people who lived in and around Tula, a city in central Mexico. Their civilization existed from around AD950 to AD1150.

tortillas Corn pancakes.

tribute Taxes paid in goods by conquered people.

tumpline A band of cloth, worn over the shoulders. The tumpline helped porters carry heavy loads.

turquoise A beautiful blue-green semi-precious stone.

U

uictli A Mesoamerican digging stick used like a spade.

V

volador An Aztec religious ritual in which four men spun around and around a tall pole.

Y

yucca A desert plant with long, fleshy leaves.

INCAS

*The world of the Incas and their ancestors, including
the Nazca, Moche and Chimú, was filled with
fabulous golden treasure. The Incas became rulers of
the most spectacular empire America has ever seen.
People lived in villages and towns, and built stepped
pyramid-platforms and temples.*

PHILIP STEELE

CONSULTANT:
DR. PENNY DRANSART

Peoples of the Andes

SNOWY PEAKS AND GLACIERS rim the skyline above high, open plateaus. Cold lakes reflect the blue sky. These are the South American Andes, stretching for about 4,700 miles from Colombia to southern Chile. To the west, plains and deserts border the Pacific Ocean. To the east, steamy rainforests surround the Amazon River.

Humans settled here in about 11,000 B.C., or even earlier. Their ancestors crossed into North America from Asia and moved south. As the climate became warmer, tribes settled in the Andes and on the coast. They learned to farm and build villages. From about 1000 B.C., the seven civilizations of the Parácas, Chavín, Nazca, Moche, Tiwanaku, Wari and Chimú rose and fell. Last of all, from around A.D. 1100 to 1532, came the Inca Empire.

WORKERS OF GOLD
Hollow golden hands from a Chimú tomb may have been used as incense holders. The Chimú people came to power in northern Peru about 400 years before the Incas. Their smiths became very skilled at working gold. These craftsmen were later employed by the Incas.

IN THE HIGH ANDES
Alpacas cross a snowfield, high in the Andes. These woolly animals are related to the South American llama, guanaco and vicuña. Their wild ancestors may have been tamed in the Andes as early as 5400 B.C. Herding and farming were developed by the Incas with great skill.

DIGGING UP THE PAST
Archaeologists work near Sipán, in Peru's Lambayeque Valley. Burials of a warrior-priest and of Moche royalty, dating from about A.D. 300, have been found there. The ancient Andean peoples kept no written records, so all we know of them comes from archaeology.

TIMELINE 11,000 B.C.–A.D. 1

Thousands of years before the Inca Empire was founded, people had settled on the Peruvian coast and in the Andes. The ruins of their cities and temples still stood in Inca times. They were part of the Inca world.

*c.*11,000 B.C. People settle at Monte Verde, Chile.

*c.*10,000 B.C. Stone tools are in use in Peru.

*c.*9000 B.C. The climate becomes warmer, and glaciers retreat.

stone tools

*c.*8600 B.C. Beans, bottle gourds and chile peppers are cultivated.

*c.*7500 B.C. Guanaco, vicuña and deer become common in the Andes and are hunted for food.

*c.*5400 B.C. Alpacas, and probably llamas, are herded.

Farming spreads along the coast and in the highlands.

*c.*4500 B.C. Andean farmers cultivate squash.

llama

*c.*3800 B.C. Corn, manioc and cotton are grown in the Andes.

*c.*3500 B.C. Llamas are used as pack animals to transport goods.

*c.*3200–1500 B.C. Mummification is used to preserve the bodies of dead people in the north of Chile.

*c.*2800 B.C. Pottery is made in Ecuador and in Colombia.

*c.*2600 B.C. Temples are built on platform mounds on the Peruvian coast.

11,000 B.C.   8600 B.C.   3800 B.C.   2500 B.C.

NAZCA PUZZLES

Mysterious markings on the ground were made on the desert on a gigantic scale by the Nazca people. Their civilization grew up on the coast of southern Peru, a thousand years before the Incas. The lines may have marked out routes for religious processions.

VALLEY OF MYSTERY

The Urubamba River winds through steep, forested gorges. In 1911, an American archaeologist named Dr. Hiram Bingham came to the area in search of Inca ruins. He discovered a lost city on the slopes of Machu Picchu, high above the river valley.

ANCIENT PEOPLES

This man is one of the Aymara people who live around Lake Titicaca, on the high border between Peru and Bolivia. Some historians believe they are descended from the builders of a great city called Tiwanaku. Others say that they arrived from the Cañete Valley after Tiwanaku was abandoned in about 1250. Although their way of life has changed over the ages, the Aymara have kept a distinctive identity.

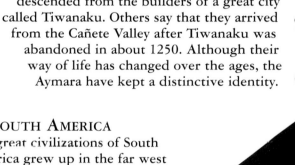

IN SOUTH AMERICA

The great civilizations of South America grew up in the far west of the continent. The area is now occupied by the modern countries of Colombia, Ecuador, Peru, Bolivia, Chile and Argentina.

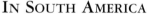

---

c.2500 B.C. A temple with stepped platforms is built at El Paraíso on the coast of Peru.

Backstrap looms are used.

Potatoes and *kinua* are cultivated.

There is widespread fishing along the Peruvian coast and the northern coast of Chile.

kinua   Andean farmers use irrigation.

backstrap loom

c.2000 B.C. The farming of corn, which first developed on the south-central coast and the north coast, is now widespread along the Peruvian coast and in the highlands.

c.1800 B.C. Pottery-making develops along the coast of Peru.

c.1500 B.C. Metal-working develops in Peru.

c.1000 B.C. Large-scale settlement takes place in the Andes.

c.900 B.C. The Chavín culture develops. The temple complex at Chavín de Huantar is built.

c.700 B.C. The Parácas culture begins to thrive.

c.200 B.C. The Chavín culture comes to an end.

The Nazca culture develops on the coast of southern Peru. Gigantic Nazca lines are marked on the surface of the deserts.

Chavín stone head

2000 B.C.   900 B.C.   A.D. 1

The Great Empire

WHO WERE THE INCAS and where did they come from? If you had asked them, they would have told you proudly that their first great ruler, Manko Qapaq, was sent to earth by his father Inti, the sun. Manko Qapaq's queen, Mama Okllo, was believed to be the daughter of the moon.

The Incas believed that they were superior to all other peoples. In reality, they were just the last link in a long chain of civilizations. They shared many beliefs with these peoples, often taking over their technology and crafts. From their mountain homeland, they learned how to live in the same landscapes and make use of them, ruling coast, desert and rainforest. The Incas started out as just one of many small tribes living in the Peruvian Andes in the 1100s. In the 1300s, led by their ruler Mayta Qapaq, they began to conquer neighboring lands. During the 1400s, Inca armies and officials created a huge empire. Although the Incas themselves only numbered about 40,000, they ruled a total population of about 12 million. Of the 20 languages that were spoken in the Inca Empire, the most important was Quechua, which is still widely spoken in the Andes mountains today.

This vast empire seemed as if it would last for ever. In 1532, something happened to change that. Spanish soldiers landed in Peru, greedy for gold and land.

Moche stirrup-spout po

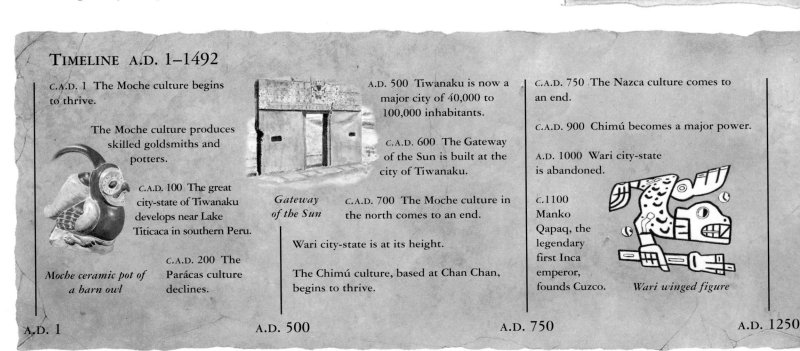

TIMELINE A.D. 1–1492

c.A.D. 1 The Moche culture begins to thrive.

The Moche culture produces skilled goldsmiths and potters.

c.A.D. 100 The great city-state of Tiwanaku develops near Lake Titicaca in southern Peru.

Moche ceramic pot of a barn owl

c.A.D. 200 The Parácas culture declines.

Gateway of the Sun

A.D. 500 Tiwanaku is now a major city of 40,000 to 100,000 inhabitants.

c.A.D. 600 The Gateway of the Sun is built at the city of Tiwanaku.

c.A.D. 700 The Moche culture in the north comes to an end.

Wari city-state is at its height.

The Chimú culture, based at Chan Chan, begins to thrive.

c.A.D. 750 The Nazca culture comes to an end.

c.A.D. 900 Chimú becomes a major power.

A.D. 1000 Wari city-state is abandoned.

*c.*1100 Manko Qapaq, the legendary first Inca emperor, founds Cuzco.

Wari winged figure

A.D. 1   A.D. 500   A.D. 750   A.D. 1250

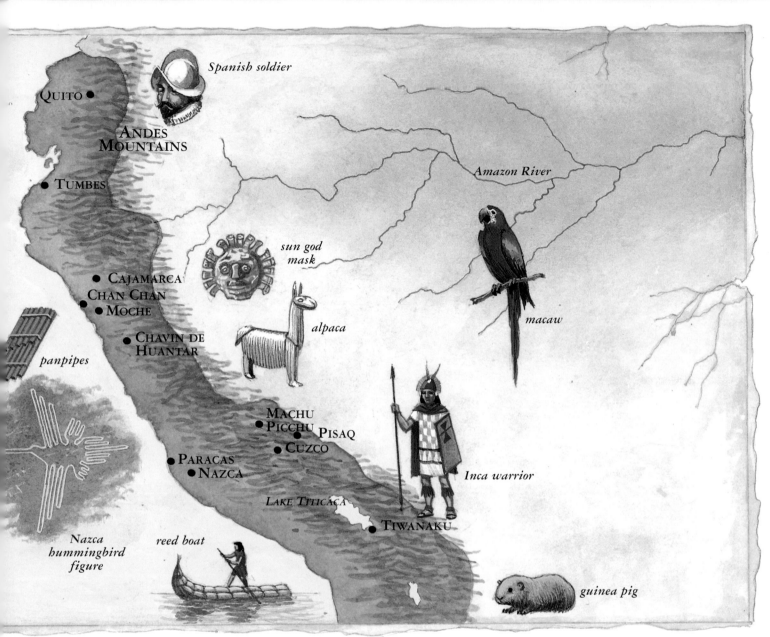

Spanish soldier

QUITO

ANDES MOUNTAINS

TUMBES

Amazon River

sun god mask

CAJAMARCA
CHAN CHAN
MOCHE

CHAVIN DE HUANTAR

panpipes

alpaca

macaw

MACHU PICCHU
PISAQ
CUZCO

Inca warrior

PARACAS
NAZCA

LAKE TITICACA

TIWANAKU

Nazca hummingbird figure

reed boat

guinea pig

c.1250 The once-great city of Tiwanaku is abandoned, perhaps because of changes in the climate.

c.1300 Sinchi Roka is the first emperor to use the title *Sapa Inca*.

1370 Chimor, the empire of the Chimú people, expands.

c.1410 The Incas make new alliances under the emperor Wiraqocha.

1437 Wiraqocha's son Yupanki conquers the mountain state of Chanca.

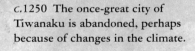

Chimú gold funeral mask

1438 Wiraqocha backs another son, Urqon, as the next emperor.

Yupanki proclaims himself emperor of a rival Inca State and renames himself Pachakuti.

Urqon is killed, and his father Wiraqocha dies.

The Inca State is reunited under Pachakuti.

c.1440 The powerful emperor, Minchançaman, rules Chimú.

c.1445 Pachakuti's brother, Qapaq Yupanki, explores the coastline to the south.

c.1450 Incas build Machu Picchu high in the Andes.

1450 The Inca Empire grows by conquest. Cuzco is rebuilt.

1470 Incas conquer Chimor.

1471 Topa Inka Yupanki becomes emperor. A great age of road building begins.

Chimú ritual knife

A.D. 1438

A.D. 1445

A.D. 1492

Makers of History

Because Inca history was not written down at the time, much of it has to be pieced together from chronicles and diaries recorded in the years after the Spanish conquest in the 1500s. Many accounts describe the everyday lives of ordinary people in the days of the Inca Empire. The names of the people who dug the fields and built the roads are mostly forgotten. Only the names of the Inca royal family and the nobles are known.

The first eight emperors recalled in Inca folklore probably did exist. However, over the centuries, their life stories, passed on from parent to child over generations, became mixed up with myths and legends. The last 100 years of Inca rule, beginning when Pachakuti Inka Yupanki came to the throne in 1438, were fresh in people's memories when the Spanish invaded. As a result, we know a good deal about the greatest days of the Inca Empire.

MAMA OKLLO
This painting from the 1700s imagines the Inca empress, Mama Okllo, carrying a moon mask. She reigned in the 1100s. In some Inca myths, she and her brother Manko Qapaq were said to be the children of the sun and the moon. Mama Okllo married her brother, who became the first ruler of the Incas. They had a son named Sinchi Roka.

ON THE ROAD TO RUIN
An Inca emperor and empress are carried around their empire. The Inca rulers had almost unlimited power, but were destroyed by bitter rivalry within the royal family. When the Spanish invaders arrived in 1532, Tawantinsuyu was divided between supporters of Waskar and his brother Ataw Wallpa.

TIMELINE A.D. 1492–1781

1492 The Incas conquer northern Chile.

1493 Wayna Qapaq becomes emperor.

1498 Wayna Qapaq conquers part of Colombia and the Inca Empire reaches its greatest extent.

c.1523 A ship-wrecked Spaniard named Alejo García enters Inca territory from the east with raiding Chiriquana warriors. He dies during his return journey.

quipu used for government records

1525 Wayna Qapaq dies without an agreed successor. His son Waskar is chosen and crowned as the twelfth *Sapa Inca* in Cuzco. Waskar's brother, Ataw Wallpa, claims the imperial throne.

War breaks out in the Inca Empire, as the brothers battle for power.

1526–7 A Spanish naval expedition sights Inca rafts off the Pacific coast.

Inca warrior

1529 The Spanish king approves a plan by Francisco Pizarro to conquer Peru.

1532 Waskar is defeated by his brother Ataw Wallpa.

The Spanish, under Francisco Pizarro, enter the inland city of Cajamarca and kill 7,000 Incas.

1533 Ataw Wallpa and his sister, Asarpay, are killed by the Spanish.

Inca rope bridge

A.D. 1492   A.D. 1525   A.D. 1529   A.D. 1535

LLOQE YUPANKI

The son of Sinchi Roka, Lloqe Yupanki was chosen to be ruler of the lands around Cuzco instead of his older brother. He was a wise ruler, and his reign in the 1200s was peaceful. His son Mayta Qapaq was more warlike. He expanded his empire by conquering neighboring peoples.

PACHAKUTI INKA YUPANKI (REIGNED 1438–71)

Inka Yupanki was still a prince when he proved himself in war by conquering the Chanca people. However, his father Wiraqocha chose another son, Inka Urqon, as the next emperor. Yupanki claimed the throne, calling himself Pachakuti, which means "the world turned upside down." Urqon was killed, and his father died soon after.

ATAW WALLPA (REIGNED 1532–3)

Known as Atahuallpa or Atabaliba to the Spanish, Ataw Wallpa was the son of the great emperor Wayna Qapaq, who died unexpectedly in 1525. When his brother Waskar was crowned in Cuzco, Ataw Wallpa stayed with the army in the north, and a bitter war followed. By 1532, Waskar had been imprisoned, and Ataw Wallpa was ruler. But before the empire could recover from the war, the Spanish invaded. Ataw Wallpa was captured and executed the following summer.

FRANCISCO PIZARRO (c.1478–1541)

In 1532, this Spanish soldier sailed to the Inca city of Tumbes with just 180 men and 37 horses. They marched inland to Cajamarca. Pizarro used treachery to capture and kill the Inca emperor, Ataw Wallpa. This army went on to loot Inca gold and bring Peru under Spanish rule. Resistance from the local people was fierce—but not as fierce as the rivalry and greed of the Spanish. Pizarro was murdered by one of his fellow countrymen fewer than ten years later.

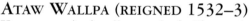

1535 The Incas rebel against Spain.

1536 Incas lay siege to the city of Cuzco. The city is burned to the ground by the Incas.

The Inca Empire collapses.

1537 A last Inca State is formed by Cura Okllo and Manko Inka, based at Vilcabamba.

1538 The Spanish invaders fight among themselves at Las Salinas, near Cuzco.

Inca messenger with conch shell

1539 Cura Okllo, the successor to Asarpay and the sister-wife of Manko Inka, is executed by the Spanish.

1541 Pizarro is assassinated.

1545 Manko Inka is assassinated.

1572 Inca resistance under Tupac Amaru I is finally defeated, and he is executed. He is the last Inca ruler.

Vilcabamba and Machu Picchu are abandoned.

1742 Resistance to the Spanish grows. Calls for restoration of the Inca Empire.

1780 Major uprising of indigenous peoples under José Gabriel Condorcanqui He adopts the name of his ancestor and declares himself Tupac Amaru II. He aims to restore the Inca Empire.

1781 Tupac Amaru II is captured and tortured to death.

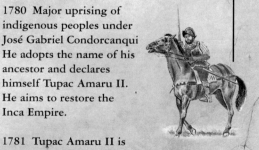

Spanish conquistador

A.D. 1539

A.D. 1742

A.D. 1781

Lords of the Sun

MANY OF THE EARLY TRIBES that lived in the Andes and on the Pacific coast were small groups of hunters and farmers. As cities and kingdoms grew in size, they began to need strong leadership. By about A.D. 900, the state of Chimor was headed by powerful kings.

The Inca emperor was called *Sapa Inca* (Only Leader). As a descendant of the sun, he was regarded as a god. He had complete power over his subjects, but he always had to be on his guard. There were many rivals for the throne among his royal relations. Each emperor had a new palace built for himself in the royal city of Cuzco. Emperors were treated with the utmost respect at all times and were often veiled or screened from ordinary people.

The empress, or *Quya* (Star), was the emperor's sister or mother. She was also thought to be divine and led the worship of the moon goddess. The next emperor was supposed to be chosen from among her sons. An emperor had many secondary wives. Waskar was said to have fathered eighty children in just eight years.

RELIGIOUS LEADERS
Sacrifices of llamas were made to the gods each month, at special festivals and before battle. The *Sapa Inca* controlled all religious activities. In the 1400s, the emperor Wiraqocha Inka declared that worship of the god Wiraqocha, the Creator (after whom he was named), was more important than worship of Inti, the sun god. This made some people angry.

A CHOSEN WOMAN
Young girls, the *akllakuna*, were educated for four years in religious matters, weaving and housekeeping. Some became the emperor's secondary wives or married noblemen. Others became priestesses or *mamakuna* (virgins of the sun). Figurines like this wore specially made clothes, but these have perished or been lost over the years.

A FEATHER FAN
You will need: pencil, card stock, ruler, scissors, paints in bright colors, paintbrush, water container, masking tape, batting, white glue, burlap or sackcloth, needle, thread, string or twine.

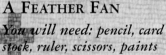

1 Draw a feather shape 1-in. long onto card stock and cut it out. The narrow part should be half of this length. Trace the shape on card stock nine times.

2 Carefully paint the feathers with bright colors. Use red, orange and yellow to look like rainforest birds. Let the paint dry completely.

3 Cut out each feather and snip along the sides of the widest part to give a feathery effect. When the paint is dry, paint the other side as well.

COMMANDER IN CHIEF

The emperor sits on his throne. He wears a tasselled wool headdress or *llautu*, decorated with gold and feathers, and large gold earplugs. He carries a scepter. Around him, army chiefs await their orders. Emperors played an active part in military campaigns and relied on the army to keep them in power.

COOL SPRINGS

At Tambo Machay, to the south of Cuzco, fresh, cold water is channeled from sacred springs. Here, the great Pachakuti Inka Yupanki would bathe after a hard day's hunting.

THE LIVING DEAD

The dead body of an emperor, preserved as a mummy, is paraded through the streets. When each emperor died, his palace became his tomb. Once a year, the body was carried around Cuzco amid great celebrations. The picture is by Guamán Poma de Ayala, who was of Inca descent. In the 1600s, he made many pictures of Inca life.

Feathers from birds of the tropical forests to the east of the Andes were used to make fans for the emperor.

4 Hold the narrow ends of the feathers and spread out the tops to form a fan shape. Use masking tape to secure the ends firmly in position.

5 Cut a rectangular piece of batting 3½ in. high and long enough to wrap around the bottom of the feathers several times. Use glue on one side to keep it in place.

6 Cut a strip of burlap or sackcloth about 2 in. wide. Starting at the bottom of the feathers, wrap the fabric around the stems. Hold it in place with a few stitches.

7 Wind string or twine firmly around the burlap to form the fan's handle. Tuck in the ends and use glue at each end to make sure they are secure.

The Inca State

FAMILY CONNECTIONS PLAYED an important part in royal power struggles and in everyday social organization in the Inca world. The nobles were grouped into family-based corporations called *panakas*. Members of each *panaka* shared rights to an area of land, its water, pasture and herds. Linked to each *panaka* was a land-holding *ayllu* (or clan)—a group of common people who were also related to each other.

The Incas managed to control an empire that contained many different peoples. Loyal Incas were sent to live in remote areas, while troublemakers from the regions were resettled nearer Cuzco, where they could be carefully watched. Conquered chiefs were called *kurakas*. They and their children were educated in Inca ways and allowed to keep some of their local powers.

The Inca system of law was quite severe. State officials and *kurakas* (conquered chiefs) acted as judges. Those who stole from the emperor's stores of grain, textiles and other goods faced a death sentence. Torture, beating, blinding and exile were all common punishments. The age of the criminal and the reason for the crime were sometimes taken into account.

A CLEVER CALCULATOR
One secret of Inca success was the *quipu*. It was used by government officials for recording all kinds of information, from the number of households in a town to the amount of goods of various kinds in a warehouse. The *quipu* was a series of strings tied to a thick cord. Each string had one or more colors and could be knotted. The colors represented anything from types of grain to groups of people. The knots represented numbers.

ONE STATE, MANY PEOPLES
The ancestors of these Bolivian women were subjects of the Incas. The Inca Empire was the largest ever known in all the Americas. It included at least a hundred different peoples. The Incas were clever governors and did not always try to force their own ideas upon other groups. Conquered peoples had to accept the Inca gods, but they were allowed to worship in their own way and keep their own customs.

A ROYAL INSPECTION

Topa Inka Yupanki inspects government stores in the 1470s. In the Inca world, nearly all grain, textiles and other goods were produced for the state and stored in warehouses. Some extra produce might be bartered, or exchanged privately, but there were no big markets or shops.

topaynga yupanqui

depocatos del ynga

PUBLIC WORKS

Laborers build fortifications on the borders of the Inca Empire. People paid their taxes to the Inca State in the form of labor called *mit'a*. This might be general work on the land. Men were also conscripted to work on public buildings or serve in the army. The Spanish continued to operate the *mit'a* as a form of tax long after they conquered the Inca Empire.

OLLANTAYTAMBO

This building in Ollantaytambo, in the Urubamba Valley, was once a state storehouse for the farm produce of the region. Ollantaytambo was a large town, which was probably built about 550 years ago. It protected the valley from raids by the warriors who lived in the forests to the east. Buildings dating from the Inca Empire were still being lived in by local people when the American archaeologist Dr. Hiram Bingham passed through in 1911.

Nobles and Peasants

INCA SOCIETY was strictly graded. At the top were the *Sapa Inca* and his *Quya*. The High Priest and other important officials were normally recruited from members of the royal family.

If noblemen were loyal to the emperor, they might receive gifts of land. They might be given gold or a beautiful *akllakuna* as a wife. They could expect jobs as regional governors, generals or priests. Lords and ladies wore fine clothes and were carried in splendid chairs, called litters.

Next in rank were the conquered non-Inca rulers and chiefs, the *kurakas*. They were cleverly brought into the Inca political system and given traditional honors. They served as regional judges.

Most people in the empire were peasants. They were unable to leave their villages without official permission. They had no choice but to stay and toil on the land, sending their produce to the government stores.

CRAFT AND CLASS
A pottery figure from the Peruvian coast shows a porter carrying a water pot on his back. In the Inca Empire, craft workers such as potters and goldsmiths were employed by the state. They formed a small middle class. Unlike peasants, they were never made to do *mit'a* (public service).

A MOCHE NOBLEMAN
The man's face on this jar is that of a noble. It was made by a Moche potter on the north coast of Peru between 1,500 and 2,000 years ago. The man's headdress sets him apart as a noble, perhaps a high priest.

A WATER JAR
You will need: self-drying clay, cutting board, rolling pin, ruler, water, water container, acrylic paints, paintbrush.

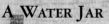

1 Roll out a piece of clay on the board. Make a circle about 6¾ in. in diameter and ½ in. thick. This will form the base of your water jar.

2 Roll some more clay into long sausages, about as fat as your little finger. Dampen the bottom with water and carefully place a sausage around the edge.

3 Coil more clay sausages on top of each other to build up the jar. Make each coil slightly smaller than the one below. Water will help them stick.

A PEASANT'S LIFE

A woman harvests potatoes near Sicuani, to the south of Cuzco. Then, as now, life was hard for the peasant farmers of the Andes. Both men and women worked in the fields, and even young children and the elderly were expected to help. However, the Inca State did provide some support for the peasants, supplying free grain in times of famine.

PLUGGED IN

This Chimú earplug is made of gold, turquoise and shell. It was worn as a badge of rank. Inca noblemen wore such heavy gold earplugs that the Spanish called them *orejones* (big ears). Noblewomen wore their hair long, covered with a head-cloth.

LAND AND SEASONS

One third of all land and produce belonged to the emperor, one third to the priests and one third to the peasants. It was hardly a fair division. A peasant's life, digging, planting and harvesting, was ruled by the seasons. Each new season was celebrated by religious festivals and ceremonies.

Children were expected to help their parents by fetching water from the wells and mountain springs.

4 When you reach the neck of the pot, start making the coils slightly bigger again to form a lip. Carefully smooth the coils with wet fingertips.

5 Use two more rolls of clay to make handles on opposite sides of the pot. Smooth out the seams carefully to make sure the handles stay in place.

6 Let the clay dry completely. Then paint the jar all over with a background color. Choose an earthy reddish brown to look like Inca pottery.

7 Let the reddish brown color dry. Use a fine paintbrush and black paint to draw Inca designs on the jar like the ones in the picture above.

On Land and Water

PERU TODAY is still criss-crossed by the remains of cobbled roads built by the Incas. Two main paved highways ran north to south, one following the coast and the other following the Andes. The first was about 2,200 miles long, the second even longer. The two roads were joined by smaller roads linking towns and villages. The roads crossed deserts, mountains and plateaus. Markers measured out distances in *topos*, units of about 4½ miles.

Despite these great engineering works, most people in the empire were not allowed to travel at all. These fine roads were strictly for use by people on official business. Messages to and from the emperor were carried by trained relay runners called *chasquis*, who were stationed in stone shelters along the way. In one day, a message could travel 150 miles. Government rest-houses called *tambos* were built on the chief routes.

The Incas were very inventive, but they had no wheeled transport. Baggage and goods were carried by porters or on the backs of llamas. Nobles traveled in richly decorated litters, carried by four or more men.

THE WATER CARRIER
A porter carries a jar on his head. Steep mountain roads must have made such work very tiring. The state road network allowed crops, food, drink, precious metal ores and textiles to be brought to the royal court from far-flung regions of the empire.

TRAVELING TO WAR
A litter, carried at shoulder height by four strong men, carries the emperor Wayna Qapaq to war. One purpose of the Inca road network was to make sure that armies could be moved quickly from one end of the empire to the other. Depots and food stores for army use were built along the highways. Depot managers were kept in a state of readiness by royal officials.

THE ROAD GOES ON
An old Inca road zigzags up steep, terraced slopes near Pisaq. Inca engineers laid down about 9,900 miles of roads in all. Some highway sections were up to 22 ft across. Most were just broad enough for a llama—about 3 ft wide. The steepest sections were stepped.

BOATS OF REEDS

These modern boats were made by the Uru people of Lake Titicaca. The Incas made boats and rafts for travel on lakes, rivers and the ocean. Because there was a shortage of timber in most areas, they made them from a type of reed called *totora*. These were cut, trimmed and tightly bound in bundles. They were light, buoyant and strong, and could be bent into curved shapes to form the prow and stern of a boat.

HIGHWAY PATROL

The governor of bridges watches as a porter carrying goods on his back crosses a rope bridge across a mountain river. Bridges had to be able to take considerable stress and strain, caused by the tramp of marching armies and by hundreds of heavily burdened llamas. Officials inspected roads and bridges and could order local workers to repair them under the *mit'a* system of conscripted labor.

BRIDGES OF ROPE

Rope bridges are still made from braided mountain grasses by the Quechua people. This one crosses a gorge of the Apurimac River in Peru. Inca engineers built long rope bridges like this one, as well as stone bridges, causeways over marshy ground and tunnels through rock. Sometimes people crossed rivers in baskets hauled across the water on ropes.

Master Masons

THE ROCKS of the Andes mountains provided high quality granite that was used for impressive public buildings. These included temples, fortresses, palaces, holy shrines and aqueducts (stone channels for carrying water supplies).

The *mit'a* labor system provided the workforce. In the quarries, massive rocks weighing up to 120 tons were cracked and shifted with stone hammers and bronze crowbars. They were hauled with ropes on log rollers or sleds. On site, the stones were shaped to fit and rubbed smooth with water and sand. Smaller stone blocks were used for upper walls or lesser buildings.

The expert Inca stonemasons had only basic tools. They used plumblines (weighted cords) to make sure that walls were straight. They used no mortar or cement, but the stones fitted together perfectly. Many remain in place to this day. Most public buildings were on a grand scale, but all were of a simple design.

BUILDING THE TEMPLE
These rectangular stone blocks were part of the holiest site in the Inca Empire, the *Coricancha* (Temple of the Sun). Inca stonework was deliberately designed to withstand the earthquakes that regularly shake the region. The original temple on this site was badly damaged by a tremor in 1650.

BRINGER OF WATER
This beautifully engineered stone water-channel was built across a valley floor by Inca stonemasons. Aqueducts, often covered, were used both for irrigation and for drinking supplies. Irrigation schemes were being built in Peru as early as around 4,500 years ago.

AN INCA GRANARY
You will need: ruler, pencil, beige, dark and cream card stock, scissors, white pencil, paints, paintbrush, water container, compass, masking tape, white glue, hay or straw.

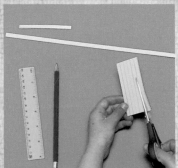

1 Use a ruler and pencil to mark eight strips 3½ in. long and ⅛ in. wide, and one strip 12½ in. long and ⅛ in. wide on beige card stock. Cut them out.

2 On the dark card stock, draw a curved shape 13½ in. along the base, 4½ in. in height and 12 in. along the top. Cut it out. Cut out a doorway 2½ in. high.

3 Paint another piece of card stock a stone color. Let it dry. Cut it into "blocks" about ¾ in. high. Glue them one by one onto the building shape.

HISTORY IN STONE

Stone walls and streets, such as these fine examples still standing in Ollantaytambo, survive to tell a story. Archaeology is much more difficult in the rainforests to the east, where timber structures rot rapidly in the hot, moist air. That is one reason we know more about the way people lived in the Andes than in the Amazon region.

INCA DESIGN

A building in Machu Picchu shows an example of typical Inca design. Inca stonemasons learned many of their skills from earlier Peruvian civilizations. Openings that are wider at the bottom than the top are seen only in Inca buildings. They are said to be trapezoid.

Storehouses were built of neat stone blocks. They kept precious grain dry and secure.

A MASSIVE FORTRESS

Llamas still pass before the mighty walls of Sacsahuaman, at Cuzco. This building was a fortress with towers and terraces. It also served as a royal palace and a sacred shrine. Its multi-sided boulders are precisely fitted. It is said to have been built over many years by 30,000 laborers. It was one of many public buildings raised in the reign of Pachakuti Inka Yupanki.

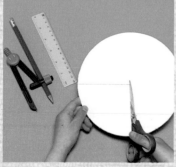

4 Use a compass to draw a circle 7 in. across on cream card stock. Cut it out and cut off one quarter. Tape the straight cut edges together to form a cone.

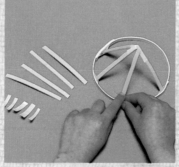

5 Make a circle by joining the ends of the 14½-in. strip with masking tape. Then attach the eight 3½-in. strips around the edge and in the middle as shown.

6 Glue short lengths of straw or hay all over the cardboard cone to form the thatched roof of the granary. The thatch should all run in the same direction.

7 Attach the edges of the walls with masking tape. Fold in the sides of the doorway. Place the rafters on top. The thatched roof fits on the rafters.

Town Dwellers

WATER ON TAP
At Machu Picchu, water was channeled into the town from the mountain springs that bubbled up about a mile outside the city walls. The water ran into stone troughs and fountains, and it was used for bathing and drinking.

GREAT CITIES had been built in Peru long before the Incas came to power. In about A.D. 600, the city of Tiwanaku, near Lake Titicaca, may have had a population of nearly 100,000. A hundred years later, the Chimú capital of Chan Chan covered 9½ square miles of the coastal plain.

The Inca capital, Cuzco, was ringed by mountains and crossed by two rivers that had been turned into canals, the Huatanay and the Tullamayo. Cuzco became dominated by fine public buildings and royal palaces when it was rebuilt in about 1450. At its center was the great public square, known as *Waqaypata* (Holy Place). At festival time, this square was packed with crowds. Roads passed from here to the four quarters of the empire. They were lined by the homes of Inca nobles, facing in upon private compounds called *canchas*. The center of the city was home to about 40,000 people, but the surrounding suburbs and villages housed another 200,000. Newer Inca towns, such as Pumpo, Huanuco and Tambo Colorado, were planned in much the same way as Cuzco, but adapted to the local landscape.

THE PAST REVEALED
Archaeologists record every detail of what they find with the greatest care. Here at an old Inca town near Cuzco, they are using precision instruments to note the exact position of everything they uncover. Excavations in Inca towns have unearthed pottery and jars, fragments of cloth, jewelry, knives and human burials. They are constantly adding to what we know about the Inca civilization.

STEEP STREETS
Machu Picchu was built on a steep slope, using *mit'a* labor. Some of its buildings were set into the rock, while many more were built on raised terraces of stone. Its streets had steps in many places. Incas may have fled to this mountain retreat from Cuzco after the Spanish invaded in 1532. It was abandoned within 40 years and soon covered by creepers and trees.

RUINS OF CHAN CHAN

Chan Chan, capital of Chimor, was built in the north, at the mouth of the Moche River. It was the biggest city of ancient Peru. Far from the granite of the Andes, Chan Chan was constructed with adobe (bricks made from sun-baked mud). The city was laid out in a grid pattern, with 36-ft-high compound walls marking out the homes of royalty, nobles and craft workers.

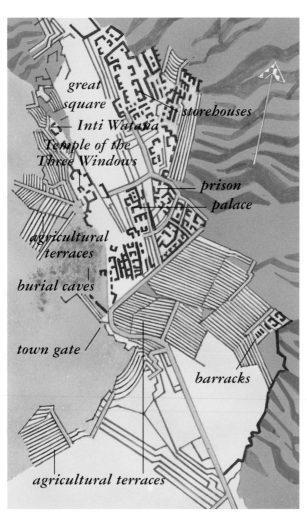

great square
storehouses
Inti Watana
Temple of the Three Windows
prison
palace
agricultural terraces
burial caves
town gate
barracks
agricultural terraces

LIVING IN THE CLOUDS

The small but spectacular Inca town of Machu Picchu clings to a high mountain ridge beneath the peak of Wayna Picchu. In about 1450, it had its own ceremonial square, temples and burial caves. The town also had army barracks, public stores, a prison, housing for craft workers and farmers, and a palace for visiting royalty. The town was defended from attack by a twin wall and a ditch.

A PLAN OF THE TOWN

The long and narrow layout of Machu Picchu was decided by its ridge-top location at 9,000 ft above sea level. The great square was the religious and political center of town.

An Inca House

A TYPICAL HOUSE in an Inca town such as Machu Picchu was built from blocks of stone. White granite was the best, being very hard and strong. The roof of each house was pitched at quite a steep angle, so that heavy mountain rains could drain off quickly. Timber roof beams were lashed to stone pegs on the gables, and supported a wooden frame. This was thatched with a tough grass called *ichu*.

Most houses had just one story, but a few had two or three, joined by rope ladders inside the house or by stone blocks set into the outside wall. Most had a single doorway hung with cloth or hide, and some had an open window on the gable end.

Each building was home to a single family and formed part of a compound. As many as half a dozen houses would be grouped around a shared courtyard. All the buildings belonged to families who were members of the same *ayllu*, or clan.

MUD AND THATCH
Various types of houses were to be seen in different parts of the Inca Empire. Many were built in old-fashioned or in regional styles. These round and rectangular houses in Bolivia are made of mud bricks (adobe). The houses are thatched with *ichu* grass.

upper story

inside hearth

courtyard

FLOATING HOMES
These houses are built by the Uru people, who fish in Lake Titicaca and hunt in the surrounding marshes. They live on the lake shore and also on floating islands made of matted *totora* reeds. Their houses are made of *totora* and *ichu* grass. Both these materials would have been used in the Titicaca area in Inca times. The reeds are collected from the shallows and piled onto the floor of the lake. New reeds are constantly added.

PICTURES AND POTTERY
Houses with pitched roofs and windows appear as part of the decoration on this pottery from Pacheco, Nazca. To find out about houses in ancient Peru, historians look at surviving towns and ruins, at housing styles still in use today and at old pictures and designs on objects.

SQUARE STONE, ROUND PEG
Squared-off blocks of stone are called ashlars. These white granite ashlars make up a wall in the Inca town of Pisaq. They are topped by a round stone peg. Pegs like these were probably used to support roof beams or other structures, such as ladders from one story to another.

gable

roofbeam

roof peg

wall niche

BUILDING MATERIALS
The materials used to build an Inca house depended on local supplies. Rock was the favorite material. White granite, dark basalt and limestone were used when possible. Away from the mountains, clay was made into bricks and dried hard in the sun to make adobe. Roof beams were formed from timber poles. Thatch was made of grass or reed.

clay

white granite

thatch

timber

BUILDING TO LAST
The Incas built simple, but solid, dwellings in the mountains. The massive boulders used for temples and fortresses are here replaced by smaller, neatly cut stones. See how the roof beams are lashed to the gables to support the thatch. Stone roofs were very rare, even on the grandest houses. Timber joists provide an upper story. The courtyard is used just as much as the inside of the house for everyday living.

Inside the Home

L ET'S VISIT THE HOME of an Inca mountain farmer. The outer courtyard is busy, with smoke rising from cooking pots into the fresh mountain air. An elderly woman stacks firewood, while her daughter sorts out bundles of alpaca wool. A young boy brings in a pot of fresh water, splashing the ground as he puts it down.

Pulling aside the cloth at the doorway, you blink in the dark and smoky atmosphere. Cooking has to be done indoors when the weather is poor. The floor of beaten earth is swept clean. There is no furniture at all, but part of the stone wall juts out to form a bench. In one corner there is a clutter of pots and large storage jars. Cloaks and baskets hang from stone pegs on the wall. Niches, inset in the wall, hold a few precious objects and belongings, perhaps a pottery jar or some shell necklaces. Other items include a knife and equipment for weaving or fishing.

POT STOVES
Cooking stoves of baked clay, much like these, have been used in Peru for hundreds of years. Round cooking pots were placed on top of these little stoves. The fuel was pushed in through a hole in the side. Pot stoves are easily carried and can be used outside. Inside the house, there might be a more permanent hearth, made of clay or stone.

DRINK IT UP!
The shape of this two-handled jar and its simple coloring are typically Inca, but the geometric patterns suggest it may have been the work of a Chimú potter. A jar like this might have been used to carry *chicha* (corn beer) made by the *mamakuna* for one of the great religious festivals. People drank far too much *chicha* on these occasions, and drunkenness was common.

INSIDE STORY
What was it like to live in Machu Picchu 500 years ago? The insides of the remaining buildings give us many clues. Even though the thatched roofs and timbers have been lost over the years, some have been restored. Well over half the buildings in Machu Picchu were homes for ordinary people.

REED MATTING

Totora reed matting, used by the Uru people today, is rolled up in bales by Lake Titicaca. In Inca times, reed mats were used as bedding by most people. They slept fully dressed on the ground. Even the emperor and the nobles slept on the floor, but they had blankets and rugs of the finest cloth to cover themselves. Like the Incas, the Uru people have many household uses for *totora* reed. It is a fuel, its flower is used to make medicines and some parts of it may be eaten.

HOUSEHOLD GOURDS

Decorated gourds are still sold in the highlands of Peru. Gourds are pumpkin-like plants bearing fruits with a hard shell. Gourds were often hollowed out and dried and used by the Incas as simple containers for everyday use around the house. They served as water bottles or jars.

FUEL SUPPLIES

In many parts of the Inca Empire, timber was scarce, and its use was officially limited. Brushwood, sticks and a mountain plant called *llareta* were collected for tinder and fuel. Llama dung was also widely used as a fuel for cooking or for firing pottery. Fires were started with drills. These were sticks rotated at such high speed against another piece of wood that they became very hot indeed and began to smoke.

timber

brushwood

Hunting and Fishing

THE INCAS hunted wild animals for sport as well as for food. Every four years, there was a great public hunt, at which beaters would form a line many miles long and comb the countryside for game. The hunters closed in on the animals with dogs. Dangerous animals were hunted, such as bears and pumas (South American cougars or mountain lions), as well as important sources of food such as deer, guanaco (a wild relative of the llama) and partridges. After the hunt, the meat was cut into strips and dried in the sun. Hunting was a pastime of royalty and nobles, but ordinary people could hunt with permission. Every child learned how to use a sling—ideal for killing small birds. Nets were used to catch wildfowl on lakes and marshes. Spears, clubs, bows and arrows were also used.

BEAK AND TACKLE
The Moche fisherman shown on this jar is using a pelican to catch fish for him with its great pouch of a beak. Fishing crews of the coast used cotton lines, fish hooks of copper or bone, harpoons, or cotton nets with gourd floats.

BEYOND THE SURF
A fishing boat made of bound *totora* reed is steered toward the surf at Huancacho, to the north of Trujillo on Peru's north coast. This sight would have been much the same in the days of the Inca Empire. The first view Spanish explorers had of the Inca Empire was of fishing boats and rafts at sea.

SPEARS OF THE NAZCA
A painting on a pottery vase shows two hunters attacking vicuña with spears. It dates from the Nazca civilization, which lasted from about 200 B.C. to A.D. 750. The first Peruvians lived by hunting, but the Inca State depended mainly on farming and fishing for its food. Hunting had become a pastime.

A REED BOAT
You will need: dry straw or hay, scissors, ruler, strong thread or twine, pencil, darning needle, plastic lid, white glue, paintbrush.

1 Take a fistful of straw or hay and gather it together as shown. Trim one end to make a bundle 8 in. long. Make another 8-in. bundle and two more 7 in. long.

2 Tie a length of thread or twine around one end of a bundle. Then wind it along at 1¼-in. intervals. Bind into a point at one end and tie a knot.

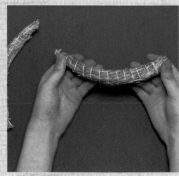

3 Gently bend the bound bundle into a banana shape. Tie and bend the remaining three bundles in exactly the same way. Keep the thread tight.

A DAY'S FISHING

Two Moche fishermen sit on a sea-going raft, drinking beer and arguing, no doubt, about the "fish that got away." Fishing was already a major occupation on the Peruvian coast about 4,500 years ago. Later coastal peoples, such as the Chimú, specialized as fishermen, supplying the inland cities with their catches. In Inca times, freshly caught fish from the coast were hurried by special messenger to the royal palace at Cuzco.

FISHING IN LAKE AND OCEAN

The cool currents that sweep up the west coast of Peru provide some of the best fishing in all the Pacific Ocean. Small fish such as sardines and anchovies swarm through these waters. Larger fish and shellfish may also be taken. Inland lakes such as Lake Titicaca are also a rich source of fish.

sardines

anchovies

THE CHASE

A picture painted on a *kero* (wooden beaker), shows an Inca hunter bringing down a guanaco. His weapon is the *bola*, a heavy cord weighted with three balls. It was hurled at the guanaco's legs in order to entangle it. The *bola* was also used in Argentina in the 1800s by the cowboys called *gauchos*.

The curving sides and pointed prow of a reed boat were designed to cut through the waves.

4 Draw a boat shape on plastic, 5½ in. long, 2½ in. at the widest point and 1½ in. wide at the stern. Cut it out. Prick holes ½ in. apart around the edge as shown.

5 Thread the needle and carefully sew one of the shorter bundles to one side of the boat. Repeat on the other side of the boat with the matching bundle.

6 Use white glue to attach the longer straw or hay bundles on top of the first ones. Curve the uncut ends upward slightly to form the prow of the boat.

7 Paint the hull of the boat with glue to make it waterproof. Let it dry completely before testing your sea-going craft in a bowl of water!

Living on the Land

THE MOUNTAINS, windy plateaus and deserts of Peru are very difficult to farm. Over thousands of years, humans struggled to tame these harsh landscapes. They brought water to dry areas, dug terraced fields out of steep slopes and improved wild plants such as the potato until they became useful food crops. In Inca times, two-thirds of the farmers' produce was set aside for the emperor and the priests, so there was little personal reward for the people who did the hard work.

Royal officials decided the borders of all the fields and of the pastures for llama and alpaca herds. The soil was broken with hoes and plow-like spades called *takllas*. These simple tools were made of hardened wood. Some were tipped with bronze. The Incas knew how to keep the soil well fertilized, using llama dung in the mountains and guano (seabird droppings) on the coast. In dry areas, the Incas built reservoirs called *qochas* to catch the rain. They were experts at irrigation, carefully controlling water-flow through the fields.

FREEZE-DRIED POTATOES
A woman of the Tinqui people lays out potatoes on the ground, just as farmers would have done in the days of the Incas. Over two hundred potato varieties were grown in the Andes. They were preserved by being left to dry in the hot daytime sun and cold overnight frosts. Dried, pressed potato, called *chuño*, just needed to be soaked to be ready for cooking.

A SAFE HARVEST
The farmer uses his sling to scare hungry birds from the new corn, while his wife harvests the crop. March was the month when the corn ripened, and April was the month of harvest.

A HIGHLAND CROP
Kinua ripens in the sun. This tough crop can be grown at over 12,400 ft above sea-level, and can survive both warm days and cold nights. *Kinua* was ideal for the Andes. Its seeds were boiled to make a kind of porridge, and its leaves could be stewed as well.

AN ANCIENT PATTERN

Painstaking work over many years created these terraced fields, or *andenes*, near the Inca town of Pisaq. All the soil had to be brought up in baskets from the valley floor far below. Terracing aims to provide a workable depth of level soil, while retaining walls prevent earth from being washed away by the rains. The bottom of each terrace was laid with gravel for good drainage. The Pisaq fields belonged to the emperor and produced corn of the highest quality.

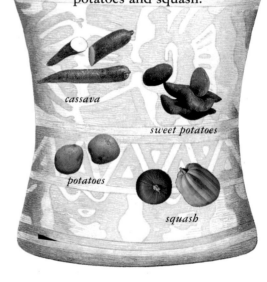

ALL-AMERICAN CROPS

Crops that were once grown in just one part of the world are now grown in other continents as well. Many of the world's most common crops were first grown in the Americas. These include potatoes, tomatoes, corn, cassava, sweet potatoes and squash.

cassava

sweet potatoes

potatoes

squash

MOTHER EARTH

This gold plate, made by the Chimú people, shows the earth goddess surrounded by Peruvian crops, each grouped according to its growing season. They include corn, sweet potato and cassava. The earth goddess was called Pachamama, and she played an especially important part in the religious beliefs of farming villages in the Andes. Most farmers in the Inca Empire spent their lives trying to tame a hostile environment. The fertility of the land was important in religious as well as economic terms.

Food and Feasts

A REGIONAL GOVERNOR might entertain a royal visitor with a banquet of venison (deer meat), roast duck, fresh fish from the lakes or the ocean, and tropical fruits such as bananas and guavas. Honey was used as a sweetener.

Peasants ate squash and other vegetables in a stew, and fish was also eaten where it was available. Families kept guinea pigs for their meat, but most of their food was vegetarian. The bulk of any meal would be made up of starchy foods. These were prepared from grains such as corn or *kinua*, or from root crops such as potatoes, cassava or a highland plant called *oca*. A strong beer called *chicha* was made from corn. The grains were chewed and spat out, then left to ferment in water.

MIXED SPICES
This pottery mortar and pestle may have been used for grinding and mixing herbs. It is about 1,000 years old and was made by the Chimú people. Peruvian dishes were often hot and spicy, using eye-watering amounts of hot chile peppers. Chile peppers were one of the first food plants to be cultivated. Peppers of various kinds were grown on the coast and foothills.

MEALS AND MANNERS
Inca nobles ate and drank from wooden plates and painted beakers called *keros*. These continued to be made after the Spanish conquest. Pottery was also used to make beautiful cups and dishes. Most peasants drank and ate from gourds. There were no tables, so food was eaten sitting on the ground. Two main meals were eaten each day, one in the morning and one in the evening.

BEAN STEW
You will need: 8½ oz dried navy beans, 4 tomatoes, 18-oz pumpkin, 2 tbsp paprika, mixed herbs, salt, black pepper, 3½ oz corn, bowl, large and medium saucepans, knife, cutting board, measuring cup, spoon.

1 Wash the beans in plenty of cold water. Place them in a large bowl and cover them with cold water. Let them soak for 3 or 4 hours.

2 Drain the beans and put them in a large saucepan. Cover them with cold water. Bring to a boil. Simmer for 2 hours or until just tender.

3 While the beans are cooking, chop the tomatoes finely on the cutting board. Peel the pumpkin and cut the flesh into ½-in. cubes.

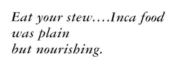

A TROPICAL MENU

The mountains were cool because they were high. Down on the lowlands it was much hotter, and tropical crops could be grown wherever there was enough water. These included tomatoes, avocados, pears, beans, pumpkin-like squashes, chile peppers, peanuts and fruits such as guava.

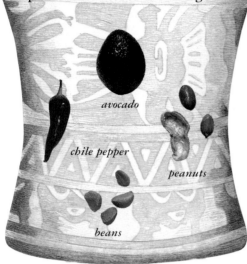

avocado

chile pepper

peanuts

beans

CORN ON THE COB

This corn plant was crafted in Inca silver. The real corn crop would have been almost as precious. Corn could be ground into the flour we call cornmeal, and this was used to make porridge, pancake-like bread and dumplings. Corn could also be toasted, boiled or puffed up into popcorn.

Eat your stew....Inca food was plain but nourishing.

TO THE LORD OF MAIZE

This corn left in a pottery dish in a Nazca grave is an offering to the Lord of the Corn. Corn played such an important part in the life of Central and South America that it had its own gods, goddesses and festivals.

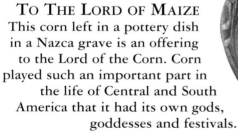

4 Heat ½ cup water in a medium saucepan. Stir in the paprika and bring to a boil. Add the tomatoes and a sprinkling of herbs, salt and pepper.

5 Simmer for 15 minutes, until thick and well blended. Drain the beans and return to the large pan with the pumpkin and the tomato mixture. Stir well.

6 Simmer for 15 minutes. Add the corn and simmer for 5 more minutes, until the pumpkin has almost disintegrated and the stew is thick.

7 Taste (but be careful, it's hot!). Add more salt and pepper if necessary. Serve in bowls. Cornbread or tortillas would be an ideal accompaniment.

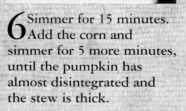

Textiles and Tunics

IN ALL THE CIVILIZATIONS of the Andes, spinning and weaving were the main household tasks of women of all ranks. Girls learned to weave at an early age, and men wove too. There was a long tradition of embroidery, using bone needles. In Inca times, weaving reached an incredibly high standard. Weaving textiles formed part of the labor tax, like farming or building. Woven cloth was stored in government warehouses and used to pay troops and officials.

Inca men wore a loincloth around the waist, secured by a belt. Over this was a simple knee-length tunic, often made of alpaca wool. On cold nights, they might wear a cloak as well. Women wrapped themselves in a large rectangular cloth of alpaca wool, with a sash around the waist and a shawl. There were many kinds of regional headdresses, caps of looped wool, headbands, hats and feathers. Sandals were made of leather or woven grasses.

INCA FASHION
About 500 years ago, this fine tunic belonged to an Inca nobleman from the south coast of Peru. Its design is simple, but it is beautifully decorated with flower and animal designs. Dress was a status symbol in the Inca Empire. The shape of clothes was much the same for all social classes, but the more important you were, the finer the cloth and the decoration.

PINNED IN STYLE
A long decorative pin called a *tupu* was used by the Incas to fasten dresses and shawls. It might be made from copper, silver or gold. This *tupu* was found at the Sacsahuaman fortress in Cuzco.

AN INCA TUNIC
You will need: blue felt 26 x 64 in., red felt 16-in. square, white glue, brush, tape measure, scissors, ruler, pencil, thread or yarn, needle, cream calico fabric, acrylic or fabric paints, paintbrush, water container.

1 Place the blue felt flat on the table. Position the red felt in the center of it to form a diamond shape. Glue the red felt carefully in place.

2 For the neck opening, cut a slit 8¾ in. long through the center of both layers of material as shown, with the long side of the blue felt toward you.

3 Fold the tunic in half along the slit. Halfway along the slit, cut a 4¾-in. slit at right angles to the first. Only cut through one double layer of fabric.

FIBERS AND DYES

Highland animals provided warm woollen fibers. Llamas had the coarsest wool, and vicuñas the softest. Alpaca wool was the one most commonly used. Cotton was grown in the hot lowland regions and was widely worn for its coolness. Plants were used to dye either the yarn or the finished textiles. A scarlet dye called cochineal was obtained from the dried bodies of insects.

alpaca wool   *cotton cloth*

dyed cotton yarn

SHIMMERING GOLD

For a religious festival, Inca nobles and priests might wear spectacular costumes. This is part of a tunic made of woven alpaca wool decorated with fine gold work. It comes from Peru's south coast. Clothes like these were produced by craftsmen in special workshops. One Chimú tunic was studded with no fewer than 13,000 pieces of gold!

Many Inca tunics were brightly colored and decorated with geometric patterns.

BACKSTRAPPERS

This Moche painting shows people weaving with backstrap looms. The upright or warp threads are tensioned between an upright post and a beam attached to the weaver's waist. The cross or weft threads are passed in between. Backstrap looms are still used in Central and South America today.

4 Using the colored thread or yarn, sew together the sides of the tunic with large stitches. Leave enough space for armholes at the top.

5 Draw plenty of 2-in. squares in pencil on the cream fabric. Paint them in colorful, geometric Inca designs. Look at the patterns here for ideas.

6 Let the paint dry completely. Then carefully cut out the squares and arrange them in any pattern you like on the front of your tunic.

7 When you have a pattern you are happy with, glue the squares in position. Wait until the glue is dry before trying on your unique Inca tunic.

Jewels and Feathers

FESTIVAL COSTUMES in the Andes today come in dazzling pinks, reds and blues. In the Inca period it was no different. People loved to wear brightly colored braids, threads and ribbons. Sequins, beads, feathers and gold were sewn into fabric, while precious stones, red shells, silver and gold were made into beautiful earplugs, necklaces, pendants, nostril-rings and disks. However, it was only the nobles who were allowed to show off by wearing feathers, jewels and precious metals. Some of the most prized ornaments were gifts from the emperor for high-ranking service in the army.

Much of the finest craft work went into making small statues and objects for religious ceremonies, temples and shrines. During the Inca period, craft workers were employed by the state. They produced many beautiful treasures, but some of the best of these were the work of non-Inca peoples, particularly the Chimú. Treasures shipped to Spain after the Conquest astounded the Europeans by their fine craftsmanship.

PLUMES OF THE CHIEF
An impressive headdress like this would have belonged to a high-ranking Inca official or general in northern Chile over 500 years ago. The hat is made from coils of dyed llama wool. It is decorated with bold designs, and topped by a spray of feathers.

A SACRED PUMA
This gold pouch in the shape of a puma, a sacred animal, was made by the Moche people between 1,300 and 1,700 years ago. It may have been used to carry *coca* leaves. These were used as a drug during religious ceremonies. The pattern on the body is made up of two-headed snakes.

A GOLD AND SILVER NECKLACE
You will need: self-drying clay, cutting board, ruler, large blunt needle, gold and silver paint, paintbrush, water container, card stock, pencil, scissors, strong thread.

1 Form pieces of clay into beads in the shape of peanuts. You will need 10 large beads (about 1½ x ¾ in.) and 10 smaller beads (about 1 x ½ in.).

2 Use the needle to mark patterns on the beads, so that they look like nut shells. Then carefully make a hole through the middle of each bead. Let dry.

3 Paint half the shells of each size gold and half of them silver. You should have 5 small and 5 large gold beads, and 5 small and 5 large silver beads.

PRECIOUS AND PRETTY

The most valued stone in the Andes was blue-green turquoise. It was cut and polished into beads and disks for necklaces, and inlaid in gold statues and masks. Blue lapis lazuli, black jet and other stones also found their way along trading routes. Colombia, on the northern edge of the Inca Empire, mined many precious stones and metals. Seashells were cut and polished into beautiful beads.

emerald   turquoise

lapis lazuli

BIRDS OF A FEATHER

Birds and fish decorate this feather cape. It was made by the Chancay people of the central Peruvian coast between the 1300s and 1500s. It would have been worn for religious ceremonies. Feather work was a skilled craft in both Central and South America. In Inca times, the brilliantly colored feathers of birds called macaws were sent to the emperor as tribute from the tribes of the Amazon forests.

Necklaces made of gold, silver and jewels would only have been worn by Inca royalty, perhaps the Quya *herself.*

TREASURE LOST AND FOUND

A beautifully made gold pendant created in the Moche period before the Incas rose to power. After the Spanish conquest of Peru, countless treasures were looted from temples or palaces by Spanish soldiers. Gold was melted down or shipped back to Europe. A few items escaped by being buried in graves. Some have been discovered by archaeologists.

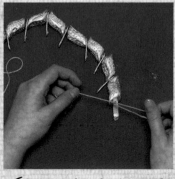

4 Paint some card stock gold on both sides. On it draw 11 rectangles (1¼ x ½ in.) with rounded ends. Cut them out and carefully prick a hole in each end.

5 Thread the needle and make a knot 4 in. from the end of the thread. Then thread the card stock strips and large beads alternately, using the gold beads first.

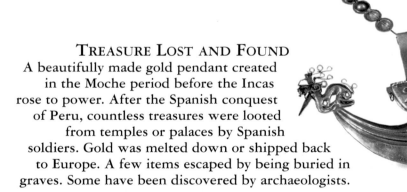

6 Start and end with card stock strips. When you have finished, knot the thread tightly next to the last card stock strip. Cut the thread 4 in. from the knot.

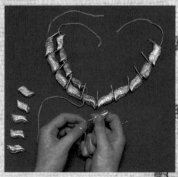

7 Repeat steps 5 and 6 using more thread and the small beads, so that the beads are joined as shown. Finally, knot the ends of the two threads together.

Everyday Crafts

MANY BEAUTIFUL OBJECTS produced in the Inca Empire were not made of gold and jewels but of simpler, more down-to-earth materials. Baskets and reed mats were made in early prehistoric times by braiding and twining various materials. All kinds of small objects, such as bowls, pins, spoons and figures, were carved from bone, stone and wood.

Pottery was being made in Peru by about 2000 B.C., which was later than in the lands to the north and east. It had a great effect on the way people lived because it affected the production, storage, transportation and cooking of food.

South American potters did not shape their pottery on a wheel. They built them up in layers from coils of clay. The coils were smoothed out by hand or with tools, marked or painted, dried in the sun and then baked until hard.

Many of the pre-Incan civilizations of the Andes produced beautiful pottery. The Nazca often used bold geometric patterns, while the Moche loved to make jars in the shape of animals and people. Many pieces were specially made for religious ceremonies.

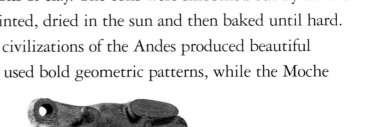

POLISHED WOOD

This fine black *kero* (drinking vessel) was made by an Inca craftsman. It is carved and polished wood. Timber was always scarce in the Inca Empire, but wood was widely used to make plates and cups. Rearing up over the rim is a fierce-looking big cat, perhaps a puma or a jaguar.

MODELED FROM CLAY

A fierce puma bares his teeth. He was made from pottery between A.D. 500 and 800. The hole in his back was used to waft clouds of incense during religious ceremonies in the city of Tiwanaku, near Lake Titicaca.

A TIWANAKU POTTERY JAGUAR

You will need: chicken wire, wire-cutters, ruler, newspaper, scissors, white glue, masking tape, flour, water, card stock, paint, water container, paintbrush.

1 Cut a rectangle of chicken wire about 5½ in. long and 8 in. wide. Carefully wrap it around to form a sausage shape. Close one end neatly.

2 Squeeze the other end of the sausage to form the jaguar's neck and head. Fold over the wire at the end to make a neat, round shape for his nose.

3 Make rolls of newspaper about 1 in. long to form the jaguar's legs. Use strips of paper and glue to attach them securely to the jaguar's body as shown.

PRETTY POLLY

This pottery jar, like many from Peru, comes with a handle and a spout. It is shaped and painted to look like a parrot and was made, perhaps 1,000 years before the Incas, by the Nazca potters of southern Peru.

WATER OF LIFE

This Inca bottle is carved with a figure inside a tower collecting water. No community could survive very long without a good supply of fresh water. Many pottery, bottles and beakers from the South American civilizations are decorated with light-hearted scenes of everyday activities. They give us a vivid idea of how people used to live.

IN THE POTTER'S WORKSHOP

The potter needed a good supply of sticky clay and plenty of water. He also needed large supplies of firewood or dung for fuel. The potter would knead the clay until it was soft and workable. Sometimes he would mix in sand or crushed shells from the coast to help strengthen the clay. Colors for painting the pottery were made from plants and minerals.

shells *sand*

clay

The handle and spout design of your Tiwanaku jaguar is known as a stirrup pot, because the arrangement looks like the stirrup of a horse.

4 Mix the flour and water into a paste. Use it to glue a layer of newspaper strips all over the jaguar's body. Let this layer dry. You will need 3 layers.

5 Cut ears from card stock. Attach with masking tape. Tape on rolls of newspaper to make the handle, spout and tail, as in the finished one above.

6 Set the model in a warm and airy place to dry. Then paint it all over with reddish brown paint. Let the paint dry completely.

7 Use black paint and a fine brush to decorate the jaguar, as shown in the picture. When the paint is dry, varnish with white glue, if desired.

Metals and Mining

THE WHOLE REGION of the Andes had a very long history of metalworking. A stone bowl that was discovered in the Andahuaylas Valley was nearly 3,500 years old. It contained metalworking equipment and finely beaten gold foil. Braziers found at the town of Machu Picchu, from the end of the Inca period, included traces of molten metal.

The Incas often referred to gold as "sweat of the sun" and to silver as "tears of the moon." These metals were sacred not only to the gods but also to their descendants on earth, the *Sapa Inca* and the *Quya*. At the Temple of the Sun in Cuzco, there was a whole garden made of gold and silver, with golden soil, golden stalks of corn and golden llamas. Imagine how it must have gleamed in the sunshine. Copper, however, was used by ordinary people. It was made into cheap jewelry, weapons and everyday tools. The Incas' love of gold and silver eventually led to their downfall, for it was rumors of their fabulous wealth that lured the Spanish to invade the region.

A SICAN LORD
A ceremonial knife with a crescent-shaped blade is called a *tumi*. Its gold handle is made in the shape of a nobleman or ruler. He wears an elaborate headdress and large disks in his ears. It was made between 1100 and 1300. The knife is in the style of the Sican civilization, which grew up after the decline of the Moche civilization in the A.D. 700s.

A CHIMÚ DOVE
Chimú goldsmiths, the best in the empire, made this plump dove. When the Incas conquered Chimor in 1470, they forced many thousands of skilled craftsmen from the city of Chan Chan to resettle in the Cuzco area and continue their work.

A TUMI KNIFE
You will need: card stock, ruler, pencil, scissors, self-drying clay, cutting board, rolling pin, modeling and cutting tools, white glue, gold paint, paintbrush, water container, blue metallic paper.

1 On card stock, draw a knife shape as shown and cut it out. The rectangular part should be 3½ x 1½ in. The rounded part is 2¾ in. across and 1¼ in. high.

2 Roll out a slab of clay about 1½ in. thick. Draw a *tumi* shape on it as shown. It should be 5 in. long and measure 3½ in. across the widest part at the top.

3 Use the cutting tool to cut around the shape you have drawn. Carefully remove the surrounding. Make sure the edges are clean and smooth.

MINERAL WEALTH

To this day, the Andes are very rich in minerals. The Incas worked with gold, silver, platinum and copper. They knew how to make alloys, which are mixtures of different metals. Bronze was made by mixing copper and tin. However, unlike their Spanish conquerors, the Incas knew nothing of iron and steel. This put them at a disadvantage when fighting the Europeans.

copper *silver*

gold

INCA FIGURES

Small ritual figures of women and men from about 2½ in. high were often made in the Inca period. They were hammered from sheets of silver and gold and were dressed in miniature versions of adult clothing. They have been found on mountain-top shrine sites in the south-central Andes, in carved stone boxes in Lake Titicaca and at important temples.

PANNING FOR GOLD

A boy laborer in modern Colombia pans for gold. Some Inca gold was mined, but large amounts also came from panning mountain rivers and streams in the Andes. The river bed was loosened with sticks, and then the water was sifted through shallow trays in search of any flecks of the precious metal that had been washed downstream.

The Chimú gold and turquoise tumi *was used by priests at religious ceremonies. It may have been used in sacrificial rituals.*

4 Cut a slot into the bottom edge of the clay shape. Lifting it carefully, slide the knife blade into the slot. Use glue to make the joint secure.

5 Use a modeling tool to mark the details of the god onto the clay. Look at the finished knife above to see how to do this. Let everything dry.

6 When the clay has hardened, paint the whole knife with gold paint. Let it dry completely before painting the other side as well.

7 The original knife was decorated with turquoise. Glue small pieces of blue metallic paper onto the handle as shown in the picture above.

Gods and Spirits

THE FIRST PERUVIANS worshiped nature spirits and creatures such as condors, snakes and jaguars. Later peoples began to believe in gods. Some said the world had been created by the god Wiraqocha, the "old man of the sky". He had made the sun, moon and stars, and the other gods. He had carved stone statues and made them live, creating the first humans. Myths tell that he sailed away across the Pacific Ocean.

To the Inca people, the most important god was Inti, the sun. He was the bringer of warmth and light and the protector of the Inca people. Inti's sister and wife was Mamakilya, the silver moon goddess.

Other gods included Pachamama the earth goddess, Mamacocha goddess of the sea, Kuychi the Rainbow god and Apu Illapu, god of thunder.

THE GATEWAY GOD
Tiwanaku's 1,400-year-old Gateway of the Sun, in Bolivia, is carved from solid rock and is over 10 ft high. The figure may represent the Chavín Staff god or Wiraqocha. It may be a sun god, for his headdress is made up of rays.

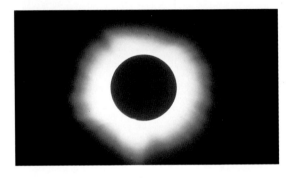

END OF THE WORLD?
The Incas believed that Inti, the sun god, dropped into the ocean each evening, swam underneath the earth and appeared next morning in the east, above the mountains. An eclipse of the sun was a terrifying experience, a warning that Inti was abandoning the emperor and his people.

SPIRITS OF THE MAIZE
On this pottery jar, three gods are shown bursting out of bundles of corn cobs. The jar was made by Moche potters between A.D. 300 and A.D. 700. To all the South American peoples, the world of nature was filled with spiritual forces. They believed that the success of the harvest depended on the good will of the gods.

A GOLD SUN GOD MASK

You will need: large piece of cardboard, pencil, ruler, scissors, white glue, paintbrush, water container, gold and black paint.

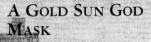

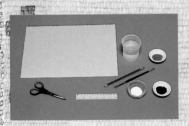

1 Draw the mask shape on cardboard as shown. It should be 24 in. wide and 24 in. high overall. The side pieces are 16 in. high. The narrowest part is 3 in. wide.

2 Draw zigzag patterns all around the edge of the mask as shown in the picture above. These patterns represent the powerful rays of the sun.

3 Carefully cut out the whole mask shape. Then cut out the rays around the edge, making sure you don't snip all the way through by mistake.

ANCIENT SECRETS

A mysterious figure, carved from a great stone pillar, stands amid the ruined temples of Tiwanaku. It holds a banded *kero* or drinking cup in its left hand and a scepter in its right. Is this the figure of an ancient god? The monument is 24 ft tall and was excavated in 1932. It dates back over 1,500 years to the days when Tiwanaku became a great religious center.

A GOLDEN MASK

Gold face-masks were made by several Peruvian peoples, including the Nazca and the Inca. Some were used during festivals in honor of the sun. Others were laid on the faces of the dead, just as they were in ancient Egypt. This fine mask was made by Moche goldsmiths in about A.D. 400.

Hail to Inti, the sun god! Your mask will look as if it is made from shining gold, the magical metal of the sun.

WORSHIPPING THE SUN

A golden face in a sunburst represents Inti, god of the sun. This picture from the 1700s imagines how the *Coricancha*, the Temple of the Sun, in Cuzco, must have appeared 200 years earlier. It shows the *Sapa Inca* making an offering of maize beer to Inti in the great hall.

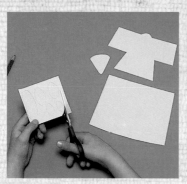

4 Cut out a rectangle of cardboard 6 x 5 in. Cut a T-shaped piece 5½ in. across and 4½ in. high. Also cut out the shapes of eyes, a nose and a mouth.

5 Glue the shapes onto the center of the mask to form the sun god's face as shown. Leave the mask flat until the glue is completely dry.

6 Make sure your table top is protected. Cover the whole surface of the mask with gold paint. The rays around the edge are difficult to paint.

7 Finally, use black paint and a fine brush to draw the face. Add ears and teeth. Decorate the top part with black paint, too.

Temples and Sacrifices

THE INCAS had many *waq'as* (holy places). Some of these shrines were simply streams, rocks or caves that had been visited by pilgrims for thousands of years. Others were wayside idols, or temples built long before the Incas came to power. In Chavín de Huantar, temples were built between 900 and 200 B.C. They were decorated with carvings of fantastic jaguars and birds of prey. Massive pyramid temples and platforms had been built on the coastal plains. Huaca del Sol, at the Moche capital of Cerro Blanco, was made from over 100 million mud bricks. The Incas themselves built many temples dedicated to the gods Inti, Mama Killa, Wiraqocha and Apu Illapa.

The *Willak Umu* (Inca High Priest) was a member of the royal family. Priests made offerings to the gods and took drugs that gave them dreams and visions. They looked for omens—signs to help them see the future.

HUACA EL DRAGON
Fantastic figures in dried mud decorate Huaca el Dragon, a pyramid burial site to the northwest of Chan Chan. It was a religious site of the Chimú people about 800 years ago, before the Inca Empire.

OFFERINGS TO THE GODS
Llamas are chosen to be sacrificed to the gods. White llamas were offered to the sun god, Inti, brown ones to the creator god, Wiraqocha, and spotted ones to Apu Illapa, a thunder god. Their entrails were examined for omens. Guinea pigs were also sacrificed. Other offerings to the gods included food, *chicha* beer, corn and cloth. Many offerings were burned on a fire.

GATEWAY OF THE SUN
The city of Tiwanaku, with its great ceremonial arch, was the center of many religious activities. It had a raised platform, 50 ft high, and archaeologists have found the remains of offerings and human sacrifices there. Tiwanaku beliefs seem to have been similar to those of the Wari city-state.

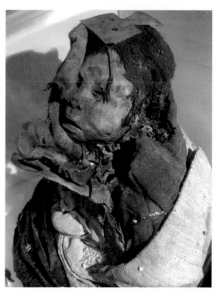

AT PACHACAMAC

Pachacamac, near Lima, was a site of pilgrimage in Inca times. It was named after Pachacamac, a much older creator god. Under Topa Inka, the Incas adopted Pachacamac as their own, worshipping him as a god of fire. They came to Pachacamac to have their fortunes told by an oracle. The site had a pyramid and many shrines. This is the Temple of the Virgins.

HUMAN SACRIFICE

When a new emperor came to the throne, or during times of crisis, Inca priests sacrificed hundreds of people. Victims had to be pure and perfect to please the gods. Boys or girls, *akllakuna*, or sometimes adults were chosen. This girl was one of three sacrificed on a peak in northern Argentina. Her remains were discovered in 1999.

TEMPLES OF THE SUN

The *Coricancha*, or Temple of the Sun, in Cuzco, was the holiest shrine in the Inca Empire. Its remains are seen here topped by a Christian church that was built by the Spanish in 1650. Inca priests believed that power lines called *ceques* radiated out from the *Coricancha*, linking holy sites across the empire. There were other great sun temples, too. One was on an island in Lake Titicaca, another was at Vilcashuaman, and a third was near Aconcagua, the highest peak in all the Americas.

Festivals and Rituals

THE INCAS loved to celebrate the natural world and its changing seasons. They marked them with special festivals and religious rituals. Some celebrations were held in villages and fields, others took place at religious sites or in the big cities. It is said that the Incas had as many as 150 festivals each year.

The biggest festival of all was *Inti Raymi*, the Feast of the Sun. It was held in June, to mark midwinter in the southern part of the world. *Qapaq Raymi*, the Splendid Festival, was held in December to mark the southern midsummer. This was when boys were recognized as adult warriors, and young nobles received their earplugs. Crop festivals included the Great Ripening each February, Earth Ripening each March and the Great Cultivation each May. The sowing of new corn was celebrated in August. The Feast of the Moon, held in September, was a special festival for women, while the Day of the Dead, in November, was a time to honor one's ancestors.

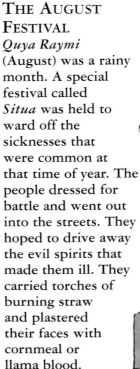

FEAST OF THE SUN
The Quechua people of Peru have revived the ancient festival of *Inti Raymi*. They gather each year at Sacsahuaman fortress, Cuzco, to celebrate the light and warmth of the sun during the southern midwinter. In Inca times, a golden bowl was raised to the rising sun. The sun's rays would be used to make fire.

BRINGER OF RAIN
Drought was feared throughout the empire, especially in the dry lands of the coast. If rain failed to fall, the life-giving irrigation channels dried up. In desperation, people visited the temples of Apu Illapu, bringer of rain. The priests made offerings and sacrifices, and the pilgrims prayed. The purpose of most Inca ceremonies and festivals was to prevent disaster and to ensure that life carried on.

THE AUGUST FESTIVAL
Quya Raymi (August) was a rainy month. A special festival called *Situa* was held to ward off the sicknesses that were common at that time of year. The people dressed for battle and went out into the streets. They hoped to drive away the evil spirits that made them ill. They carried torches of burning straw and plastered their faces with cornmeal or llama blood.

DANCERS AND MASKS

Drums, music and dance were always an important part of *Inti Raymi*, the Sun Festival. The Incas played rattles and whistles, drums and hand-drums, flutes and panpipes to help them celebrate the festival. Musicians played all day long without taking a break, and some of their ancient tunes are still known. Today, masks representing the Spanish invaders are added to the festivities. The modern festival proves that the old way of life has not been forgotten. Modern Peruvians are proud of their Inca past.

THE EMPEROR'S DAY

The modern festival of *Inti Raymi* attracts thousands to Cuzco. In the days of the Incas, too, nobles poured into the Inca capital from every corner of the empire. Their aim was to honor the emperor as much as the sun god. They came carrying tributes from the regions and personal gifts, hoping for the Emperor's favor in return.

FIESTA TIME

A drawing from the 1700s shows Peruvian dancers dressed as devils. Many of them are playing musical instruments or carrying long whips. After the conquest, festivals were known by the Spanish term, *fiestas*, and officially celebrated Christian beliefs. However, many of the festivities were still rooted in an Inca past. The dances and costumes often had their origins in Inca traditions.

Flutes, Drums and Dice

ABOY HERDING ALPACAS in the misty fields picks out a tune on a bone whistle. Drums rattle and thump as excited crowds gather in Cuzco for a great festival. The Inca world is full of music.

Music and dance played a very important part in the everyday lives of the Incas. They did not use stringed instruments, but drums and hand-drums, rattles, flutes, whistles and panpipes. Instruments were made from wood, reeds, pottery and bone. At festivals, musicians would play all day without a break. Large bands walked in procession, each panpipe player picking out a different part of the tune. Ancient tunes and rhythms live on in the modern music of the Andes.

The Incas did not have books, but they enjoyed listening to poets and storytellers. They liked tales about the gods, spirits and magic, or princesses and warriors. They enjoyed running races and, like other peoples of the Americas, they loved to gamble. They played games of flicking seeds and rolling dice.

SOUND OF THE PANPIPES
Panpipes made of cane, pottery or bone have been found at many ancient sites in the Inca lands. They are also found in other parts of the world, but their breathy, melodious sound has become very much linked to the Andes. Panpipes are played by blowing across the open end of a sealed tube. They come in many different sizes. In Peru, they are called *antaras* or *zampoñas*.

WHISTLE LIKE A BIRD
A flute is carved to resemble a bird's head and decorated with patterns. It is made from bone and was probably the treasured possession of a Moche musician around A.D. 700.

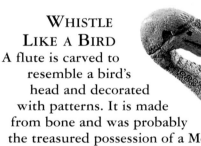

AN INCA HAND-DRUM
You will need: cardboard, pencil, ruler, scissors, masking tape, cream calico fabric, white glue, paintbrush, paints, water container, batting, 12-in. length of dowel, colored yarn.

1 Use a pencil and ruler to mark two rectangles, measuring 3½ x 34 in., on the cardboard. Cut them out carefully. They will form the sides of the drum.

2 Bend one rectangle into a circle and use masking tape to attach the ends together. It may be easier to ask a friend to help you do this.

3 Lay the cardboard ring on the calico fabric. Draw a circle around it, leaving a gap of about ¾ in. Remove the ring and cut out the fabric circle.

CUZCO DRUMMERS

A modern street band in Cuzco plays the haunting music of the Andes, which has become popular around the world. Local peoples such as the Aymara and Quechua took up new instruments after the Spanish conquest, including various kinds of harp and guitar. However, there are still traces of the Inca musical tradition.

SOUND OF THE CONCH

A Moche noble is shown on this pottery made in about A.D. 500. He is blowing a conch at some royal or religious ceremony. Conches are large seashells, which in many parts of the world are blown as trumpets. The Incas called them *wayllakipa*. Conch trumpets were also carried by royal messengers on the Inca roads. They were blown to warn the next relay station they were on the way. Communication was an important part of running the Inca Empire.

Women played hand-drums like this at festivals in Inca times. Drums were sometimes suspended from wooden frames.

4 Paint glue around the edge of the fabric circle. Turn the fabric over. Carefully stretch it over the cardboard ring. Keep it taut and smooth the edges.

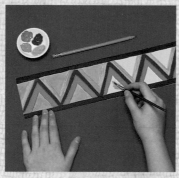

5 Draw a geometric Inca pattern on the remaining strip of cardboard. Use paints to decorate it in bright colors. Lay it flat and let it dry.

6 Wrap the painted strip around the drum. Use masking tape to attach one edge to the drum, then use glue to stick down the rest of the patterned strip.

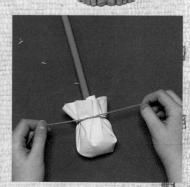

7 Cut out a calico circle 8 in. in diameter. Make a beater by wrapping batting and the calico around one end of the dowel. Tie it with yarn.

Medicine and Magic

L IKE MOST PEOPLES in the world five hundred years ago, the Incas and their neighbors had some idea of science or medicine. However, curing people was believed to be chiefly a matter of religious rituals and magical spells. No doubt some of these did help people to feel better. Curing sick people was the job either of priests, or of the local healer or medicine man.

As in Europe at that time, Inca healers used fasting and blood-letting (allowing blood to flow from a cut) for many cures. They also tried blood transfusion (putting new blood into someone's body). They succeeded in this far earlier than doctors in other parts of the world, because peoples of the Andes shared the same blood group. The Incas could also set broken bones, amputate limbs, treat wounds and pull teeth. Medicines were made from herbs, roots, leaves and powders.

THE MEDICINE MAN
This Moche healer or priest, from about A.D. 500, seems to be going into a trance and listening to the voices of spirits or gods. He may be trying to cure a sick patient, or he may be praying over the patient's dead body.

MAGIC DOLLS
Model figures like this one, made from cotton and reed, are often found in ancient graves in the Chancay River region. They are often called dolls, but it seems unlikely that they were ever used as toys. They were probably believed to have magical qualities. The Chancay people may have believed that the dolls helped the dead person in another world.

CARRYING COCA
Small bags like these were used for carrying medicines and herbs, especially coca. The leaves of the coca plant were widely used to stimulate the body and to kill pain. Coca is still widely grown in the Andes today. It is used to make the illegal drug cocaine.

MEDICINE BAG

You will need: scissors, cream calico fabric, pencil, ruler, paintbrush, water container, acrylic or fabric paints, black, yellow, green and red yarn, white glue, needle and thread, masking tape.

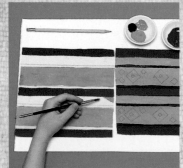

1 Cut two 8-in. squares of fabric. Draw a pattern of stripes and diamonds on the fabric and use acrylic or fabric paints to color them.

2 For the tassels, cut about 10 pieces of yarn 3¼ in. long. Fold a piece of yarn 6 in. long in half. Loop it around each tassel as shown above.

3 Wind a matching piece of yarn, 20 in. long, around the end of the tassel. When you have finished, knot the yarn and tuck the ends inside.

HERBAL REMEDIES

Drugs widely used in ancient Peru included the leaves of tobacco and coca plants. A yellow-flowered plant called calceolaria was used to cure infections. Cinchona bark produced quinine, a medicine we use today to treat malaria. That illness only arrived in South America after the Spanish conquest. However, quinine was used earlier to treat fevers. Suppliers of herbal medicines were known as *hampi kamayuq*.

cinchona tree   *tobacco plant*

SKULL SURGERY

Nazca surgeons were able to carry out an operation called trepanation. This involved drilling a hole in the patient's skull in an attempt to relieve pressure on the brain. The Incas believed this released evil spirits. A small silver plate was sometimes fitted over the hole as a protection.

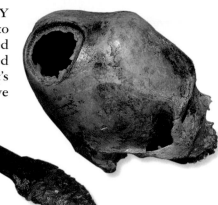

Doctor on call! An Inca medicine chest took the form of a woven bag, carried on the shoulder.

A BAD OMEN

A comet shoots across the night sky. The Incas believed such sights would bring plague or disease in their wake. Other common causes of illness were believed to include witchcraft, evil spirits and a failure to please the gods. People tried to make themselves better by making offerings to the gods at *waq'as* (local shrines). Healers used charms or spells to keep their patients free from evil spirits.

4 Make nine tassels in all. Place them in groups of three along the bottom of the unpainted side of one of the pieces of fabric. Use glue to stick them in place.

5 Let the glue dry. Place the unpainted sides of the fabric pieces together. Sew around the edges as shown. Leave the top edge open.

6 Make a strap by braiding together strands of yarn as shown. Cross each outer strand in turn over the middle strand. Tape will help keep the work steady.

7 Knot the ends of the strap firmly. Attach them to both sides of the top of the bag with glue. Make sure the glue is dry before you pick the bag up.

Inca Knowledge

INCA MATHEMATICIANS used the decimal system, counting in tens. To help with their arithmetic, people placed pebbles or grains of corn in counting frames. These had up to twenty sections. *Quipu* strings were also used to record numbers. Strings were knotted to represent units, tens, hundreds, thousands or even tens of thousands.

The Incas worked out calendars of twelve months by observing the sun, moon and stars as they moved across the sky. They knew that these movements marked regular changes in the seasons. They used the calendar to tell them when to plant crops. Inca priests set up stone pillars outside the city of Cuzco to measure the movements of the sun.

As in Europe at that time, astronomy, which is the study of the stars, was confused with astrology, which is the belief that the stars and planets influence human lives. Incas saw the night sky as being lit up by gods and mythical characters.

FORTUNES FROM THE STARS AND PLANETS

An Inca astrologer observes the position of the sun. The Incas believed that careful watching of the stars and planets revealed their influence on our lives. For example, the star pattern or constellation that we call the Lyre was known to the Incas as the Llama. It was believed that it influenced llamas and those who herded them.

THE SUN STONE

A stone pillar called *Inti Watana* (Tethering Post of the Sun) stood at the eastern edge of the great square in Machu Picchu. It was like a giant sundial and the shadows it cast confirmed the movements of the sun across the sky—a matter of great practical and religious importance.

A QUIPU

You will need: scissors, rope and string of various thicknesses, a 36-in. length of thick rope, paints, paintbrush, water container.

1 Cut the rope and string into about 15 lengths measuring from 8 in. to 32 in. Paint them in various bright colors. Let them dry completely.

2 To make the top part of the *quipu*, take a piece of thick rope, about 36 in. long. Tie a knot in each end as shown in the picture above.

3 Next, take pieces of thinner rope or string of various lengths and colors. Tie them along the thicker rope, so that they all hang on the same side.

THE MILKY WAY

On dark nights, Inca priests looked for the band of stars that we call the Milky Way. They called it *Mayu* (Heavenly River) and used it to make calculations about seasons and weather conditions. In its darker spaces they saw the shadow of the rain god Apu Illapu. The shape of the Milky Way was believed to mirror that of the Inca Empire.

SUN WATCH

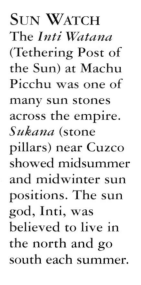

The *Inti Watana* (Tethering Post of the Sun) at Machu Picchu was one of many sun stones across the empire. *Sukana* (stone pillars) near Cuzco showed midsummer and midwinter sun positions. The sun god, Inti, was believed to live in the north and go south each summer.

KEEPERS OF THE QUIPU

Vast amounts of information could be stored on a *quipu*. A large one might have up to 2,000 cords. The *quipu* was much like an Inca version of the computer, only the memory had to be provided by the operator's brain rather than a silicon chip. Learning the *quipu* code of colors, knots, and major and minor strings took many years. Expert operators were called *quipu-kamayuq.*

You have now designed a simple quipu. Can you imagine designing a system that would record the entire population of a town, their ages, the taxes they have paid and the taxes they owe? The Incas did just that!

4 Tie knots in the thinner ropes or strings. One knot you might like to try begins by making a loop of rope as shown in the picture above.

5 Pass one end of the rope through the loop. Pull the rope taut but don't let go of the loop. Repeat this step until you have a long knot. Pull it tight.

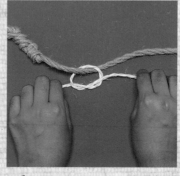

6 Make different sizes of knots on all the ropes or strings. Each knot could represent a family member, school lesson or other important detail.

7 Add some more strings to the knotted strings. Your *quipu* may be seen by lots of people. Only you will know what the ropes, strings and knots mean!

Married Life

WEDDINGS WERE SOME of the happiest occasions in an Inca village. They offered a chance for the whole community to take time off work. The day was celebrated with dancing, music and feasting. The groom would probably be 25 years of age, at which point he was regarded as an adult citizen, and his bride would be younger—about 20.

For the first year of the marriage, a couple did not have to pay any tax either in goods or labor. However, most of their lives would be spent working hard. When they were elderly, they would still be expected to help with household chores. Later still, when they became too old or sick to look after themselves, they received free food and clothes from the state warehouse. They would then be cared for by their clan or family group.

Not everyone was expected to get married. The *mamakuna* (virgins of the sun) lived much like nuns, in a special convent in Cuzco. They wove fine cloth and carried out religious duties. No men were allowed to enter the *mamakuna's* building.

WEDDING CLOTHES
An Inca nobleman would get married in a very fine tunic. This one is from the southern coast of Peru. Commoners had to wear simpler clothes, but couples were presented with free new clothes from the state warehouses when they married.

REAL PEOPLE
This jar from the Moche period is over 1,300 years old. Unlike the portraits on many jars, it seems to show a real person sitting down and thinking about life. It reminds us that ancient empires were made up of individuals who fell in love, raised children and grew old, just as people do today.

MARRIAGE PROSPECTS
Two Inca noble women are painted on the side of this *kero* (wooden beaker). Women of all social classes were only allowed to marry with the approval of their parents and of state officials. They were expected to remain married for life and divorce was forbidden. If either the husband or wife was unfaithful, he or she could face trial and might even be put to death.

A ROYAL MARRIAGE

A prince of the emperor's family marries in Cuzco. The scene is imagined by an artist of the 1800s. An emperor had many secondary wives in addition to his sister-empress. Between them they produced very many princes and princesses. Inca royal families were divided by jealousy and by complicated relations, which often broke out in open warfare. The emperor ordered his officials to keep tight control over who married whom. His own security on the throne depended on it.

A HOME OF THEIR OWN

When a couple married, they left their parents' houses and moved into their own home, like this one at Machu Picchu. The couple now took official control of the fields they would work. These had been allocated to the husband when he was born. Most couples stayed in the area occupied by their own clan, so their relatives would remain nearby.

HIS AND HERS

The everyday lives of most married couples in the Inca Empire were taken up by hard work. Men and women were expected to do different jobs. Women made the *chicha* beer and did the cooking, weaving and some field work. Men did field work and fulfilled the *mit'a* labor tax in service to the Inca State. They might build irrigation channels or repair roads.

Land of the Dead

ARCHAEOLOGISTS HAVE FOUND many burial sites in the Andes. Bodies are most easily preserved in very dry or very cold conditions, and this region has both. As early as 3200 B.C., the Andean peoples learned how to embalm or mummify bodies. The insides were often removed and buried. The rest of the body was dried, and the eyes were replaced with shells. When an Inca emperor died, his mummified body was kept in his former palace. The body was waited on by his descendants and even taken out to enjoy festivals! Respect for ancestors was an important part of Inca religious beliefs.

Inca funerals were sad occasions with slow music. Women cut off their long hair as a sign of grief. When the emperor died, some of his wives and servants were killed. The Incas believed that good people went to *Hanakpacha*, the Empire of the Sun, after death. Bad people had a wretched afterlife, deep in the earth.

FACING THE NEXT WORLD

Many South American mummies were buried in a sitting position. Their knees were drawn up and bound into position with cord. Over their faces were masks of wood, clay or gold, depending on their status. This mask, perhaps from the pre-Incan Nazca period, was decorated with colored feathers.

THE LORD OF SIPÁN

In 1988, a Peruvian archaeologist named Dr. Walter Alva opened up a royal tomb at Sipán, near Chiclayo in northern Peru. The "Lord of Sipán" had been buried there with his servants, amid treasures made of gold, silver, copper and precious stones. The tomb belonged to the Moche civilization, which flourished between A.D. 1 and 700.

A CHANCAY GRAVE DOLL

You will need: scissors, cream calico fabric, pencil, ruler, paints, paintbrush, water container, black yarn, white glue, batting, 20 red pipe cleaners, red yarn.

1 Cut two rectangles of fabric 6½ x 4½ in. for the body. Cut two shield-shaped pieces 2¾ in. wide and 3¼ in. long for the head. Paint one side as shown.

2 Cut 35 strands of black wool, each 7¼ in. long, for the doll's hair. Glue them evenly along the top of the wrong side of the unpainted face shape.

3 Cut a piece of batting slightly smaller than the face. Glue it on top of the hair and face below. Then glue the painted face on top. Let dry.

TOWERS OF THE DEAD

Various South American peoples left mummies in stone towers called *chullpas*, such as these ones at Nina Marca. Goods were placed in the towers for the dead person to use in the next life. These included food and drink, pins, pots, knives, mirrors and clothes. Discoveries of the goods left in graves have helped archaeologists find out about everyday life long ago.

FACE OF THE MUMMY

This head belonged to a body that was mummified over 1,400 years ago in the Nazca desert. The skin is leathery, and the mouth gapes open in a lifelike manner. Most extraordinary is the skull's high, domed forehead. This shows that the dead person had his head bound with cloth as a small child. An elongated head was a sign of status amongst the Nazca people.

DEATH WITH HONOR

This face mask of beaten gold dates back to the 1100s or 1200s, during the Inca Empire. Its eyes are made of emerald, and it is decorated with pendants and a nose ornament. The crest on top, decorated with animal designs, serves as a crown or headdress. This mask was made by a Chimú goldsmith and laid in a royal grave.

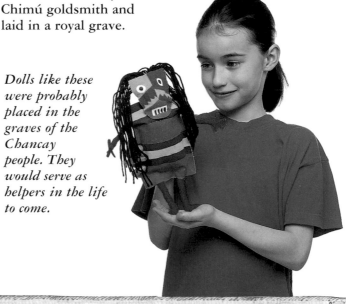

Dolls like these were probably placed in the graves of the Chancay people. They would serve as helpers in the life to come.

4 For each arm, take five pipe cleaners and cut them to 4½ in. Twist them together to within ½ in. of one end. Splay this end to make fingers.

5 Make legs in the same way, but this time twist all the way and bend the ends to make feet. Wind yarn around the arms and legs to hide the twists.

6 Assemble the doll as in the picture. Use glue to attach the arms and legs and batting between the body pieces. Glue the front piece of the body in place.

7 Use glue to attach the head to the front of the body, making sure the hair does not become caught. Let the doll dry completely before picking it up.

Warriors and Weapons

THE INCA EMPIRE was brought about and held together by military force. Its borders were defended by a string of forts. The cities served as walled refuges when the surrounding countryside was under attack from enemies. There was a standing army of some 10,000 elite troops, but the great bulk of soldiers were conscripts, paying their state dues by serving out their *mit'a*. Badges and headdresses marked the rank of officers. In the 1500s women joined in the resistance to the Spanish conquest, using slings to devastating effect. The Incas were fierce fighters, but they stood no chance against the guns and steel of the Spanish.

TAKE THAT!
This star may have looked pretty, but it was deadly when whirled from the leather strap. It was made of obsidian, a glassy black volcanic rock. Inca warriors also fought with spikes set in wooden clubs, and some troops favored the *bolas*, corded weights that were also used in hunting. Slings were used for scaring the birds. However, in the hands of an experienced soldier, they could be used to bring down a hail of stones on enemies and crack their heads open.

WAITING FOR THE CHARGE
A Moche warrior goes down on one knee and brings up his shield in defense. He is bracing himself for an enemy charge. All South American armies fought on foot. The horse was not seen in Peru until the Spanish introduced it.

IN THE BARRACKS
Many towns of the Inca Empire were garrisoned by troops. These restored barrack blocks at Machu Picchu may once have housed conscripted soldiers serving out their *mit'a*. They would have been inspected by a high-ranking general from Cuzco. During the Spanish invasion, it is possible that Machu Picchu became a base for desperate resistance fighters.

AN INCA HELMET
You will need: scissors, cream calico fabric, ruler, balloon, white glue, paintbrush, paints, water container, yellow and black felt, black yarn.

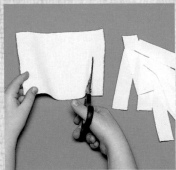

1 Cut the fabric into strips about 3¼ x ¾ in. as shown in the picture. You will need enough to cover the top half of a blown-up balloon three times.

2 Blow up the balloon to the same size as your head. Glue the strips of fabric over the top half. Let each layer dry before adding the next.

3 When the last layer is dry, pop the balloon and carefully pull it out. Use scissors to trim around the edge of the helmet. Paint it a reddish orange.

KINGS OF THE CASTLE

The massive fortress of Sacsahuaman at Cuzco was built on a hill. One edge was formed by a cliff and the other defended by massive terraces and zigzag walls. The invading Spanish were excellent castle-builders. They were awestruck by Sacsahuaman's size and defenses. The Incas regarded warfare as an extension of religious ritual. Sacsahuaman was certainly used for religious ceremonies. Some historians claim that the Inca capital was laid out in the shape of a giant puma, with Sacsahuaman as its head.

SIEGE WARFARE

An Inca army takes on the enemy at Pukara, near Lake Titicaca. Most South American cities were walled and well defended. Siege warfare was common. The attackers blocked the defenders' ways of escape from the town. After the conquest, in 1536, Inca rebels under Manko Inka trapped Spanish troops in Cuzco and besieged them for over a year.

Inca helmets were round in shape and made of wood or cane. They were decorated with braids and crests.

4 Take the felt. Measure and cut a 1¼-in. yellow square, a yellow circle with a diameter of 1¼ in., a 3½-in. yellow square and a 2¼-in. black square.

5 Glue the felt shapes onto the helmet as shown above. Glue a ¾-in.-wide strip of yellow felt along the edge of the helmet to neaten the edge.

6 Take 12 strands of black yarn, each 12 in. long. Divide them into 3 hanks of 4 strands. Knot the ends together, then braid to the end.

7 Knot the end of the finished braid. Make two more. Glue them inside the back of the helmet. Wait until it is dry before trying it on.

Eclipse of the Sun

IN NOVEMBER 1532, the emperor Ataw Wallpa met the Spanish invaders, under Francisco Pizarro, in the great square of Cajamarca. The *Sapa Inca* was riding in a litter that was covered in feathers. Surrounding him were troops glinting with gold. The sound of conch trumpets and flutes echoed around the buildings. The Spanish were amazed by the sight, and the Incas looked uneasily at the strangers with their fidgeting horses.

Within just one hour, thousands of Incas had been killed, and their emperor was in the hands of the Spanish. Ataw Wallpa was arrested. He offered to raise a ransom to secure his release. Silver and gold arrived by the ton, filling up a whole room. The Spanish gained unimagined riches. Even so, in the summer of 1533 they accused Ataw Wallpa of treason, and he was garroted (executed by strangulation). Resistance to the Spanish continued for another 39 years, but South American civilization had changed forever that day.

THE WORD OF GOD?
When emperor Ataw Wallpa met the Spanish invaders in Cajamarca, he was approached by a Christian priest named Vincente de Valverde. The priest raised a Bible and said that it contained the words of God. Ataw Wallpa grabbed the book and listened to it. No words came out, so he hurled it to the ground. The Spanish were enraged, and the invasion began.

CONQUEST AND SLAVERY
The Spanish conquest was a disaster for all the native peoples of the Americas. Many of them were murdered, enslaved or worked to death in the mines. The Spanish introduced money into Inca life, trading in silver, gold, farm produce and coca. But it was mostly the Spanish settlers who became wealthy, not the native people.

"SANTIAGO!"
Before the 1532 meeting with Ataw Wallpa in the great square of Cajamarca, the Spanish invader Francisco Pizarro had hidden troops behind buildings. When he shouted the pre-arranged signal of *"Santiago!"* (St. James), they began to shoot into the crowd. Chaos broke out as the emperor was seized and taken prisoner.

SUFFERING FOR SILVER

In 1545, the Spanish discovered silver at Potosí in the Bolivian Andes and began to dig mines. The wealth was incredible, but the working conditions were hellish. Local people were forced to work as slaves. Mule trains carried the silver northward to Colombian ports, making Spain the richest country in the world.

THE TREASURE FLEETS

The Spanish plundered the treasure of the Incas and the minerals of the Andes. Big sailing ships called galleons carried the gold and silver back to Europe from ports in Central and South America. The region was known as the Spanish Main. Rival European ships, many of them pirates from England, France and the Netherlands, began to prey on the Spanish fleets. This led to long years of warfare. Between 1820 and 1824, Spain's South American colonies finally broke away from European rule to become independent countries, but most of the region's native peoples remained poor and powerless.

DESCENDANTS OF THE EMPIRE

Christians of Quechuan and mixed descent take part in a procession through Cuzco. In the Andes, over the past few hundred years, many Inca traditions, festivals and pilgrimages have become mixed up with Christian ones. Indigenous peoples today make up 45 percent of the total population in Peru, 55 percent in Bolivia, and 25 percent in Ecuador.

Glossary

A

akllakuna Girls selected for special education and training in the Inca capital.

alloy Any metal made from a mixture of other metals.

alpaca A llama-like animal, valued for its wool.

aqueduct A channel carrying water supplies. It may take the form of a bridge when it crosses a valley.

archaeology The study of ancient remains and ruins.

ashlar A squared-off block of stone, used for building.

astrology The belief that the stars, planets and moon influence the way we live on earth.

astronomy The observation and scientific study of the stars, planets and other heavenly bodies.

ayllu A land-holding clan, made up of people descended from the same ancestor.

B

backstrap loom A system of weaving in which the upright (warp) threads are stretched between a post and a belt around the weaver's waist.

barracks Buildings used to house soldiers.

barter To exchange one item for another, to swap. This is the way in which goods may be acquired in societies that have no money.

blood-letting Cutting a patient to release blood, for medical reasons.

bola Three heavy balls tied to cords. It was used by soldiers as a weapon and by hunters and herders to bring down birds and running animals.

bronze A metal alloy, made by mixing copper with tin.

C

cassava A starchy root crop, first grown for food in the Americas. It is also called manioc.

chicha Strong beer made from fermented corn.

chullpa A burial chamber in the form of a tower.

coca A South American plant whose leaves were used by the Incas as a mild drug, as a medicine and for fortune-telling.

compound An enclosed yard surrounding a building or group of buildings.

conch A large seashell that makes a booming sound when it is blown.

conscription A term of service to the state, in which people have to work as laborers or soldiers.

D

distaff A cleft stick used to dispense fiber for spinning.

drill A length of wood that is rotated rapidly against another. The friction makes it so hot that it can be used to start a fire.

drop-spindle A hand-held weight used to draw out fiber and spin it into yarn.

E

empire A group of lands ruled or governed by a single country.

G

gables The pointed ends of a house, supporting the roof.

garrison A force of soldiers posted to guard a fortress or a town.

gourd A hard-skinned plant, often hollowed out for use as a container.

guanaco A wild relative of the llama, commonly hunted.

I

incense A gum or any other material which is burned to produce sweet-smelling smoke during religious ceremonies.

indigenous Originating from a country, native.

irrigation Bringing water to dry lands so that crops can be grown.

K

kero A drinking vessel.

kinua A plant whose seeds can be used to make a sort of porridge and whose leaves can be cooked like spinach.

kuraka One of the local chiefs of lands conquered by the Incas.

L

litter A chair or platform in which someone is carried.

llama A camel-like creature of South America. It is used as a pack animal, shorn for its wool and was sacrificed in religious ceremonies by the Incas.

loom A piece of equipment used to weave cloth.

M

mamakuna Virgins of the sun, selected from the *akllakuna* to remain unmarried and lead religious lives.

manioc A starchy root crop, first grown for food in the Americas. It is also called cassava.

mit'a Conscripted labor, owed to the Inca State as a form of tax.

mummy A dead body preserved by being dried out in the sun, by extreme cold or by using mixtures of chemicals.

N

niche A hollow inset in a wall.

nobles People who are high in social rank.

O

omen A sign of good or bad fortune in the future.

oracle A mysterious telling of one's fortune, or a shrine.

overseer A supervisor or boss.

P

panaka A land-holding corporation made up of nobles who were related to each other.

panpipes A series of pipes, normally of cane, joined to make a single musical instrument. Sounds are produced by blowing over the open ends.

pendant A piece of jewelry that hangs down, usually from the neck.

plateau Geographical feature of high, flat land, usually among mountains.

plumbline A weighted cord, held up to see if a wall or other construction is vertical.

pyramid A large monument with a square base, rising to a point or with steps up to a platform.

Q

quipu A series of knotted, colored cords used to record information.

Quya The Inca empress, who was the sister-wife or mother of the emperor.

S

sacrifice Ritual killing of people or animals to please the gods.

Sapa Inca One of the titles taken by some Inca emperors, meaning "Only Leader."

sling A length of cord used to hurl stones or other missiles.

smelt To heat rock to a high temperature, melting and extracting the metal that is contained within it.

squash Vegetable important to the Incas as a food source.

T

textile Cloth produced by weaving threads together.

topos A unit of measurement used in the Inca Empire, equal to about 4 miles.

trapezoid Having four sides, of which only two are parallel. The Incas often used trapezoid shapes when designing windows and doors.

trepan Boring a hole in someone's skull for medical or religious reasons.

tribute Taxes paid in goods by conquered people.

tumi A ceremonial knife with a semi-circular blade.

tupu A long pin used by women to fasten clothing together. The Incas did not have buttons.

V

vicuña A llama-like animal whose wool was used to make the finest cloth.

W

wa'qa A shrine, a holy place or holy object.

NORTH AMERICAN INDIANS

The Sioux, the Blackfoot and other native American tribes roamed the Great Plains, setting up camp in tipis and hunting for bison. There were hundreds of different tribes and languages in the vast land of North America.

MICHAEL STOTTER

CONSULTANT: MICHAEL JOHNSON

The First Americans

DESCENDANTS OF THE ANASAZIS, who were among the earliest known North American Indians, have colorful tales of their origins. One story tells how their ancestors climbed into the world through a hole. Another describes how all of the tribes were created from a fierce monster who was ripped apart by a brave coyote. The early history of the many nations or tribes is not clear, though archaeological finds have helped to build a picture of their way of life. If you could step back to before A.D. 1500, you would find that the United States and Canada were home to hundreds of different native tribes. Each had its own leader(s) and a distinctive language and culture. Some tribes were nomadic, some settled permanently in large communities. Remains of pottery, woodcarvings and jewelry show how many of the North American peoples developed expert craft skills.

KEEPING THE PAST ALIVE
Descendants of the different tribes survive throughout North America, passing down stories and traditions to new generations. This boy in Wyoming is dressed in ceremonial costume for a modern powwow. He is helping to preserve his tribe's cultural history.

BRIDGING THE GAP
Archaeological evidence suggests that the first American Indians traveled from Asia. They crossed ice and land bridges formed at the Bering Strait around 13,000 B.C. or earlier. From here, they moved south, some settling along the coasts.

TIMELINE 32,000 B.C.–A.D. 1400

Most historians believe that hunters walked to North America from Siberia. Evidence suggests there may have been two migrations—one around 32,000 B.C., the second between 28,000 B.C. and 13,000 B.C. Some historians think there may have been earlier ancient populations already living there. More research is needed to support this theory. The hunters spread out, each group, or tribe, adapting their way of life to suit their environment. Later, some gave up the nomadic hunting life and began to settle as farmers.

serpent mound of the Hopewell culture

3000 B.C. Inuit of the Arctic are probably the last settlers to come from Asia.

1000 B.C. Early cultures are mound builders such as the Adena and later, the Hopewell people. The Hopewell are named after the farmer on whose Ohio land their main site was found.

1000 B.C. Farming cultures develop in the Southwest with agricultural skills brought from Mexico.

black and yellow corn

300 B.C.–A.D. 1450 Cultures, such as the Hohokam, use shells as currency.

A.D. 200 (or before) There is evidence of corn being grown by the mound-building people, probably introduced from Mexico.

A.D. 700–900 Pueblo people bury their dead with black and white painted Mimbres pots.

burial pot

32,000 B.C.   3000 B.C.   300 B.C.

FALSE FACE

Dramatic, carved masks were worn by several tribes to ward off evil spirits thought to cause illnesses. This one is from the Iroquois people. It was known as a False Face mask because it shows an imaginary face. False Face ceremonies are still performed in North America today.

BUCKSKIN RECORD

Tales of events were painted on animal skins, such as this one, created by an Apache. The skins serve as a form of history book. North American Indians had no real written alphabet, so much of the evidence about their way of life comes from pictures.

DIGGING UP EVIDENCE

Hopewell Indians made this bird from hammered copper. It dates back to around 300 B.C. and was uncovered in a burial mound in Ohio. The mounds were full of intricate trinkets buried alongside the dead. Finds like this tell us about the crafts, materials and customs of the time.

ANCIENT TOWN

Acoma *(right)* is one of the oldest continuously inhabited traditional Pueblo settlements in the Southwest. It is still partly inhabited by Pueblo descendants. The Pueblo people were given their name by Spaniards who arrived in the area in 1540. *Pueblo* is a Spanish word meaning village. It was used to describe the kind of tribe that lived in a cluster of houses built from mud and stone. Flat-roofed homes were built in terraces, two or three stories high.

A.D. 700

A.D. 700 Mound-building cultures build temples at Cahokia near the Mississippi River. The city holds the largest population in North America before the 1800s.

A.D. 900 Earliest Anasazis (ancient people) on the Colorado Plateau live in sunken pit homes. Later, they build their homes above the ground but keep pit dwellings as kivas, which are their religious buildings.

kiva (underground temple) of the Anasazis

A.D. 982 First Europeans reach Greenland (northeast of Canada) under the Viking, Erik the Red.

A.D. 1002 Leif Eriksson lands in Newfoundland, Canada, and creates the first European settlements.

Vikings arrive

A.D. 1100 Anasazi people move into the mountains, building settlements in cliffs.

Mesa Verde, a cliff palace

A.D. 1200 The Calusa in Florida are skillful carvers and craftsmen who trade extensively.

1270s–1300 Anasazis abandon many of their prehistoric sites and stone cities—many move eastward.

1300 Beginnings of the Pueblo tribes (Hopi and Zuni) in the Southwest. Many of these are descendants of the Anasazis.

A.D. 1400

Inhabiting a Vast Land

The first North Americans were hunters who followed musk oxen, bison and other animals to the grassland interior of the huge continent. Early settlements grew up in the rugged, hostile terrain of the Southwest where three dominant cultures evolved. The Mogollon (Mountain People) are thought to be the first Southwest dwellers to build houses, make pottery and grow their own food, starting around 300 B.C. The Hohokam (Vanished Ones) devised an extensive canal system to irrigate the desert as early as 100 B.C., while the Anasazi (Ancient Ones) were basket makers who built their homes high among the cliffs and canyons. In contrast, the eastern and midwestern lands abounded with plant and animal life. Here, tribes such as the Adena (1000 B.C. to A.D. 200) and the Hopewell (300 B.C. to A.D. 700), created huge earth mounds to bury their dead. The central Great Plains was home to over 30 different tribes, who lived by hunting bison. In the far north, the Inuit had a similar existence, relying on caribou and seals for their food and clothes. Europeans began to arrive around A.D. 982 with the Vikings. Then, in the 1500s, Spanish explorers came looking for gold, land and slaves. Over the next 400 years, many other foreign powers laid claim to different parts of the land. By 1910, the native population was at its lowest, about 400,000, and many tribes had been forced from their homelands on to reservations.

Aleut

orca (killer whale)

TRIBAL HOMELANDS
In the 1400s, there were more than 300 tribes, or nations, spread across North America (between two and three million people). These are often divided into ten cultural areas based on the local environment:
1 Arctic
2 Subarctic
3 Woodlands
4 Southeast
5 Great Plains
6 Southwest
7 Great Basin
8 Plateau
9 Northwest Coast
10 California.

TIMELINE A.D. 1400–1780

Columbus

1400 Apaches arrive in the Southwest, probably by two routes—one from the Plains after following migrating buffalo, the other via the Rockies.

1492 Christopher Columbus sails from Spain to the Bahamas, where he meets the peaceful, farming Arawaks.

1510 The powerful Calusas of Florida abandon their ancient center, Key Marco, an island made from shells, possibly after hearing of foreign invaders.

1513 Calusas drive off Ponce de León.

1541 Zuni people get a first glimpse of horses when Spain's Francisco Vasquez de Coronado travels to the Southwest.

1541 Caddo people of the Plains oppose Spanish Hernando de Soto's soldiers.

1542 The large Arawak population that Columbus first encountered has been reduced to just 200 people. Ten years later the Arawaks die out due to mistreatment.

shell wampum belt celebrates the League of Five Nations

1550 League of Five Nations is formed by the Seneca, Cayuga, Mohawk, Oneida and Onondaga tribes in the northeast to create a strong government. They are referred to as the Iroquois.

1585 Sir Walter Raleigh reaches the northeast coast and, ignoring the rights of the Secotan natives, claims the land for the English, calling it Virginia.

1590 Raleigh and John White return to Virginia, but the colony has disappeared. White draws pictures documenting Secotan life.

1400   1540   1550   1595

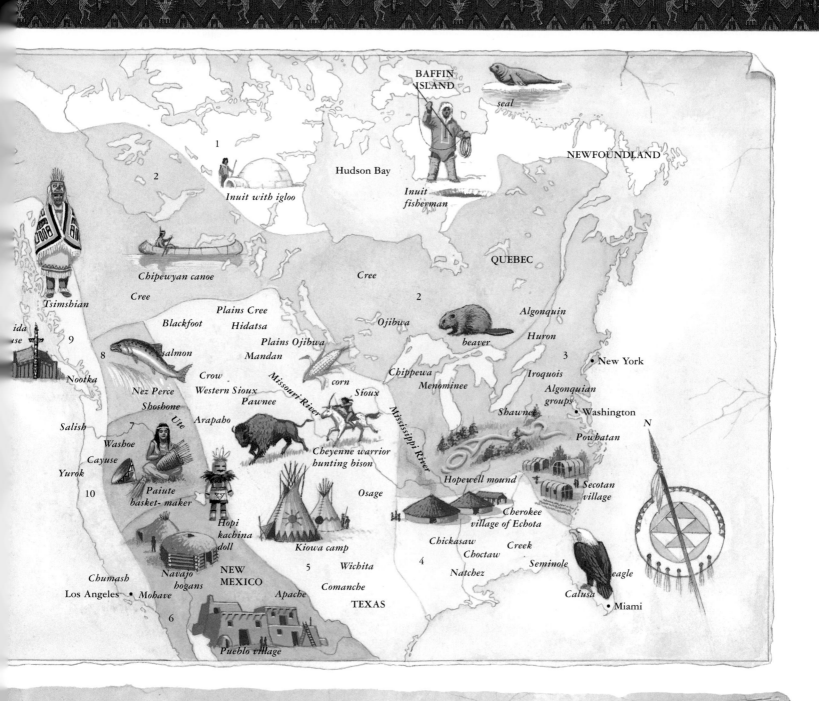

BAFFIN ISLAND

seal

NEWFOUNDLAND

1

2

Hudson Bay

Inuit with igloo

Inuit fisherman

QUEBEC

Chipewyan canoe

Cree

Cree

2

Ojibwa

Algonquin

Plains Cree

Hidatsa

beaver

Huron

Tsimshian

Blackfoot

Plains Ojibwa

3

New York

ida
se

9

salmon

Mandan

Chippewa

Iroquois

8

Crow

corn

Menominee

Algonquian
groups

Nootka

Western Sioux

Sioux

Washington

Nez Perce

Pawnee

Shawnee

Salish

Shoshone

Arapaho

Powhatan

Ute

N

Washoe

Missouri River

Cayuse

Mississippi River

Yurok

10

Paiute
basket- maker

Cheyenne warrior
hunting bison

Hopewell mound

Secotan
village

Hopi
kachina
doll

Osage

Cherokee
village of Echota

Chickasaw

Creek

Chumash

Navajo
hogans

NEW
MEXICO

Kiowa camp

Choctaw

Seminole

Los Angeles

Mohave

5

Wichita

4

Natchez

eagle

Apache

Comanche

Calusa

6

TEXAS

Miami

Pueblo village

1598 Juan de Onate founds the first Spanish colony on Pueblo Indian land.

1600s Shoshone acquire horses from the Southwest (brought there by Spanish invaders), and they spread across the Great Plains.

horses on the Plains

1607 Jamestown colony is founded on Powhatan land.

1607 Pamunkey members of the Powhatan Confederacy take John Smith prisoner.

1620 The Mayflower Pilgrims arrive on the east coast and are helped by the Wampanoag.

willow bow

1650 Guns from European traders (at first flintlocks, later rifles) begin to take the place of traditional weapons.

1707 A Russian expedition reaches the Northwest Coast to discover that it is inhabited.

coup stick

rifle

1722 League of Five Nations increases to six when the Tuscarora join the group.

1774 Juan Perez sails to the Northwest Coast to take the land for Spain. Smallpox, from the Europeans, almost wipes out the Haida people.

Around 1750, Sioux tribes move to the Plains.

1771 Five Franciscan missions are set up on Chumash land in California (this leads to a revolt in 1824).

1620

1710

Haida totem pole

Brave and Bold

MANY NORTH AMERICAN Indians who have earned a place in history lived around the time that Europeans reached North America. They became famous for their dealings with explorers and with the white settlers who were trying to reorganize the lives of American Indian nations. Some tribes welcomed the new settlers. Others tried to negotiate peacefully for rights to their own land. Those who led their people in battles, against the settlers, became the most legendary. One of these was Geronimo, who led the last defiant group of Chiricahua Apaches in their fight to preserve the tribe's homeland and culture.

POCAHONTAS (1595–1617)
The princess became a legend, and the topic of a Disney film, for protecting English Captain John Smith against her father, Chief Powhatan. The English took Pocahontas captive to force Powhatan's people to agree to their demands. She married John Rolfe, an English soldier, and in 1616 left for England with their baby. She never returned, and died of smallpox, in England, at the age of 22.

CORNPLANTER (died 1796)
In the 1700s, Cornplanter was a chief of the Iroquois Confederacy. He was a friend to the Americans and fought on their side in the Revolution of 1775–83. Seneca lands were spoiled, but Cornplanter's people were given a reservation for their help. Many Iroquois people fought on the side of the British, which split the group.

Opechancanough, Powhatan

Black Hawk, Sauk

Geronimo, Apache

Pontiac, Ottawa

Lapowinsa, Lenape

TIMELINE A.D. 1780–1924

1783 The colonists (settlers) sign a treaty with Britian, which recognizes their independence and calls them Americans. The tribes are never regarded as American.

1788 The Chinook in the Northwest have their first encounter with Europeans when they meet Englishman, John Mears.

1789 Explorers encounter Kutchin and other Subarctic tribes, who later set up trade with the Hudson's Bay Company (formed in 1831).

1795 Tecumseh refuses to sign the Treaty of Greenville giving up Shawnee land.

William Clark and Meriwether Lewis

1803 The United States federal government buys Mississippi land from the French, squeezing out the tribes even more.

1804 Sacawagea guides Lewis and Clark on the first overland journey from Mississippi to the Pacific Coast.

1830–40s Painters such as Frederic Remington, George Catlin and Karl Bodmer, document lifestyles of the Plains Indians.

1832 Sauk chief, Black Hawk, leads a final revolt against the United States and is defeated.

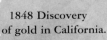

George Catlin painting a Mandan chief

1848 Discovery of gold in California.

coming of the train

1848–58 Palouse tribe of the Plateau resist white domination, refusing to join a reservation.

1780   1803   1848

SARAH WINNEMUCCA (1844–1891)

Sarah was from the Paviotso Paiutes of northern Nevada. Her grandfather escorted British Captain John Fremont in his exploration of the West in the 1840s. But in 1860 her mother, sister and brother were all killed in the Paiute War against white settlers. Sarah acted as a mediator between her people and the settlers to help improve conditions. She later wrote a book, *Life Among the Paiutes,* telling of the suffering of the tribe and her own life.

SITTING BULL (1831–1890)

The Hunkpapa Sioux had a spiritual leader, a medicine man known as Sitting Bull. He brought together sub-tribes of the Sioux and refused to sign treaties giving up the sacred Black Hills in South Dakota. He helped to defeat of General Custer at Little Bighorn.

TECUMSEH (Died 1813)

A great chief of the Shawnees, Tecumseh, tried to unite tribes of the Mississippi valley, Northwest and South against the United States. He even fought for the British against the United States in the 1812–14 war. The picture shows his death.

Oscelo, Seminole

Red Cloud, Sioux

Chief Joseph

PROTECTING THEIR TRIBES

These eight North American chiefs are some of the most famous. Not all fought. Lapowinsa of Delaware, was cheated out of land when he signed a contract allowing settlers as much land as they could cover in a day and a half. Pontiac traded with the French but despised English intrusion. Chief Joseph tried to negotiate peacefully for land for the Nez Perce tribe but died in exile. Red Cloud successfully fought to stop gold seekers invading Sioux hunting grounds.

1850s–80s Railways open up the West to settlers.

1850 The Navajo sign their third treaty with the United States, but hostilities continue.

1864 The Long Walk—Navajo people and animals are massacred by United States troops, their homes burned. Survivors are forced to walk 300 mi. to Fort Sumner.

1864 Sand Creek Massacre—300 Cheyenne women and children are killed by United States soldiers.

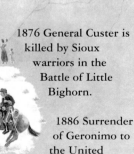

Sand Creek Massacre

1876 General Custer is killed by Sioux warriors in the Battle of Little Bighorn.

1886 Surrender of Geronimo to the United States. He is a prisoner.

1890 Ghost dance springs up as Sioux tribes mourn their dead— it worries the white settlers who see it as provocation.

1890 Sitting Bull is killed at Standing Rock reservation by American Indian police hired by the United States.

1890 Sioux chief Big Foot and many of his tribe are killed in the Massacre of Wounded Knee. This ends the Sioux's struggle for their homelands.

Buffalo coin

1924 United States citizenship granted to American Indians and marked by a coin bearing a buffalo.

Ghost dance shirt

1870

1924

Nomadic Life

MANY TRIBES, such as the Cheyenne and Arapaho of the Great Plains, were nomadic. Their life was regulated by the bison who supplied them with their food, clothing and shelter. There were also semi-nomadic tribes such as the Pawnee, who spent part of their time in permanent lodges but sometimes wandered onto the Plains to hunt bison. Others, like the Inuit in the Arctic and the Pima of the Southwest, lived in villages but moved with the changing seasons. American Indians believed that the land was a source of life, filled with spirits. They lived in harmony with nature, adapting themselves to their surroundings. In contrast, the white settlers believed that they owned the land, and built

permanent towns that changed the landscape.

FOLLOWING THE HERD
A hunter on horseback catches up with two bison. Before the 1700s, there were massive herds of bison. The Great Plains were virtually treeless, with vast areas of grass to feed the large animals. The Plains covered an area of about 750 mi. by 1,250 mi. and hunters often had to travel for days to glimpse a herd.

FREE LIVING ON THE PLAINS
Groups of women and children moving home across the Great Plains were a common sight. The men would often travel behind the convoy to guard the families from surprise attacks. A travois (carrying frame) was one of the most effective ways of carrying tepees and clothes. It was simply two long poles tied together. Bundles of possessions were strapped in the center, and sometimes children sat on it.

MAKE A TEPEE
You will need: *an old double sheet (or fabric measuring approx 8 x 3 ft), scissors, pencil, ruler/tape measure, large and small paintbrushes, yellow, blue and red acrylic paints, water bowl, 12 bamboo sticks 10 ft long, rope or string, three small sticks, large stones (optional).*

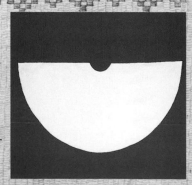

1 Lay the sheet flat. In the center of one longer edge, cut a semicircle 18 in. across and 8 in. deep. Cut the fabric into a semicircle 5 ft deep all around.

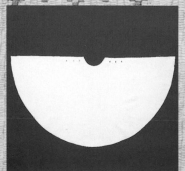

2 Measure, then make, three evenly spaced small holes on each of the straight edges. Start 2½ in. in from the center and 1 in. in from the flat edge.

3 Using a pencil and ruler, draw a geometrical pattern of triangles, lines and circles. Make it bold and simple. Paint it, then let dry.

Camping on the Shores of Lake Huron

A group of Ojibwas go about their everyday business in a camp by Lake Huron. A woman is pounding corn in preparation for making corn mush. The men are resting by their birchbark canoes after a fishing trip. Their simple home is a conical form of the birchbark wigwam. Families would always try to pitch their homes near water.

Whale Knife

This knife has a bone spear tip and shell blades. It was used by the Makah and Nootka whale hunters of the Northwest Coast who used it to cut blubber off whales.

Treasured Memories

An Arctic Inuit carved pictures on a walrus's tusk to record a great day of hunting caribou. Color was added by rubbing a mixture of charcoal and grease into the etched lines.

Moving On

This family of Blackfoot Indians are migrating to Canada. They have few possessions. The homes of the nomadic tribes were easy to construct and easy to pack when it was time to move on.

Your tepee is a simplified version of the Plains tepees. These were large, heavy constructions made of buffalo skin. They had a built-in smoke flap and a cut-out hole for the door.

4 Take three of the bamboo sticks and join them together at the top. Arrange them on the ground to form a tripod. Tie them securely.

5 One by one, lean the rest of the bamboo sticks against and around the tripod. Remember to leave a gap which will be your tepee entrance.

6 Now take the painted sheet (your tepee cover) and wrap it around the frame. Overlap the two sides at the top of the frame so that the holes join up.

7 Insert a small stick through the two top holes to join them. Do this for each of the other holes. Place stones around the bottom to secure your tepee.

Travel and Transport

NORTH AMERICAN INDIANS were often on the move, although walking was at first their only form of land transport. Hunting and trade were the main reasons for traveling. Young infants were carried in cradleboards, while Inuit babies were put into the hoods of their mothers' parkas. Travois were popular among those living on the Plains. These were frames dragged by dogs and later, horses. One strong dog could pull a load of 50 pounds. In the late 1600s, the Spanish introduced horses, which the Crees called big dogs. This transformed Plains life, as tribes could travel greater distances to fresh hunting grounds.

WATER WAYS
A Kutenai Indian uses his birchbark canoe to paddle out to a clump of rushes. Much of North America is covered with rivers, streams and lakes, and tribesmen were skilled boatbuilders. There were kayaks (Arctic), bark canoes (Woodlands) and large cedar canoes (Northwest Coast).

ANCIENT TRACKS
Traveling over land was traditionally by foot. American Indians made carrying pouches from animal skins, which were tied to their backs by leather strips. For thousands of years, ancient trade routes connected villages that were hundreds of miles apart. Paths and trails were mainly formed by animals, either migrating or looking for food and water. Hunters found and used these trails, which were often no bigger than the width of one person.

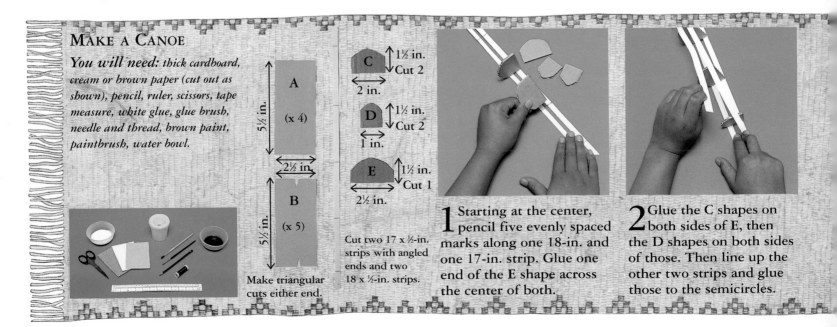

MAKE A CANOE
You will need: thick cardboard, cream or brown paper (cut out as shown), pencil, ruler, scissors, tape measure, white glue, glue brush, needle and thread, brown paint, paintbrush, water bowl.

A (x 4) 5½ in.

2½ in.

B (x 5) 5½ in.

Make triangular cuts either end.

C 1½ in. Cut 2 2 in.

D 1½ in. Cut 2 1 in.

E 1½ in. Cut 1 2½ in.

Cut two 17 x ½-in. strips with angled ends and two 18 x ½-in. strips.

1 Starting at the center, pencil five evenly spaced marks along one 18-in. and one 17-in. strip. Glue one end of the E shape across the center of both.

2 Glue the C shapes on both sides of E, then the D shapes on both sides of those. Then line up the other two strips and glue those to the semicircles.

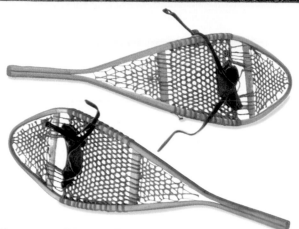

KEEPING YOUR BALANCE

In the north, walking on snow was aided by snowshoes, so that even in deep snow a hunter could pursue his prey. Inuit, in the Subarctic and Arctic, used test sticks, similar to ski poles, to test the strength of ice.

TRAVOIS TRAVEL

Chief Eagle Calf is getting ready for a trip. The long poles of the travois are made into a V–shape and attached to the horse's saddle with leather thongs. The open ends drag on the ground. A carrying platform made of animal skin is stretched across the middle and lashed to the frame. This could be piled with goods or children. It took two horses to carry the poles and covers of a single tepee.

SLEDDING

Sleds were essential in ice and snow. Runners were made of wood or whalebone with antlers for crosspieces. Strips of rawhide helped to cushion the rider and make the ride less bumpy. Sleds were pulled by husky dogs either singly or in teams of up to eight.

COLD HOMECOMING

In the snowy Arctic, Inuit used dogs to pull sleds. Dogs were no use over ice floes, so the Inuit pulled his own sled.

Birchbark canoes were made by the Chipewyan tribe in the Subarctic. They were used for crossing lakes and streams, but also for fishing, farming and gathering rushes and wild rice.

3 Glue the two 18-in. strips together, then the two 17-in. strips, at both ends. Glue shapes B to the frame, making sure the triangular cuts fit over C, D and E.

4 Neaten the ends by gluing the excess paper around the frame. Place the A shapes over the gaps, then glue to the top of the frame.

5 Continue sticking on the rectangles of paper, until all of the boat is covered. Now, carefully fold over and glue the tops of the paper all around.

6 Thread the needle. Using an overlapping stitch, sew all around the top edge of the boat to secure the flaps. Now you can paint your boat.

Tribal Society

Asingle tribe could be as small as ten families or stretch to thousands. Neighboring tribes would come together in times of war, for ceremonies and for trading, or to form powerful confederacies (unions). Some Algonquin people formed the Powhatan Confederacy, named after their leader, and controlled the coastal region of present-day Virginia. Other northeastern groups formed the League of the Iroquois to prevent conflict between local tribes. In the Southeast, the Creek, Seminole, Cherokee, Choctaw and Chickasaw were known by Europeans as the Five Civilized Tribes because of their system of law courts and land rights developed from European influences.

MAGNIFICENTLY COSTUMED
American Horse of the Oglala Sioux wears a double-trail war headdress. His painted shirt shows he was a member of the Ogle Tanka'un, or Shirt Wearers, who were wise and brave.

COMMITTEE MEETING
A Sioux council gathers to hear the head chief speak. Councils were made up of several leaders or chiefs. They elected the head chief, whose authority came from his knowledge of tribal lore and skill as a warrior.

MAKE A HEADDRESS
You will need: ruler, 3 ft x ½-in. red ribbon, red upholstery tape (30 x 2½ in.), masking tape, needle, cotton string, scissors, white paper, black paint, paintbrushes, water bowl, 3mm diameter balsa dowel, white glue, 6 feathers (optional), white, red, yellow, light and dark blue felt, beads (optional), red paper, 8 x ½-in. lengths of colored ribbon.

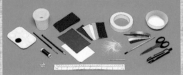

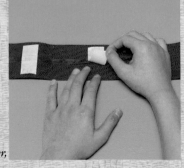

1 Lay the 3-ft length of red ribbon along the middle of the upholstery tape. Leave 5-in. lengths at each end. Tape it in place while you sew it on.

2 Next, make the feathers. Cut 26 feathers from the white paper. They need to be 7 in. long and 1½ in. at their widest point. Paint the tips black.

3 When the black paint is dry, use the scissors to make tiny cuts around the edges of the paper feathers. This will make the paper look more like feathers.

WOMEN IN SOCIETY

The Iroquois women attended council meetings, but in most tribes women did not join councils or become warriors. Women held a respected place in society. In many tribes, such as the Algonquian, people traced their descent through their mother. When a man married, he left his home to live with his wife's family.

DISPLAYS OF WEALTH

Potlatch ceremonies could last for several days. The gathering was a lavish feast celebrated by tribes on the Northwest Coast. Gifts would be exchanged and the status of a tribe judged by their value.

IN COMMAND

This chief comes from the Kainah group of Blackfoot Indians. The Kainah were also known by Europeans as the Blood Indians because of the red face paint they wore. The Blackfoot headdress had feathers that stood upright as opposed to the Sioux headdress, which sloped backward sometimes, with trailing eagle feathers.

FEATHER PIPE OF PEACE

North American Indians had a long tradition of smoking pipes. Plants were often smoked for religious and ritual reasons. Early peace talks involved passing around a pipe for all to smoke to show they had good intentions of keeping agreements.

   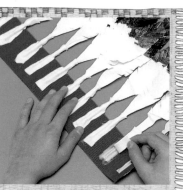

4 Cut the balsa dowel into 26 lengths of 5½ in. long. Carefully glue a stick to the center of the back of each feather, starting just below the black tips.

5 If you are also using real bird feathers, tie them with cotton to the bottom of six of the paper feathers. These will be at the front of the headdress.

6 Glue and tape the feathers to the front of the red band, overlapping the feathers slightly. Position them so that the six real feathers are in the center.

7 Cut ½ x 2½-in. lengths of white felt. Glue them over each of the sticks.

Instructions for the headdress continue on the next page...

Dress and Identity

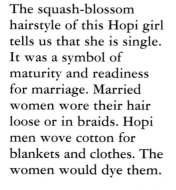

ONE OF THE MOST POPULAR images of a North American Indian is that of a warrior dressed in fringed buckskin with a war headdress and decorated with body paint and beads. That was just one style of dress mainly used by the Plains Indians. Each nation, or tribe, had its own identity and distinctive clothing. Hunters dressed in animal skins and furs.

In areas where agriculture dominated, cloth was woven from wild plant fiber or cultivated cotton. Tribes, such as the Navajo, began to use wool when the Spanish introduced sheep in the 1600s. Climate also dictated what was worn. In the cold north, the Inuit wore mittens, boots and hooded coats called parkas. These were made of seal or caribou skins with the fur worn on the inside. Many east coast and Woodlands men wore just loin cloths or leggings, while women wore fringed skirts.

HOPI GIRL
The squash-blossom hairstyle of this Hopi girl tells us that she is single. It was a symbol of maturity and readiness for marriage. Married women wore their hair loose or in braids. Hopi men wove cotton for blankets and clothes. The women would dye them.

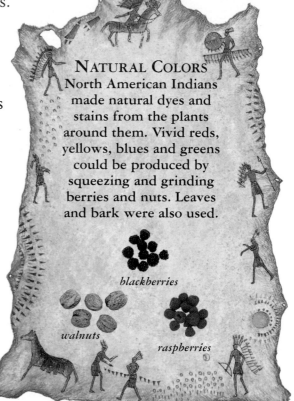

NATURAL COLORS
North American Indians made natural dyes and stains from the plants around them. Vivid reds, yellows, blues and greens could be produced by squeezing and grinding berries and nuts. Leaves and bark were also used.

blackberries

walnuts

raspberries

8 Cut out ½ x ⅓-in. pieces of red felt. Cut 3 for 10 of the feathers (5 each end) and 2 for the rest. Glue to the white felt to make stripes.

9 Cut out a 16 x 1½-in. yellow felt band. Decorate it by gluing on triangles of light and dark blue felt, and small squares of red felt.

10 You can also decorate it with beads. Carefully glue these onto the centerpiece, in the middle of the felt squares and triangles.

11 Very carefully glue the centerpiece to the red band, using a ruler to help you place it in the middle. Some feathers will show on either side.

VERSATILE HAT

This early, woven spruce-root hat was worn by the Nootka on the Northwest Coast. It could also be used for carrying, storage or even as a fish trap. To make it, bundles of fiber were woven together, then coiled into a spiral shape.

TRADITIONAL CRAFTS

This woman wears a modern version of a cape. Woodlands and Plains people particularly liked the red and blue cloth brought by European traders.

WORN WITH PRIDE

Scalplocks of human hair hang down the front of this hide shirt. These show that the Plains warrior who owned it had surpassed himself in battle. He would wear it with pride on ceremonial occasions. The shirt has been made from two deerskins stitched together.

BEADED VEST

To decorate this man's vest the Sioux would have traded goods for glass beads brought to North America from Italy. Beads were traded by weight or by length, in strings. Before beads, the Sioux used porcupine quills to decorate their ceremonial dress.

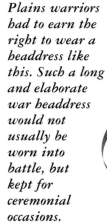

Plains warriors had to earn the right to wear a headdress like this. Such a long and elaborate war headdress would not usually be worn into battle, but kept for ceremonial occasions.

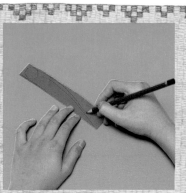

12 Draw a circle 1 in. in diameter on the red paper. Then draw a 6-in. tail starting at the circle. It should measure ½ in. across and taper to a point.

13 Draw eight of these and cut them out. Glue them to the ends of the feathers on the middle of the band so that the points stick into the air.

14 Cut out two circles of yellow felt, 2 in. in diameter, and decorate with red and white felt shapes. Glue the colored ribbons to the back of the circles.

15 Finally, glue or stitch the felt circles on to the headdress on top of the decorative band. The ribbons should hang down on either side of your ears.

Ornament and Decoration

J EWELRY, BODY PAINT and tattoos were worn by both men and women. Haida women tattooed their faces, bodies and the backs of their hands with family symbols. The people of the Yuma wore minimal clothing so that they could display their tattoos with pride. Tattoos could be simple or elaborate, such as the designs that decorated Timucua adults. These were colored black, red and blue. A tattoo revealed status or was worn to gain protection from a spirit. A less permanent and painful form of skin decoration was created with face and body paints. Hairstyles also carried meanings. A particular style could indicate that a young man was unmarried, belonged to a military society or was a brave warrior. Woodlands men had a distinctive hairstyle. They braided their hair at the front and decorated it with turkey feathers. Some Plains warriors, such as the Pawnee and Iowa, shaved their heads completely, leaving a long tuft on top.

WAR PAINT
Mato-Tope, the chief of the Mandan people, put on his war paint just to have his picture painted. He was posing for the artist Karl Bodmer in 1834. Body paint was used to indicate a social position, and was usually applied for ceremonies and before going to war.

CHILDREN'S COSTUMES
These children were photographed in 1913. Even without being told the date, their costume gives away the era and the tribe they are from. This style of clothes was worn by the Sioux. The girl's hair is braided with a center part. This was known as the reservation style because it was popular after the tribe had been moved to official camps. Children's dress was usually a smaller version of adults' clothing.

MAKE A NECKLACE
You will need: white paper, ruler, white glue, brush for the glue, paints in blue, turquoise and red, paintbrush, water bowl, scissors, air-drying modeling clay, wooden skewer, string.

1 Roll up strips of thin white paper into ¼-in. tubes. Glue down the outer edge to seal the tube and let dry. Make three of these paper tubes.

2 Paint the rolls of paper. Paint one roll blue, one turquoise and one red, making sure that you cover all the white. Let them dry.

3 When dried, the painted paper tubes will have hardened slightly. Carefully cut the tubes into ½-in. pieces to make little beads.

THE NATURAL LOOK

Body paints were extracted from raw materials. Red came from earth with iron in it, and copper ore was used for green and blue. Charcoal made a good black. Berries were used to stain faces and clothes.

ocher

charcoal

blueberries

MEDICINE MAN

This medicine man from New Mexico is wearing a head wrap. His beads, scarf and particularly the blanket wrap were popular among the Diné (Navajos). Other tribes wore head wraps, such as the Osage, who wore an otter-skin turban.

TATTOOED WOMAN

A Florida woman's body is covered with simple black band tattoos. They were etched by pricking the skin with needles dipped in vegetable dyes, and were worn by men and women.

DECORATIVE TEETH

An Inuit has carved ivory ornaments for this necklace. Ivory comes from the tusks (canine teeth) of the walrus or the sperm whale.
Inuits use ivory as well as wood, bone, fur and feathers for jewelry, ceremonial masks and trinkets.

Native craftmakers traditionally made beads like these from bone, stone and shell. Some of their bone beads were 3–4 in. long. It was the European traders who brought glass beads over in the 1500s.

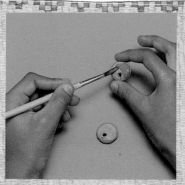

4 Make two larger clay beads by rolling the clay on a flat surface. When you are happy with their shape, pierce the center with the skewer.

5 Let the clay beads dry and harden. When they are ready, paint both of the beads blue (or your preferred color). Once again, let them dry.

6 Thread the beads onto the string. Start with the clay beads, which will hang in the centre. Then, add the blue on either side, then turquoise, then red.

7 Tie a large loop knot at each end of the string when you have finished threading, to stop the beads from falling off. Your necklace is ready to wear.

Native American Homes

URING THE WINTER months, the Inuit of the far north built their dome-shaped homes out of blocks of ice or with hard soil, wood and whale bones. Houses had to be adapted to their surroundings. Where wood was plentiful in the east, a variety of homes was built. The wikiup, or wigwam, was dome-shaped and made out of thatch, bark or hide, tightly woven across an arch of bent branches. Basic, rectangular thatched houses were built from a construction of chopped twigs covered with a mixture of clay and straw, or mud. Near the east coast, massive longhouses, up to 150 feet long, with a barrel-shaped roof, were made from local trees. Some tribes lived in different kinds of shelters depending on the season. The Plains Indians mostly lived in tepees (tents made of hide) or sometimes in earth lodges. The most similar to modern buildings were the homes of the Pueblos in the Southwest. These were terraced villages built of bricks made of mud. The Pueblo Indians also built round underground ceremonial chambers with a hidden entrance in the roof.

AT HOME
A Mandan chief relaxes with his family and dogs inside his lodge. Notice how a hole is cut in the roof to let out smoke from the fire and let fresh air in. Earth lodges were popular with Mandan and Hidatsa people on the Upper Missouri River. The layout followed strict customs. The family would sleep on the south side, guests slept on the north. Stores and weapons were stored at the back. The owner of this home has his horse inside to prevent it from being stolen while the family sleeps.

HOMES ON THE PLAINS
The hides of around 12 buffaloes were used to cover a family tepee belonging to a Plains Indian. Tepee comes from a Siouan word meaning to dwell. Hides were sewn together and stretched over wooden poles about 25 ft high. When it became too hot inside, the tepee sides were rolled up. In winter, a fire was lit in the center.

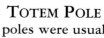

TOTEM POLE
Totem poles were usually found in the far northwest of the United States. They were carved out of wood, often from the mighty thuja (red cedar) trees. Tall totem poles were erected outside the long plank houses of the Haida people. These homes were shared by several families. The poles were carved and painted to keep a record of the family histories of the people inside. They were also sometimes made to honor a great chief.

EARTH LODGES

Mandan Indians perform the Buffalo Dance in front of their lodges. These were built by using logs to create a dome frame, which was then covered over with tightly packed earth.

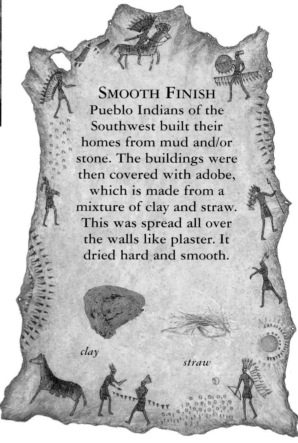

SMOOTH FINISH

Pueblo Indians of the Southwest built their homes from mud and/or stone. The buildings were then covered with adobe, which is made from a mixture of clay and straw. This was spread all over the walls like plaster. It dried hard and smooth.

clay

straw

LAYERS OF BRICK

This ruin was once part of a complex of buildings belonging to Pueblo Indians. Pueblo homes were often many-storied with flat roofs. The floors were reached by ladders. Circular brick chambers were built underground. These were the kivas used for religious and ceremonial rites.

holes in the roof to let out smoke

sleeping platform

higher platform for storing food

THE LONGHOUSE

Iroquois people of the Woodlands built long wooden houses. The frame was made of poles hewn from tree trunks with cladding made from sheets of thick bark. Homes were communal. Many families lived in one longhouse, each with their own section built around an open fire.

Groups of longhouses were built together, sometimes inside a protective fence.

Family Life

ROLES WITHIN THE FAMILY were well-defined. The men were the hunters, protectors and tribal leaders. Women tended crops, made clothes, cared for the home and the sick, and prepared the food. The children's early days were carefree, but they quickly learned to respect their elders. From an early age, young girls were taught the skills of craftwork and homemaking by their mothers, while the boys learned to use weapons and hunt from the men. Girls as young as 12 years old could be married. Boys had to exchange presents with their future in-laws before the marriage was allowed to take place. At birth most children were named by a grandparent. Later, as adults, they could choose another name of their own.

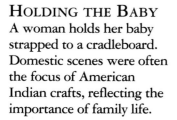

BONES FOR DINNER
This spoon was carved from animal bone. For the early family there were no metal utensils. Many items were made from bone, tusks, antlers or horns. Bone was also used to make bowls.

HOLDING THE BABY
A woman holds her baby strapped to a cradleboard. Domestic scenes were often the focus of American Indian crafts, reflecting the importance of family life.

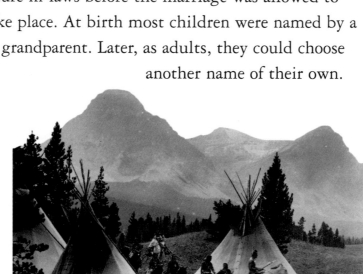

A DAY'S HUNTING
Blackfoot girls look on as men leave camp on a hunting trip. They are in search of bison. If the hunt is successful, the women will help skin the animals, then stretch out the hide to dry. Bison skins were used to make tepee covers. Softer buckskin, from deer, was used for clothing.

MAKE A KACHINA DOLL
You will need: cardboard roll, ruler, scissors, compass, pencil, thick cardboard, white glue, brush for glue, masking tape, paints in cream/yellow, green/blue, red and black, paintbrush, water bowl, red paper.

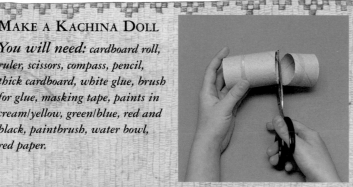

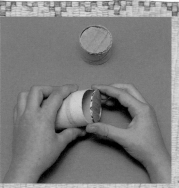

1 Take the cardboard roll and cut a section of about 1½ in. (or a third) off the top. This will form the head piece. The larger end will form the body.

2 Use the compass (or end of the cardboard roll) to draw four circles of ½-in. radius on cardboard. Then draw a smaller circle ¾-in. radius. Cut them all out.

3 Glue the larger circles to either end of both of the cardboard roll tubes. Let dry. Glue the smaller circle of cardboard on top of one end of the longer roll.

ROLE PLAY

Children love to copy their elders, and this little Sioux girl is wearing an adult's large headdress. She is holding a favorite doll to pose for the picture. Playing with dolls taught girls about their future role as a caregiver. Boys were taught to ride, shoot arrows and hunt.

FAMILY GATHERING

A Cree family in Canada enjoys a quiet evening around the fire. American Indian families were usually small, as no more than two or three children survived the harsh life. However, a lodge was often home to an extended family. There could be two or three sisters, their families and grandparents under one roof.

Kachina dolls were made by the Hopi people to represent different spirits. This is the Corn kachina. Some parents gave the dolls to their children to help them learn about tribal customs.

BABY CARRIER

For the first year of its life, a baby would spend its time strapped to a cradleboard, such as this one influenced by the eastern Woodland tribes. It was also used by eastern Sioux, Iowa, Pawnee and Osage parents. A baby could sleep or be carried in safety while laced in its cradle, leaving the mother free to work. The board was strapped to the mother's back.

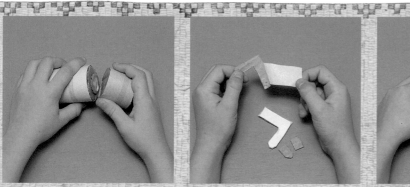

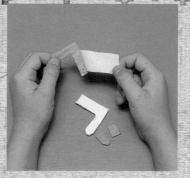

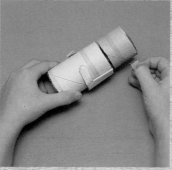

4 The smaller cardboard circle forms the doll's neck. Glue the small cardboard roll (the head) on top of the larger cardboard roll (the body).

5 Cut two small L-shapes from cardboard to form the arms. Then cut two small ear shapes from the cardboard. Cover these shapes with masking tape.

6 Glue the arms to the body and the ears to the sides of the head, so that they stick out at right angles. Paint the doll the colors shown above.

7 While the paint is drying, cut two small feather shapes from red paper. Glue these to the top of the doll's head, so that they stick into the air.

Food and Farming

FOOD BASKET

The Apaches and other people in the Southwest are renowned for making beautiful baskets. They waterproofed them with melted pinon (pine tree) gum. Versatile basket bowls were used for storing corn and carrying or serving food.

FROM THE NORTH AMERICAN Indians' earliest days, tribes have hunted, fished and gathered their own food. Archaeologists recently found evidence of a version of popcorn dating back to 4000 B.C. The area and environment tribes lived in determined their lifestyle. Inuit and coastal people fished and hunted. Calusas in Florida farmed the sea, sectioning off areas for shellfish. Tribes on the Northwest Coast took their food from the sea and so had little reason to develop farming, although they did grow tobacco. For many tribes, however, farming was an important way of life, and each developed its own agricultural skills.

The Secotan tribal name means an area that is burnt, referring to their method of setting fire to land to clear it for farming. They and other tribes on the fertile east coast planted thriving vegetable gardens. As well as the staple corn, squash and beans, they grew tomatoes, berries, vanilla beans and asparagus.

COOKING OUTSIDE

This beehive-shaped structure is a traditional outdoor oven. It was used by the Pueblo and other people of the Southwest. A fire was lit inside the dome, which heated stones placed all around the fire. The oven was used to bake corn bread or roast vegetables and meat.

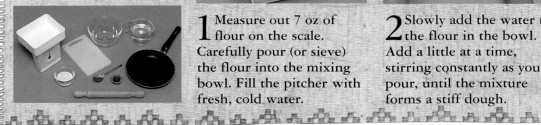

MAKE CORN CAKES

You will need: 7 oz corn tortilla flour or all-purpose flour, scale, sieve (optional), mixing bowl, cold water, pitcher, metal spoon, wooden or cutting board, rolling pin, frying pan, a little oil for cooking, honey.

1 Measure out 7 oz of flour on the scale. Carefully pour (or sieve) the flour into the mixing bowl. Fill the pitcher with fresh, cold water.

2 Slowly add the water to the flour in the bowl. Add a little at a time, stirring constantly as you pour, until the mixture forms a stiff dough.

3 Using your hands, gently knead (press) the mixture. Keep kneading until the dough is not too sticky. You may need to add a little more flour.

BAGGING WILD RICE

Two rice gatherers are sorting their harvest of rice just as their ancestors would have done. Vast areas of wild rice grew on the shores of lakes and rivers of the eastern Woodlands. Men and women would gather the stalks, bend them over the edge of a boat and strike them with a blunt tool. The grains of rice would fall into the boat. They were then gathered in bags to dry in the sun.

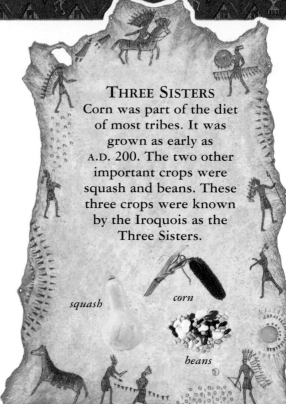

THREE SISTERS

Corn was part of the diet of most tribes. It was grown as early as A.D. 200. The two other important crops were squash and beans. These three crops were known by the Iroquois as the Three Sisters.

squash

corn

beans

PREPARING A MEAL

These Secotan people are sorting beans for a meal. American Indians grew about 60 different types of beans. Most tribes would prepare food to share.

FISH SUPPER

It was a good day's fishing for this Inuit. The fish will be hung up to be smoked and preserved. Inuit caught fish from kayaks or trapped fish in shallow water. In winter they fished through holes in the ice.

Tortillas were often eaten with beans and savory food. They also taste delicious with honey. Try them!

4 Sprinkle flour on the board. Take the dough from the bowl and knead it on the floured board for about 10 minutes. Let it stand for 30 minutes.

5 Pull off a small lump of dough. Roll it between your hands to form a flat round ball. Repeat this process until you have used all the dough.

6 Keep patting the dough balls until they form flat round shapes. Finish by using the rolling pin to roll them into flat, thin cakes, also known as tortillas.

7 Ask an adult to come and cook them with you. Heat a heavy frying pan or griddle. Gently cook the tortillas until they are lightly browned on both sides.

Hunting

THE EXCITING BUT DANGEROUS TASK of chasing the herds began only after a buffalo dance had been performed. The first signs of the bison (the real name for American buffalo) were often tracks left in the earth. Hunters followed these until the herd was spotted in the distance. Early hunters stalked the animals on foot, which was very dangerous. They made an avenue out of rocks and bushes down which the bison were driven. This led to a jump where the animals were stampeded to the edge of a steep cliff to fall to their death. When the horse came, it made hunting easier, though not always safer. A hunter had to ride in close to the herd, pick out a bison and drive it away. Bison was not the only animal hunted. The rivers to the east were once rich in beaver, much favored by fur traders, and tribes in California would hunt deer in the hills.

BUFFALO GRAVEYARD
The skulls were all that was left of the bison after a hunt. Meat was used for food, fat for glue and soup, and the hide became tepees and moccasins. Bladder and bones were made into cooking utensils, and the hair was used as stuffing.

HUNTING BEAR
This painting by George Catlin shows grizzly bears being speared by Plains warriors. Bears were sacred animals to many tribes, however, and believed to be guardian spirits. A warrior might paint symbols of the bear on his shield or red claw marks on his face for protection.

MAKE A SKIN ROBE
You will need: an old single sheet (or large piece of thin cotton fabric), scissors, tape measure or ruler, pencil, large needle, brown thread, felt in red, yellow, dark blue and light blue, white glue, glue brush, black embroidery floss (or string), red cotton thread (or other color).

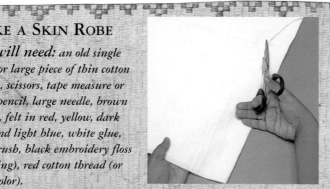

1 Take the sheet and cut out a rectangle 5 x 2 ft. Then cut out two 16 x 14-in. rectangles for the arms. Fold the main (body) piece in half.

2 At the center of the fold, draw a neckline 9 in. across and 3 in. deep. Cut it out. Roll fabric over at shoulders and stitch down with an overlapping stitch.

3 Open the body fabric out flat and line up the arm pieces, with the center on the stitched ridge. Stitch the top edge of the arm pieces onto the body.

FOOLING THE BUFFALO

Hunters have disguised themselves as wolves to sneak up close to the bison. The skin masked the hunter's own body smell, and they often tried to imitate a wolf's movements. It was essential to keep downwind because of the bison's keen sense of smell. However, the bison had very poor eyesight.

BUFFALO RUN

Hunters on horses rush at a bison trying to force it toward archers lying in wait. On a hunt, the first goal was to get all the animals to run in a circle. Then the hunters would surround them killing individual animals until they had all the meat needed. If the bison stampeded, the chase continued.

The North American Indians would have made their robes from buckskin. When the Europeans first spotted the natives wearing it, they could not figure out what the pale, soft material was made from.

BUTCHERS AT WORK

A hunt is over, and the tribe moves in to skin and butcher the kill. Often it was the women and elder children who handled the harvesting. The skin would carefully be taken off in one piece and used to make clothing. Meat would be prepared for a feast.

4 Fold the fabric in half again to see the shirt's shape. Now stitch the undersides of the sleeves. The sides of the shirt were usually not sewn together.

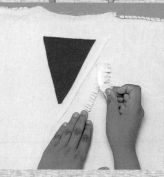

5 Your shirt is ready to decorate. Cut out strips and triangles of felt and glue them to the shirt. Make fringes by cutting into one side of a felt strip.

6 Make fake hair pieces by cutting 3-in. lengths of black thread and tying them together in bunches. Wind red thread tightly around the top, as here.

7 Glue or sew the fake hair (or scalplocks) on to your shirt. You can follow the pattern we used as shown in the picture (top), or create your own.

The Mighty Bison

For generations, the native bison (or buffalo) provided the Plains Indians with most of life's essentials, such as their food and housing materials. Although they hunted all year round, summer and autumn were the main buffalo seasons. During the summer months, large herds of thousands of animals came to the grass ranges to fatten up for winter. The arrival of the bison was marked by festive ceremonies before hunting began. The night after a successful hunt, a large feast was held with singing and dancing. A great deal of bison meat was eaten at the feast, but some had to be preserved for harder times. For this the meat was cut into narrow strips and hung over wooden racks to dry in the sun or over a fire. This is called jerky. Tougher meat was ground and mixed with bison fat and berries, a delicacy known as pemmican.

BUFFALO DANCE
Mandan men are getting themselves in the right mood for a hunt. Buffalo dances were held to bring the hunters good luck. Legend has it that the bison taught men their dance and chant. The Plains Indians believed in many spirits. They felt that if they prayed and chanted, the spirits would help them. The bull (male) head and hide robes were sacred objects worn by the shamans (medicine men) and those offering up prayers for the hunt.

OFFERING A PRAYER
A lone American Indian stands on top of the hill. He is using the sacred skull of a buffalo to call upon the great spirit of Wakan Tanka to bring buffalo herds to the Great Plains. The Sioux believed their world was full of spirits that controlled the earth, the sun, the sky, the wind—in fact, everything. Wakan Tanka controlled all of the spirits.

HUNTER VERSUS THE BISON
A large bull (male) turns on his attacker. An average male weighed more than a ton and stood more than 5 ft high at the shoulder. The lone rider is armed with a spear and guides his horse with knee pressure alone. A hunt was a chance for a warrior to prove himself. If he killed a bison, a hunter had the honor of eating the heart. The American Indians believed that this transferred the bison's spiritual power to the hunter.

STRETCHING THE HIDE

An Oklahoma man is stretching and tanning the hide in a traditional way. North American Indians stretched buffalo skin over a wooden frame or staked it out on the ground. First, the fat, flesh and fur had to be scraped off, then the skin was washed with a mixture of grease and water. Sometimes urine was used. Rawhide, the uncured animal skin with its fur scraped off, was used to make drums, shields and robes.

A HUNT GOES ON

The excitement of bison hunting is captured in this Blackfoot painting on a tepee lining. Pictures were used to record significant events in tribal life. They were painted on tepees or shields. The images described war exploits, good hunting trips or the family history. The bison here were probably eaten by the tribe.

WILD AND FREE

In 1800, there were an estimated 60 million bison roaming the Plains. These numbers fell dramatically as European settlers moved further west. Around four million bison were slaughtered in just four years. They were hunted almost to extinction. In 1872, Yellowstone National Park was the first conservation area set up to protect them.

HUNTING AS SPORT

Passengers on the Kansas Pacific Railroad shoot buffalo for sport. When railways were built in 1860, white settlers moved west of the Mississippi River and onto the Plains. They did not understand the American Indians' way of life and killed many animals, including bison. Later, the United States government encouraged white hunters to shoot herds. They thought that if the bison were destroyed, tribes would lose their livelihood and give up their land.

Language and Communication

DIFFERENT TRIBES USUALLY SPOKE widely differing languages. It is estimated that at one time more than 500 languages in 2,200 different dialects were spoken. There were a few who shared similar tongues. The seven Sioux sub-tribes spoke a Siouan language, while the Plains Crees, Ojibwas, Blackfoot and Arapaho spoke Algonquian languages. These tribes were, however, spread over a wide area, which made inter-tribal communication very difficult. The North American Indians also developed a sign language using hand gestures for inter-tribal communication. Before the Europeans arrived, there was no written alphabet. Instead, they used pictographs, which are drawings representing humans, animals or objects. An alphabet was created by Sequoya of the Cherokees in 1821 and, once accepted by the elders, it was passed on to the people. In 1828, the Cherokee Phoenix newspaper was published in Cherokee and English.

REVEALING DREAMS
These glyphs have been painted by the Chippewa people of the Woodlands. Each picture is symbolic, based on mythical figures rather than signifying real events. They were either spirits worshiped by the tribe or images the artist saw in a dream.

PAINTING ON SKIN
An elderly tribal member is painting on a buffalo skin. The dried skin was pegged out on the ground and stretched taut. The tools were sticks dipped in paints or dyes made from plants and earth. Black, yellows and reds were the most common. European traders later introduced oils, poster paints and watercolors. Hide was not the only place pictures and glyphs were painted. Records were stored on bark, bone, totem poles, and later, cloth, while Inuit carved pictographs on tusks.

MAKE A WINTER COUNT
You will need: muslin, piece of cardboard or a board, masking tape, ruler, pencil, scissors, white glue, brush for glue, sheet of 8½ x 11-in. white paper, tracing paper, thin card stock (preferably cream or white), very fine paintbrush or an ink pen, black ink or paint.

1 Stretch the muslin over a board or piece of cardboard. Tape it down. Draw a 12 x 8-in. rectangle on the muslin. Untape it and cut out the rectangle.

2 Use a brush to paint the cut edges of the muslin with white glue so that they will not fray while you work (and keep them neat afterward).

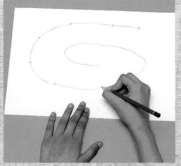

3 Draw a wide spiral in the middle of the sheet of white paper. Mark 11 points around the line of the spiral. Space the points out evenly.

KEEPING A DIARY

A Plains Indian has recorded a raid by his tribe on another camp. Pictures such as these told the history of a tribe. Some acted as a kind of visual diary and were known as Winter Counts because they were usually made, or added to, in the winter. The family and other tribal members would often gather around telling stories while one wrote them down using picture writing.

SMOKE SIGNAL

Warriors in the Plains region send a smoke signal to the rest of their tribe. A fire of damp leaves or grass would be lit, as it produced heavy smoke. This was allowed to rise in set intervals to convey an agreed message. Sioux warriors sent signals using mirrors to reflect the sun's rays. Woodland tribes developed drum signals and cries.

whooping cough

chicken pox

brings many horses

chase many horses around camp

many ice

no grass

lots of snow

white dog came

Hunka's ceremony

horse disease

visit by mixed blood

LIFE ON THE PLAINS

These drawings have been copied from a Sioux Winter Count. Unlike pictographs of the Woodland people, the Sioux Indians painted pictures showing everyday life on the Plains. Such events as bad weather and ill-health greatly affected the tribes. Icy weather meant that plant life and animals were scarce and the tribe might go hungry.

4 Draw a figure at each of the 11 points. These will describe significant events over the past year. Copy some of the real pictographs above.

5 Trace the figures onto the piece of tracing paper. Turn the tracing paper over and re-trace the figures on the other side, covering all pencil lines.

6 Tape the muslin to the cardboard. Tape the tracing paper over it. Rub a pencil over the figure outlines, then remove the paper and paint over them in ink.

Now you can paint the figures like the pictographs above, or make your own designs. You can even make another one, which tells your own family history next time.

Myths and Legends

TRIBAL LIFE WAS FILLED WITH myths and famous tales. Legends of tribal ancestors, gods and spirits were passed down through the generations. Some of the greatest legends were told in song or dance at large gatherings. They were often connected with religious beliefs, and many of the tales were an attempt to explain the origins of the tribes and the universe. The Haida, Snohomish and Quinault (of the Northwest Coast) believed that animals were the original inhabitants of the land. They thought that the coyote (a large wild dog) could take off its fur to reveal a man inside. It was the god Kwatee, who created humans from the coyote. The Iroquois believed in a sky woman and earth goddess named Ataensic. She died giving birth to twins. After her death, one of the twins created the world from her corpse. In Navajo mythology, a sea goddess known as White Shell Woman was in charge of water, and her sister was an earth goddess who made the seasons change each year.

BUSHY HEADS
Members of the Iroquois Husk Face Society wore this type of mask. They were said to have special healing powers and could handle hot ashes and rub them on the heads of patients. The masks were made of braided corn husks and nicknamed bushy heads.

LARGER THAN LIFE
The mighty Thunderbird was a powerful supernatural creature, seen here in a Haida wood carving. A flap of its wings was said to bring thunder, and lightning struck when it blinked. The Algonquins in the east called them Our Grandfathers. They could fight with other beings or grant mighty blessings.

MAKE A SPIRIT MASK
You will need: thick cardboard, scissors, pencil, masking tape, newspaper, all-purpose flour, water, bowl and fork for mixing, fine sandpaper, white and red acrylic paint, paintbrushes, water bowl, awl, elastic, twine, white glue, brush for glue.

1 Cut out an oval piece of cardboard, a little larger than your face. Make four ¾-in. cuts, two toward the top and two at the bottom, as shown above.

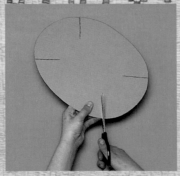

2 Overlap the cut bits of card and tape them down. This will create a 3-D shape to fit your face. Ask a friend to help mark holes for eyes and mouth.

3 Cut the eye and mouth holes, then build up the nose, cheeks and mouth. Fold bits of newspaper to make the right shapes and tape them in place.

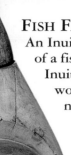

FISH FACE

An Inuit carved this mask of a fish and its spirit. Inuit and Aleut people wore masks to honor native animals such as the whale, seal, bear and caribou, which were important food sources. The people aimed to please the animal spirits who would ensure good food supplies. Some masks had animal heads with human faces. They were worn for one ceremony, then burned or buried.

SPIRIT MASK

This scary face is an Inuit mask. Creatures in the spirit world were recreated in masks, and so the masks were felt to be alive. Ordinary people wore masks during ceremonies, but shamans wore them more often. A mask carved by a shaman would give him spiritual powers to heal sick people.

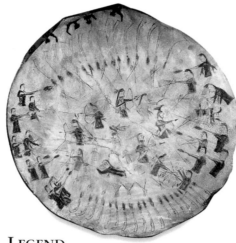

SUMMONING SPIRITS

The god of lightning is represented by this kachina doll. Hopi, Zuni and other Pueblo Indians carved many kachina dolls. They were no ordinary dolls—a kachina was a guardian spirit. The Hopi believed the spirits lived in the mountains. They came down on the winter solstice (shortest day of the year) and stayed until the summer solstice (longest day).

LEGEND IN THE MAKING

The pictographs on this Sioux war shield show that the tribe had fought in a huge battle. They are surrounded by the United States Cavalry—the figures around the edges. Many scenes of legendary battles were recorded on shields.

Your mask follows the design of a False Face Mask of the Iroquois. The wearer was a member of a False Face Society and used it during ceremonies to cure the sick.

4 Make a paste of flour and water. Tear bits of newspaper into small strips, dip them into paste and cover the mask with them. Make 2–3 layers.

5 Let the mask dry in a warm place. When dry, smooth it down with sandpaper. Coat in white paint then red, or just several layers of red.

6 When dry, add more detail using white paint. Make a hole on either side using an awl. Tie a piece of elastic to each side to hold the mask on your face.

7 Take the twine and dampen it slightly, then untwist it so you have straw-like strands. Dry them out and glue them to the mask to create hair.

Arts and Crafts

NORTH AMERICAN INDIANS were expert craftsmen and women. Beautiful pots have been found dating back to around 1000 B.C. The people of the Southwest were renowned for their pottery. Black and white Mimbres bowls were known as burial pots because they were broken when their owner died and buried along with the body. Baskets and blankets were the other most important crafts. The ancient Anasazis were known as the basket-making culture because of the range of baskets they produced. Some were coiled so tightly they could hold water. The Apaches coiled large, flat baskets from willow and plant fibers, and the Paiutes made cone baskets, which were hung on their backs for collecting food. All North American Indians made use of the materials they had on hand such as, wood, bark, shells, porcupine quills, feathers, bones, metals, hide and clay.

BASKET WEAVER
A native Arizona woman is creating a traditional coiled basket. It might be used for holding food or to wear on someone's head. Tlingit and Nootka tribes from the Northwest Coast were among those who wore cone-shaped basket hats.

POTTERY
Zuni people in the Southwest created beautiful pots such as this one. They used baskets as molds for the clay or coiled thin rolls of clay around in a spiral. Afterward, they smoothed out the surface with water. Birds and animals were favorite decorations.

DRILLING WALRUS TUSKS
An Inuit craftsman is working on a piece of ivory. He is using a drill to etch a pattern. The drill bit is kept firmly in place by his chin. This way, his hands are free to move the bow in a sawing action, pushing the drill point into the ivory.

MAKE A TANKARD
You will need: air-drying modeling clay, board, water in bowl, pencil, ruler, cream or white and black poster paints or acrylic paints, fine and ordinary paintbrushes, non-toxic varnish.

1 Roll out a round slab of clay and press it into a flat circle with a diameter of about 4 in. Now, roll out two long sausage shapes of clay.

2 Slightly dampen the edges of the clay circle. Place one end of the clay sausage on the edge of the circle and coil it around. Continue spiraling around.

3 Continue coiling with the other clay sausage. Then, use your dampened fingers to smooth the coils into a good tankard shape and smooth the outside.

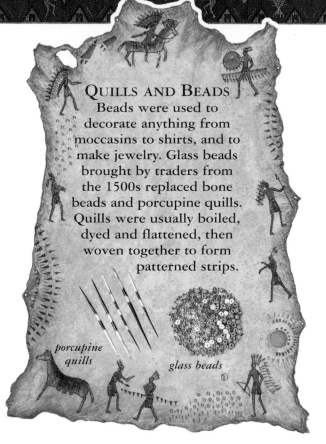

QUILLS AND BEADS
Beads were used to decorate anything from moccasins to shirts, and to make jewelry. Glass beads brought by traders from the 1500s replaced bone beads and porcupine quills. Quills were usually boiled, dyed and flattened, then woven together to form patterned strips.

porcupine quills

glass beads

TALKING BLANKET
It could take half a year for a Tlingit woman to make one of the famous Chilkat blankets. She wove cedar bark fiber and mountain goat wool with her fingers. The Tlingits said that if you knew how to listen, the blankets could talk.

FRUITS OF THE LOOM
Striped blankets were the specialty of Indians in the Southwest. This Hopi woman is using an upright loom made from poles. Pueblo people were the first North American Indians to weave like this.

Each tribe had its own pottery designs and colors. These geometric patterns were common in the Southwest.

4 Roll out another, small sausage shape of clay to make a handle. Dampen the ends and press it onto the clay pot in a handle shape. Let dry out.

5 Using a sharp pencil, mark out the design you want on your tankard. You can follow the traditional Indian pattern or make up your own.

6 Using poster paints or acrylic paints, colour in the pattern on the tankard. Use a fine-tipped brush to create the tiny checked patterns and thin lines.

7 When the paint is dry, coat your tankard in one or two layers of non-toxic varnish using an ordinary paintbrush. This will protect it.

Games and Entertainment

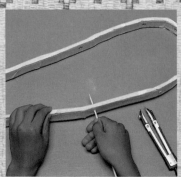

As hard as life was, the North American Indians always found time to relax by playing games and entertaining themselves. There were games of chance and gambling and games of skill. Games of chance included guessing games, dice-throwing, and hand games where one person had to guess in which hand his opponent was hiding marked bones or wooden pieces. Archery, spear throwing and juggling were favorite games to improve hunting skills, and there was a variety of stick and ball games, such as lacrosse. Children also loved to swim and take part in races. In the north, the girls and boys raced on toboggans. Active pastimes like these helped to develop skills a North American Indian needed to survive, such as strength, agility, bravery and stamina. Ritual foot races were also of ceremonial importance. Running could supposedly help the crops grow, bring rain and give renewed strength to the sun.

TEAM GAMES
The Ball Game of the Creek, Seminole, Cherokee and Choctaw people was similar to lacrosse. They used two sticks, while in lacrosse, one is used. Cherokees called it *little brother of war*, and to the Choctaw it was *stickball*.

SNOW FUN
These Inuit children are enjoying a toboggan ride in the snow. They are wrapped up in animal skins. Iroquois adults played Snow Snake to see how far a lance could be slid on ice.

MAKE A LACROSSE STICK
You will need: thick cardboard, ruler or tape measure, pencil, scissors, masking tape, compass, wooden skewer or sharp object to make holes, bamboo stick (to reach to your waist from ground level), white glue, glue brush, string, brown paint, paintbrush, water bowl, light ball.

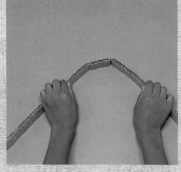

1 Measure, then cut a strip of cardboard 48 x 1 in. Fold it gently at the center to make a curve (Or cut two 24 x 1 in. pieces and tape them together).

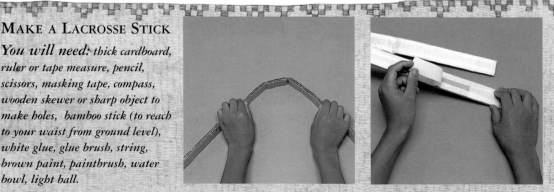

2 Cover the cardboard completely with masking tape. Start from the edges and work around, keeping the bent shape. Cover both sides.

3 Use a compass to mark two points from the center of the bend, 4 in. apart, then two, 4 in. from these and two more 4 in. down. Use a stick to make holes at these points.

GAME OF THE ARROW

Plains tribes enjoy target practice. A stationary target was made of wood, grass or bark. A more adventurous game for the archer was to throw a bundle into the air and try to shoot an arrow into it before it came down. This was a favorite with the Mandan, who tried to shoot several arrows into the air at the same time from one bow.

The aim of the game of lacrosse is to get the leather ball between two posts to score a goal. It is a bit like hockey, but instead of the ball being hit, it is scooped up in the net of the curved stick or racquet.

KEEPING THE BEAT

Songs and dance were essential during ceremonies. They inspired visions among listeners, who often chanted to the rhythmic beat.

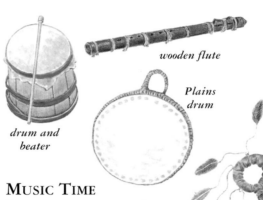

drum and beater

wooden flute

Plains drum

rattle

MUSIC TIME

Instruments were made from everyday materials. Drums were the most important. There were various types of flat or deep drums, mostly made from rawhide (untreated buffalo skin) stretched over a base of carved wood. Reed flutes were sometimes played by Sioux men when they were courting their future wives.

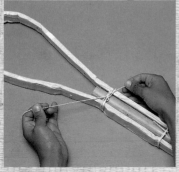

4 Glue the ends of the cardboard strip to the top of the bamboo stick, leaving a loop (as shown above). Tie string around the outside to keep it in place.

5 Pinch the cardboard together at the end of the stick, just under the loop. Tie it tightly with string and trim the ends. Paint the stick brown.

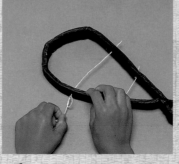

6 When the paint is dry, thread two pieces of string horizontally between the two sets of holes on the sides of the loop. Knot them on the outside.

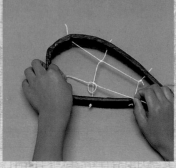

7 Now, thread two vertical strings. Start at the holes at the top of the frame and tie the string around both horizontal strings. Tie the ends. Use a light ball.

Contact with Europeans

THE VIKINGS WERE THE first Europeans to discover the existence of North America. It was other explorers arriving around 500 years later, however, who created the most impact. These Europeans claimed the land for their own countries, setting up colonies of settlers. They eventually forced many North American Indians from their homelands, killing thousands in the process. When Christopher Columbus landed in the Bahamas in 1492, he set about claiming the land for Spain. Fellow Spaniard Ponce de León landed in Florida in 1512, while Hernando Cortés had conquered the Aztecs in Central America by 1521. Tales of mountains of gold in the Southwest brought a Spanish expedition headed by Vasquez de Coronado. He encountered Apache, Hopi, Pawnee and Wichita Indians. He never did find gold. Sadly, the European explorers and colonists never regarded the American Indians as equals. They tried to force tribes to change their lifestyles, beliefs and even to adapt their traditional crafts to suit European buyers.

EARLY VISITORS
Erik the Red, the Viking king, sailed to Greenland around 982 A.D. He was probably in search of new trading partners. His son Leif later sailed to Newfoundland and established a settlement at a place now called L'Anse aux Meadows. A trade in furs and ivory was set up with northern Europe.

SETTING SAIL
Columbus and his crew prepare to set sail from Spain in 1492 in search of a trade route to India. He never reached Asia but landed on San Salvador in the Bahamas. The Arawaks there thought that Columbus and his men came from the sky and greeted them with praise. Columbus set about claiming the islands for the Spanish Empire, making many of the natives slaves.

A DISTANT LAND

This map from around 1550 shows a crude European impression of North America. Henry II of France ordered Descallier, a royal cartographer (map maker), to make a map of what Central and North America looked like. The French were eager to gain land there for themselves. Jacques Cartier, a French navigator, spent eight years exploring the St. Lawrence River area. He made contact with Huron communities. He wrote and told the king that he hoped the natives would be "easy to tame."

MAN WITH A MISSION

A Plains Indian views a missionary with suspicion. Eastern tribes were the first to meet French missionaries whom they called Black Robes. In California, many were forced to live and work in Spanish mission villages.

SAY A LITTLE PRAYER

Young girls dressed in European clothes have been separated from their families and tribal customs. Europeans could not understand the North American Indians' society and religious beliefs. They wanted to convert them to Christianity, by force if necessary. In many areas, children were taken away from their people and sent to white boarding schools, given European names and taught European religion, language and history.

European Settlers

ROM 1500, NORTH AMERICA was visited by the English, French and Spanish in increasing numbers, each establishing colonies to expand their empires. It was mostly the British and the French who stayed. At first their settlements were on the east coast and in eastern Canada, but gradually they explored further inland, meeting with more and more tribes. Europeans brought diseases previously unknown to the American Indians. The smallpox epidemic of 1837 almost wiped out the Mandan tribe. Fewer than 200 people survived, from a tribe that had once numbered over 2,500. The colonists continued to push out the North American Indians. In the 1760s to 1780s, colonists fought for independence from their empires. In 1783 the United States was officially recognized as being independent from Britain. The United States government wanted to move eastern tribes west of the Mississippi River. They bought the Louisiana Territory in 1803 for 15 million dollars from France. This doubled the size of the United States and marked the end of French rule. It didn't stop there—they continued to push their frontiers west.

LEADING THE WAY
Sacawagea, a Shoshoni girl, guides United States captains Meriwether Lewis and William Clark from Mississippi to the Pacific coast, in 1804. It took them almost one year. President Thomas Jefferson asked them to map out the land from the Mississippi River to the Rockies. This helped to pave the way for settlers to move to the far west.

ROLLING ACROSS THE PLAINS
From around 1850, wagon trains were signs that times were changing for the Plains tribes. Although settlers had been living in North America for around 300 years, they had mostly remained on the east coast. The United States government encouraged white families to move inland.

SOD HOUSE
This is a fine example of a sod house, a house literally made from sod, or turf, cut out of the ground. Settlers had to build homes from whatever material was on hand. Life was hard for the children; they had to do chores, such as feeding chickens. If they were lucky, they went to school.

NEW TOWN

Plains Indians watch a train steaming into a new town. Land was sacred to the tribes who called it their Earth Mother. The settlers thought that the tribes wasted their land and wanted to build towns and railways on it. At first, the federal government took land for settlers. Later, they bought millions of acres of tribal land in various treaties (agreements), using force if the American Indians did not agree.

PANNING FOR GOLD

A man is sifting through sand in search of gold. When gold was discovered in late 1848 in California, it started the Gold Rush. Thousands of immigrants came to the west coast from all over the world. The sheer numbers forced the tribes off their land.

TRAIN ATTACK

Plains warriors attack a train crossing their hunting grounds. The Plains tribes had always been fiercely defensive of their territory. Now they turned on the new invaders. More and more settlers were encouraged to move onto the Plains. In the 1860s, railways were constructed across tribes' lands. These were built over sacred sites and destroyed buffalo hunting grounds which were essential to the tribes' livelihood. Attacks on settlers, trains and white trading posts became more frequent.

Horse Culture

THERE WERE HORSES ROAMING wild in America during prehistoric times, but they had died out by the Ice Age. The Spanish reintroduced the horse to North America in the early 1500s when they brought the animals over on ships. As the Spanish moved north of Mexico further inland, more tribes came to contact with the horse. It was forbidden by Spanish officials to trade in horses, but gradually tribes obtained them one way or another. To go on a horse-stealing raid was counted as a great honor. The arrival of the horse on the Plains had a dramatic effect on tribal life. It meant that they could expand their hunting area, and made hunting bison much easier. It also meant that greater loads could be carried or pulled by horses, including much larger tepees. By 1700, the Crows traded horses with the Colombian Plateau tribes of the Nez Perce, Cayuse and Palouse. The Cayuse became renowned for breeding a strong type of horse, which bears their name. The Palouse were also very good at breeding horses and their name was given to the Appaloosa breed favored by the Nez Perce tribe. Tribes treated the animals with respect, and there was often a special bond between a warrior and his horse.

PLAYING THEIR PART
Horses feature prominently among the many pictures painted by Plains Indians on deer and buffalo skins. On this Blackfoot buffalo robe, the horses are shown helping warriors to victory in battle and transporting people and property to new camp sites. In a short time, horses had become crucial to the Plains people's way of life. They could never go back to life on foot.

WILD SPIRIT
An American Indian catches a horse that was roaming wild on the Plains. The new owner would spend weeks teaching the animal to accept a rider on its back. More usually, American Indians would catch horses in raids on other tribes or settlers' camps. Life on the Plains produced a strong and hardy horse.

HORSE RUSTLING
These American Indians appear to be on the lookout. Some tribes bred horses to trade, others were not so honest. The Comanche raiders in Texas would steal horses from other Texans or Mexicans and then trade them to friendly tribes.

OFF OUR LAND

A chief stands on his horse to emphasize the point he is making. The white man is probably marveling at the American Indian's ability to stay upright. Plains Indians were famed for their showmanship and riding skills. The chief's saddle blanket is made from tanned buffalo hide. Most Indian riders used blankets rather than saddles. Tribes, such as the Crow, made bridle ornaments and beaded saddlebags, while others painted symbols on the horses.

TAMING THE HORSE

These boys are attempting to break in a wild horse. When horses were first acquired by tribes, only brave young men and women rode them, although they were used to carry goods. It took about a generation for horses to be accepted.

A TEST OF HONOR

This Blackfoot Indian could be on a horse raid. Stealing horses from another tribe was one way a warrior could prove that he was brave. The raids were not thought of as a crime, more an expression of honor. The Comanche were regarded as the best horsemen and were feared by other tribes and white settlers alike.

COVETED HAIR

Horsehair adorns the head of this Iroquois False Face Mask. American Indians made use of everything around them. Horsehair was used for a variety of things. It could be braided to make rope. It was used as stuffing in a cradle to give a baby some comfortable padding. It could also add the final decoration to an eagle feather headdress.

Markets and Trade

NORTH AMERICAN INDIANS HAD a long tradition of trading. The Hopewell civilizations of about A.D. 200 brought metals and other materials to their centers around the Ohio valley. The Calusas in southern Florida had a vast trade network both inland and across the sea to the Bahamas and Cuba. Many people would travel long distances to buy and sell goods at a regular meeting place. Although some tribes used wampum (shell money), most swapped their goods. People from settled villages exchanged agricultural products such as corn and tobacco for buffalo hides, baskets or eagle feathers from nomadic tribes. When European traders arrived, in the 1600s, they exchanged furs and hides for horses, guns, cotton cloth and metal tools. Early trading posts such as the Hudson's Bay Company were built by whites. These posts were usually on rivers, which could be reached easily by canoe.

BASKETS FOR GOODS
Crafts, such as this Salish basket, were sometimes traded (or swapped) between tribes, and later with Europeans. American Indians particularly wanted wool blankets, while European traders eagerly sought bison robes.

WORDS OF A WAMPUM
A Mohawk chief, King Hendrick of the League of Five Nations, was painted on a visit to Queen Anne's court in London in 1710. He holds a wampum belt made from shells. These were made to record historic events such as the formation of the League of Five Nations of the Iroquois.

COLONIAL TRADERS
A native hunter in Canada offers beaver skins to colonial fur traders in 1777. They would probably have been made into beaver hats. Beaver fur was the most important item the Woodlands tribes had to trade, as competition between European nations for animal skins was fierce. This trade was partly to blame for many tribal conflicts. The Iroquois were renowned beaver hunters who ruthlessly guarded their hunting territory.

SHELL SHOW

A Plains Indian is holding up a wampum belt decorated with shells. The belts were usually associated with the Iroquois and Algonquian tribes who used them to trade, as currency, or to record tribal history. Quahog clam shells were strung together to make a long rectangular belt with patterns showing tribal agreements and treaties. Even colonists used them as currency when there were no coins around.

SAVING SHELLS

Instead of coins, shells or beads made from shells were the main currency. They served as tokens that were swapped for goods. Blue and white shells such as clams and periwinkles were the most prized. These were strung, like beads, on buckskin thongs.

thong *clam shell* *mussel shell*

TRADING POSTS

North American Indians would gather in the Hudson's Bay trading post. In return for bringing in pelts (animal furs), the American Indians would be given European goods. Many would be useful, such as iron tools and utensils or colored cloth. Firearms and liquor traded from around 1650 did the tribes more harm than good. As trade increased, more trappers and hunters frequented the trading posts. Later, some of the fur trade posts became military forts and attracted settlers who built towns around them.

Warriors and Warfare

MOST WARS BETWEEN TRIBES were fought over land or hunting territory, and later over horses. As Europeans began to occupy more land, many tribes fought to stop them. Each tribe had warriors, known as braves. There were military societies within the tribe, such as the Cheyenne Dog Soldiers, whose job was to protect the tribe. Warriors would paint both themselves and their horses for spiritual protection. A white stripe across a Blackfoot warrior's face meant vengeance. In the 1700s, Plains tribes traded guns with the Europeans, but they felt that blasting their tribal enemies lacked honor. Instead, warriors developed a way of fighting without killing. A warrior had to get close enough to strike his enemy with a long stick known as a counting coup, then escape unhurt. Each act of bravery earned an honor feather to be tied to the stick.

HEAVY HANDS
Crude tomahawks such as this date back to the Stone Age, but were still used by Plains warriors in the late 1800s. War clubs made from local rocks were vicious weapons, as was the wooden gunstock club, which had a large spike sticking out.

WEAPONS
This tomahawk dates back to around 1750 and once belonged to an Iroquois warrior. Before they acquired firearms, warriors had a variety of weapons of war. They used the bow and arrow, knives, or long lances, as favored by the Comanches from Texas.

HORSEMANSHIP
This Plains warrior displays excellent equestrian skills. He is riding on the side of his horse, holding on with just one foot tucked over the horse's back. This shields him from harm while his hands are free to thrust his spear. Sioux warriors believed that horses fought with their rider in battle. If a warrior died, Apaches would often kill his horse and bury it with its master's body.

MAKE A SHIELD
You will need: thick cardboard, ruler, pencil, scissors, white glue, glue brush, masking tape, two 14-in. strips of balsa wood dowel ½ in. in diameter, white cotton (or other fabric) approx 16-in. square, red, black and cream or yellow paints, paintbrush, water bowl, brown felt.

1 Cut two strips of thick cardboard measuring 1 x 46 in. Glue them together to give a double thickness. Then bend them to make a circle.

2 Glue and tape the ends together to form a circle, with about 1½ in. overlapping. The diameter should be approximately 14 in. Let dry.

3 Cross and glue the two dowel sticks together at right angles. Glue both to the frame, one from top to bottom, one horizontally. Let the base dry.

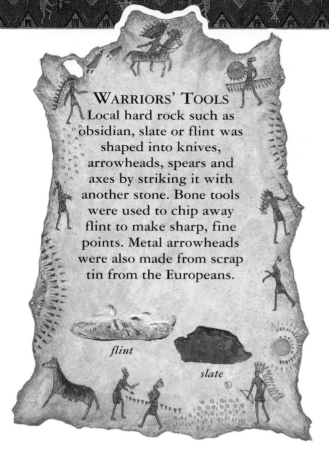

WARRIORS' TOOLS

Local hard rock such as obsidian, slate or flint was shaped into knives, arrowheads, spears and axes by striking it with another stone. Bone tools were used to chip away flint to make sharp, fine points. Metal arrowheads were also made from scrap tin from the Europeans.

flint

slate

HERO'S FRIEND

The shield was one of the warrior's most prized possessions. He felt it gave him both spiritual and physical protection. Skin from the bison's neck was used to make it, as this was the toughest part of the animal. It could be decorated with symbols and feathers or scalps.

DRESSED FOR BATTLE

Chief Quanah Parker of the Comanche is wearing his war costume. Each tribe had a war chief who was in charge of planning attacks. He was not usually the leader of the people, but had proved himself to be a brave warrior in battle. Chief Parker led his followers in battles throughout Texas. They fought against the United States in the Red River War of 1874–75. His mother, Cynthia Parker, was a white captive of the tribe.

Warriors often painted animals on their shields. A buffalo head (used here) was a symbol of strength.

4 Lay the fabric flat. Using the frame as a guide, draw around it to make a circle 1 in. wider than the frame. Cut out the circle.

5 Draw a pattern on the fabric, then paint it. A simple, bold pattern works best, or copy our shield and paint a buffalo head. Let the paint dry.

6 Stretch the fabric over the frame, keeping the pattern centered. Glue down the edges all around. Paint the edges red (background color) to neaten them.

7 Cut a strip of brown felt measuring about 1 x 16 in. Glue the ends to the top and bottom edges of the shield at the back. This is the armband.

War and Defeat

FROM 1775 TO 1783, COLONISTS fought for independence from Britain. Some Indians remained neutral in the Revolutionary War, some took sides. At first, the Iroquois League of Nations did not want to be involved in a white man's quarrel. They had, however, allied with the British against the French in other European wars. The League was split and eventually most of the tribes supported the British. In 1777, they ended up fighting some of their own people, the Oneidas, who had sided with the Americans. The United States gained independence in 1783. With new strength, the United States started pushing for more land and introduced the Indian Removal Act of 1830. The aim was to relocate eastern tribes west of the Mississippi River onto reservations (areas set aside for Indians). The Choctaws were the first tribe to be relocated in 1830, to Oklahoma.

WILD WEST
There were many conflicts between United States soldiers and different tribes, such as this attack in the 1800s. Some attempts at peaceful talks were made. However, military records show that between 1863 and 1891, there were 1,065 fights.

They were followed by the Chickasaws, Creeks and Seminoles. Many long and bitter battles were fought, as the Indians struggled to keep their homelands. Much reservation land was neither as fertile nor as productive as the old tribal land, and some tribes faced starvation.

TRAIL OF TEARS
The heartbroken Cherokee nation is being forced to leave its homelands in 1838–39. During the trek west, rain and snow fell, and soldiers made them move on too quickly. It is estimated that almost 4,000 Cherokees died from exhaustion and exposure.

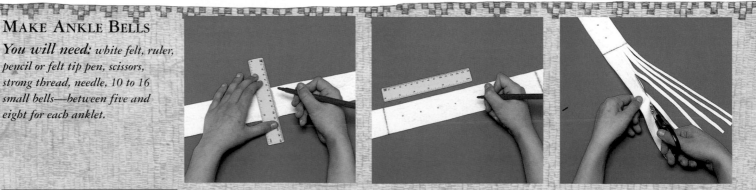

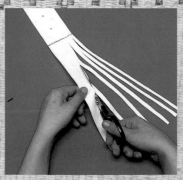

MAKE ANKLE BELLS
You will need: white felt, ruler, pencil or felt tip pen, scissors, strong thread, needle, 10 to 16 small bells—between five and eight for each anklet.

1 Cut out two strips of white felt 30 x 2 in. Measure and mark a line across the felt strips, 9½ in. in from one end. Do the same at the other end.

2 Now make a series of marks in the middle section of the strips. Start 1 in. away from one line, then mark every 1 in. This is where the bells will go.

3 Create the fringing at each end of the anklet. Do this by cutting into both ends of the band up to the penciled lines. Do the same for the other anklet.

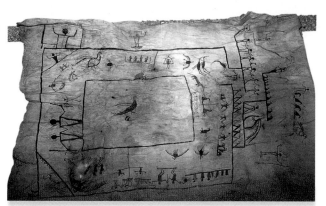

WAR BUNDLE
This buckskin was used to wrap a personal war bundle. It has been painted with the Thunderbird and other supernatural beings for spiritual protection. A bundle might carry a warrior's medicine herbs or warpaint.

THE SHIELD SURVIVED
This warrior's shield belonged to a Dakota (Sioux) warrior in the late 1800s. It may have been used in the Battle of Little Bighorn. The Sioux tribes fought in many battles with the United States around that time. In 1851 their lands were defined by a treaty. Then, when gold was found in Montana, gold hunters broke the treaties by traveling through Sioux land, and war raged again.

THE END OF GENERAL CUSTER
The Battle of Little Bighorn, in 1876, is counted as the last major victory of the North American Indian. Custer's entire 7th Cavalry was defeated by Sioux sub-tribes, after they attacked an Indian village. Sadly, this made United States soldiers even more brutal in their dealings with tribes.

WAR DANCE
Sioux warriors are performing a war dance. During the dance a medicine man would chant and ask for spiritual guidance and protection for warriors going into battle. Other dances were performed after a battle.

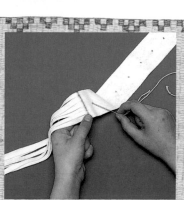

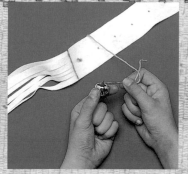

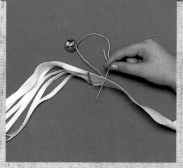

4 Thread a large needle with strong, doubled and knotted thread. Insert the needle into the fabric and pull through until the knot hits the fabric.

5 Thread the needle through the bell and slip the bell up to the felt. Then insert the needle back into the felt very near the place it came out.

6 Push the needle through and pull tight. Knot the end (opposite side of the bell) to secure and cut away the excess thread. Repeat with the other bells.

The bells of the North American Indians were sewn on to strips of animal skins. They were tied around the ankles or just under the knees, for ceremonial dances.

Beliefs and Customs

NORTH AMERICAN INDIANS DID NOT believe in a single god. They believed that the changing seasons and events surrounding them were caused by different spirits. To them, everything in the world had a soul or spirit which was very powerful and could help or harm humans. Spirits had to be treated with respect, so prayers, songs, chants and dances would be offered to please them. The most important spirit to the Sioux was Wakan Tanka, the Great Spirit or Great Mysterious, who was in charge of all other spirits. The Navajo believed in the Holy People. These were Sky, Earth, Moon, Sun, Hero Twins, Thunders, Winds and Changing Woman. Some tribes believed in ghosts. Western Shoshonis, Salish (Flathead) people and Ojibwas considered ghosts to be spirit helpers who acted as bodyguards in battle. The leader of ceremonies was the shaman (medicine man) who conducted the dances and rites. He also acted as a doctor. The shamans of California would treat a sick person by sucking out the pain, spitting it out and sending it away.

CHARMED LIFE
A whale's tusk was used to carve this Inuit shaman's charm. Spirits called tuneraks were thought to help the angakok, as the Inuit shaman was called, in his duties. The role of shaman was passed from father to son. In Padlimuit, Copper and Iglulik tribes, women could also be shamans.

BEAR NECESSITIES OF LIFE
This shaman is nicknamed Bear's Belly and belonged to the Arikara Plains tribe. Shamans were powerful, providing the link between humans and spirits. After years of training, they could cure ailments, tell the future or speak to the dead.

MAKE A RATTLE
You will need: thick cardboard, pencil, ruler, scissors, masking tape, compass, white glue, brush, two balsa wood strips 1 in. wide and about 7 in. long, raffia or string, air-drying clay, wooden skewer, cream, black, orange/red and brown paint, paintbrushes, water bowl, black thread, needle.

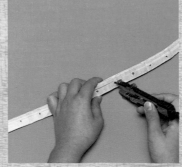

1 Cut two pieces of cardboard ½ in. wide, one 18 in. long and one 23 in. long. Cover both in masking tape. Make holes about 1 in. apart along the strips.

2 Bend each strip into a ring. Glue and tape the ends together to make two rings. Glue the two strips of balsa wood into a cross to fit across the large ring.

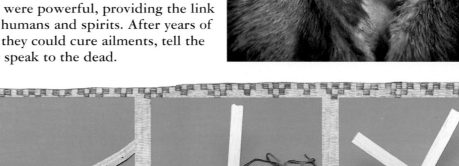

3 Glue the two sticks together, then strap them with raffia or string. Wrap the string around one side, then cross it over the center. Repeat on all sides.

NATURAL REMEDY

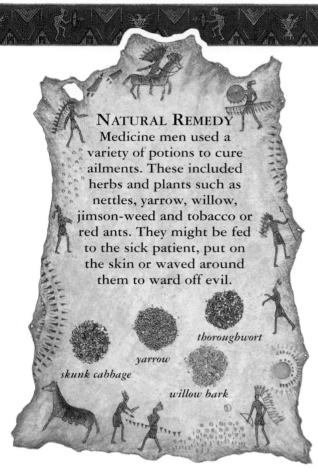

Medicine men used a variety of potions to cure ailments. These included herbs and plants such as nettles, yarrow, willow, jimson-weed and tobacco or red ants. They might be fed to the sick patient, put on the skin or waved around them to ward off evil.

skunk cabbage

yarrow

thoroughwort

willow bark

THE HAPPY COUPLE

Menominee people of the Woodlands made these dolls to celebrate the marriage of a couple. The miniature man and woman were tied face to face to keep husband and wife faithful. Dolls feature in the customs of many tribes, especially the Hopi and Zuni of the Southwest. Their kachina dolls are spirits shown in the form of animals, humans or plants.

MEDICINE BAGS

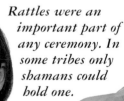

Crystals, animal parts, feathers and powders made of ground up plants and vegetables might be inside these bundles. They were used to make cures and spells by a shaman (medicine man) of the Winnebago tribe from the Woodlands.

SACRED BIRD

Rattles, such as this Thunderbird rattle from the Northwest Coast, were considered sacred objects and carved with the images of spirits. They were made of animal hoofs, rawhide or turtle shells, and filled with seeds or pebbles. Some were hand held, others were put on necklaces.

Rattles were an important part of any ceremony. In some tribes only shamans could hold one.

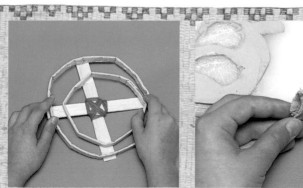

4 Glue the two cardboard rings onto the cross, as here. The larger ring sits on the outer ends of the cross. The smaller one is roughly ½–1 in. inside of that.

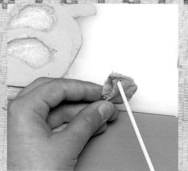

5 Roll out the clay to a ½-in. thickness. Cut out 20 to 30 semicircle shapes to resemble penguin beaks. Use a stick to make a hole at one end.

6 When the beaks are dry, paint them cream. Let dry. Paint the tips black, then paint red or orange stripes. Next, paint the two rings brown.

7 Thread the black cotton through the hole in a painted beak, then tie it through one of the holes in the rings. Repeat with each beak, filling both rings.

The Sweat Lodge and Other Rites

SWEATING PURIFIED THE BODY and mind according to North American Indians. The Sioux called it "fire without end." The sweat ritual was one of the most important and ancient of all North American religious rituals. They were among the first people to use heat to cleanse the body. But for tribe members, it was not simply a question of hygiene. The sweat lodge rite was performed before and after other ceremonies to symbolize moving in and out of a sacred world. Warriors prepared their spirits before the Sun Dance ceremony by taking a sweat bath. This was a dance to give thanks for food and gifts received during the year, and often featured self-mutilation. Sweats were also taken to purify the body and as a medical treatment to cure illness. They were often one of various customs, such as rites of passage from childhood to adulthood. A young boy who was about to make his transition into warrior-life was invited to spend time with the tribe's males. They would offer him the sacred pipe, which was usually smoked to send prayers. This was called Hunka's ceremony and showed the tribe's acceptance that the boy was ready. Some warrior initiation rites were brutal—such as the Mandan's custom of suspending young men by wooden hooks pierced through their chest, or scarring them, known as Okipa. Both girls and boys prepared for passing into adolescence by spending time alone and fasting (not eating).

STEAM AND SMOKE
A holy man, such as this Pima shaman, would be in charge of sweats. Prayers and chants were offered, and the sacred pipe was passed around each time the door was opened.

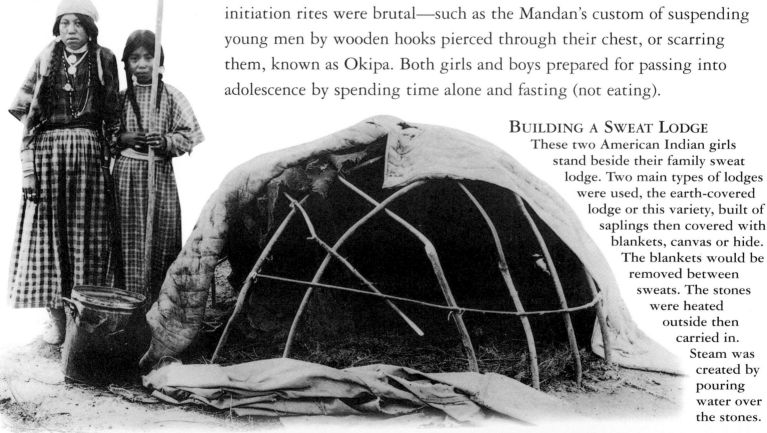

BUILDING A SWEAT LODGE
These two American Indian girls stand beside their family sweat lodge. Two main types of lodges were used, the earth-covered lodge or this variety, built of saplings then covered with blankets, canvas or hide. The blankets would be removed between sweats. The stones were heated outside then carried in. Steam was created by pouring water over the stones.

BATHS IN EARTH

An American Indian crawls out from an earth-covered sweat lodge for air. Six to eight people could sit around the hot stones inside, depending on the size of the sweat lodge. Males and females would both take part in sweats, but it was customary to do so separately. In some tribes, families built their own family lodges, and some larger sweat lodges were also used as homes or temples. Sticks and wood formed the frame. This was covered in mud or clay. The fire would be built in the lodge, causing a dry heat. It was dark, stuffy and hot, similar to the saunas used in Europe. However, a sweat lodge was used to cleanse the spirit as well as the skin.

CLEANSED AND REFRESHED

Herbs, such as sweetgrass and cedar, were often put on the hot stones inside a sweat lodge. When the water was poured over the stones, the smell and essence of the herbs were released into the lodge with the steam. Herbs helped to clear the nasal passages. They could also be selected to treat particular ailments. As the heat from the steam opened up the skin's pores, the herbs could enter the body and work at the illness or help purify the spirit. Sweating removed toxins (poisons in the body) and, the American Indians believed, forced out disease.

GROWING UP

A young Apache girl is dressed up for a modern tribal ceremony. The lives of North American Indians were filled with rituals to mark each milestone in a person's life or important tribal events. There were ceremonies for birth, for becoming an adult and to mark changing seasons.

INSTRUMENTS TELL A STORY

This Tsimshian rattle has been involved in many ceremonies. Tribes had a vast amount of ceremonial objects, from rattles to headdresses, clothing and wands. Their decorations were usually of spiritual significance. In some tribes, the frog was respected, since it would croak when danger was near. Others believed that their long tongues could suck out evil. A frog also stars in creation myths of the Nez Perce.

Sacred Dances

DANCING WAS AN IMPORTANT PART of North American Indian life. Some of the sacred dances were performed before or after great events such as births, deaths, marriages, hunts or battle, but they meant more than a big party. The Green Corn Dance was held annually to start the Creek New Year and celebrate agricultural growth. The Arikara Bear Dance hoped to influence the growth of corn and squash crops. Dancers often wore costumes. The Cheyenne Sun dancers painted their upper body black (for clouds) with white dots (for hail). The Assiniboine Clown dancers often danced and talked backward and wore masks with long noses.

DOG DANCE
A Hidatsa warrior from the Crazy Dog Soldier Society performs the Dog Dance to thank spirits for his strength. His headdress is made from magpie tail feathers with a crest of turkey tail feathers. The Hidatsa on the Missouri had many societies, including the White Buffalo Society, a women's group. The White Buffalo Woman was a mythical spirit.

SNOWSHOE DANCE
The Snowshoe Dance was performed after the first snow each winter by some Woodlands tribes. To the Indians, snow meant the passing of a year. People would speak of something happening two snows ago. Winter was a hard time, food was scarce with few animals around to hunt. The dance asked spirits for help to survive.

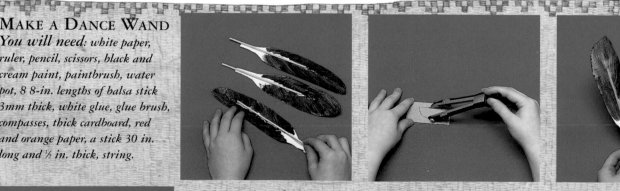

MAKE A DANCE WAND
You will need: white paper, ruler, pencil, scissors, black and cream paint, paintbrush, water pot, 8 8-in. lengths of balsa stick 3mm thick, white glue, glue brush, compasses, thick cardboard, red and orange paper, a stick 30 in. long and ½ in. thick, string.

1 Cut out eight feather shapes 8 in. long from white paper. Make cuts on the top edges and paint the tips black. Glue sticks 1½ in. from the top of the feather.

2 Use a compass to measure out two semicircles with a diameter of 2 in. on the cardboard. Cut out both semicircles. Hold the feathers by the sticks.

3 Glue the bottom end of the feathers between the two cardboard semicircles. Arrange them around the curved edge. Leave the straight edge unstuck.

PREPARING FOR WAR

Only men joined in war dances such as this Sioux ceremony. Warriors were preparing themselves for conflict. They hoped to gain favor with the spirits who would protect them from their enemies. Deer tails and feathers might hang on dance wands, but lances and spears had more grisly decorations. They displayed trophies of war such as the head of the enemy or scalps (a patch of skin and hair cut from an enemy in battle).

NATIVE KILT

This buckskin apron (or kilt) was once worn by a shaman during ceremonial dances. It is decorated with a picture of a beaver, a native North American animal. The beaver is this shaman's totem, a spirit helper. The spirit would be called upon to give the dancer strength to drive away sickness and evil spirits, and bring luck.

Ceremonial wands were carried during dances. Sometimes just one huge eagle feather or an animal tail hung from the top.

4 Draw and cut out 12 2½-in. long feathers from the red and orange paper. Make eight more red ones, 1 in. long. Make feathery cuts into the top edges.

5 Divide the 2½-in. feathers in half and glue them to each end of the long stick. Secure them with string tied around the stick and bottom of feathers.

6 Paint the semicircles cream, then dry. Bend back the two straight edges. Place the flaps on either side of the center of the stick. Glue them firmly in place.

7 Glue the smaller red feathers to the outside tips of the black feathers (one on each). Let dry. Your wand is ready, so let the dance begin.

Death and Burial

A DEATH IN THE TRIBE was followed by a solemn ceremony. North American Indians believed in spirits and often an afterlife, so the dead person had to be properly prepared for it. The Pueblo Indians would rub cornmeal on the body and place a cotton mask over the face. Cheyenne mourners would dress the dead in a pair of moccasins with beaded soles. This meant they could walk on the clouds to meet their relatives in the Always Summer Land (afterworld). Apaches would kill a warrior's horse to accompany its master. Bodies would be buried or burned depending on custom. The early Hohokam cremated their dead and placed the ashes in pots and these were buried. Some tribes, Crees of the Plains for example, buried their dead in the ground, while other clans, such as the Mandan, placed bodies under earth mounds. Stone graves, or the dead person's home were also used. The Apaches took their dead far away and placed the bodies in mountain crevices. Both the Apaches and the Navajo were very superstitious and afraid of ghosts. They burned the dead person's house and burned or broke the contents to stop the ghost from coming back to earth. Some Pueblo people smashed painted pottery and buried it with the dead body to symbolize the release of the soul.

FUNERARY DOLL
Funerary effigies, such as this doll from California, were used during the funeral ceremony and buried with the body. Some tribes had annual food offerings to keep the ghosts happy.

MORTUARY POLE
Haida people placed human remains in grave boxes. These were put on top of a short totem pole called a mortuary pole, usually carved from a red cedar tree. A potlatch ceremony (a feast where gifts were given) would be held. This material display would show that the dead person had been valued.

PROTECTED IN DEATH
This is a wooden gravemarker from the Northwest Coast. It was carved using stone tools. Many tribes carved figures for their dead. The Zuni carved effigies of the War Gods (guardians of the people) from wood that had been struck by lightning. These would be placed at the entrance of a tomb to protect it. Other figures and effigies were left to keep the dead person company.

HAIDA HEAD
A member of a Haida family is remembered in this carving. Many totem (spirit) figures were of tribal ancestors, as a way of keeping the dead person's memory alive. Other carvings of mythical figures have been found on totem and mortuary poles.

REMEMBERING THE DEAD
The death of an important tribe member has been recorded on this painted buckskin from the Kiowa and Comanche tribe. Most of the Plains tribes used the burial platform, which was usually placed in trees. The Huron people of the Woodlands also placed their dead on a platform. Later, the rotted body was carried to a cemetery, where the remains were placed in a small cabin (spirit house). The mourners put food, oil, tools and presents inside to assist the spirit in the afterworld.

HOUSE OF SPIRITS
Bright grave markers rest on an Inuit spirit house in Alaska. The Inuit believed that the souls of humans (and animals) came back into the world again as someone else. Animals could become human. When people or animals died, tribe members celebrated their spirit, including animals they had hunted.

BURIAL PLATFORM
The tall stick scaffolding in this picture is a burial platform. Bodies of the dead were placed high off the ground to prevent wolves or coyotes from eating them. They would stay there, wrapped with cloth or a buffalo robe, until the skin had rotted. The remains would be buried.

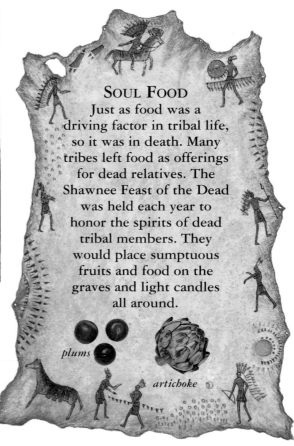

SOUL FOOD
Just as food was a driving factor in tribal life, so it was in death. Many tribes left food as offerings for dead relatives. The Shawnee Feast of the Dead was held each year to honor the spirits of dead tribal members. They would place sumptuous fruits and food on the graves and light candles all around.

plums

artichoke

North American Indians Today

R ECORDS SHOW THAT BY 1900 the American Indian population north of Mexico was down from between 2.5 and 3 million, to 400,000. Today the figure is in the region of 1,750,000. From the 1800s, many North American Indians were moved by the United States government from their homelands to areas of land known as reservations. In Canada, the lands are called reserves. There are several hundred of these, smaller in size than the United States reservations, but the American Indians were not moved. About 300 United States federal reservations still exist today, some for a single tribe, others as home to a number of groups. In the 1900s, American Indians became more politically active, helped by political groups such as the American Indian Movement (AIM). Tribes began seeking compensation for lost land. The Cherokees were awarded 15 million dollars for lands they had lost. Many reservations are now governed by the tribes. Some are run by a council with an elected chief. In a way, it is similar to traditional tribal society. However, the United States government still has control over much surviving American Indian land. Since 1970, tribes have been allowed to run their reservation schools and to teach children their ancestral history.

MODERN CEREMONIES
This couple is joining other American Indian descendants at a powwow (tribal gathering). The meetings are popular because of a recent surge of interest in the culture of the tribes. Powwows give the people a chance to dress in traditional costume, speak their native language and learn more about their tribal history.

TRIBAL PROTEST
In July of 1978 these American Indians walked for five months to Washington from their reservations to protest to Congress. At protest meetings, leaders read from a list of 400 treaties, all the promises that the United States had broken. For years, many tribes tried to get back land taken from them. In 1992, Navajo and Hopi tribes were given back 1.8 million acres of their land in Northern Arizona to be divided between the tribes.

SODA FOUNTAIN STOP
A Seminole family enjoys sodas in 1948 in a Miami store. Tribes gradually adapted to the American ways of life, but some kept their own customs and dress. Seminoles were forced from Florida to Oklahoma in 1878. Almost 300 refused to leave the Everglades, and about 2,000 live there today.

SURVIVING CRAFTS

Turquoise was found in rock in the Southwest and mined by local tribes like the Zuni and Navajo. The semi-precious stone was believed to ward off evil spirits. Turquoise is still used today. It is set into bracelets and necklaces made of silver.

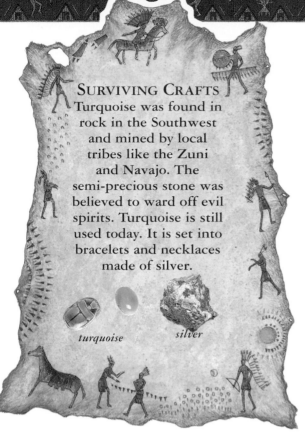

turquoise   *silver*

THE TOURIST TRAIL

A traditional Inuit scene of snowshoes propped outside an igloo. Most people in Alaska and Greenland live in modern, centrally heated homes. However, the ancient skills of building temporary shelters from ice bricks still survive. They are passed down to each generation and occasionally used by hunters or tourists eager to experience North American Indian customs.

CHEERLEADING CHIEF

Dressed in full ceremonial costume, this North American Indian helps conduct celebrations at a football stadium. It is a way of raising awareness of the existence of tribes. The cheerleading is not far removed from a war chief's tribal role of encouraging warriors in battle.

STITCHING THE PAST

Traditional American Indian crafts are still made today. The method of curing hides has remained the same. No chemicals are used during the tanning process, and the scraping is still done by hand. However, styles of crafts had already changed to suit the European market in the 1600s when traders brought in new materials.

TRADITIONAL SKILLS

An Indian craftsman produces beautiful jewelry in silver and turquoise. Zuni and Navajo people were among the finest jewelry makers in this style. Other tribes, such as the Crow, are famous for their beadwork.

Glossary

A

adobe Plaster used by Pueblo Indians on their homes. It was made from clay and straw.

Algonquian A group of many tribes (including the Secotan and Powhatan) who shared the same coastal areas in the northeast and spoke a version of the same language.

ancestor A family member who died long ago.

angakok A name for an Inuit shaman (medicine man).

archaeologist Person who studies ancient remains or ruins.

B

bark Outer layer (covering) of tree trunks.

blubber Fat of a whale, found just beneath the skin.

C

caribou Reindeer found in North America.

cavalry Soldiers on horseback.

clan A group of people who are related to each other.

colonies Communities or groups of people who settle in another land, but still keep links with their own country.

Congress Legislative branch of the United States government.

cradleboard A wooden board, usually with protective head area, to which a baby was strapped and carried around.

currency Form of exchange for goods such as money or wampum.

D

descendant Person who is descended from (born after) an individual or group of people who lived earlier.

dialects Regional accents and language variations.

dugout canoe A canoe made by hollowing out a tree trunk.

E

effigy Figure or doll representing someone.

F

frontiers Land on the border between Indian territory and land European settlers had already taken or bought.

G

glyphs Pictures that tell a message or have a meaning.

H

hunter-gatherer Person who lives by hunting animals and gathering wild roots and plants.

I

ice floes Large sheets of ice floating in the sea.

immigrants People who come to live in a land from other countries.

Inuit The native people of the North American Arctic, Canada and Greenland as distinguished from Asia and the Aleutian islands. Inuit is also the general name for an Eskimo in Canada.

Iroquois A group of tribes from the Woodlands who joined together to form a powerful government.

K

kiva Underground chamber used for religious ceremonies among Pueblo people.

Kwatee Mythical figure connected with tales of the creation of the universe.

L

lacrosse Stick and ball game played with a stick with a net on the end. The ball is scooped in the net rather than hit in the air or along the ground.

legend Ancient story that has been handed down over the years. It may be part myth and part truth.

legislation Making laws.

loom A frame used for weaving yarn into fabric and blankets.

M

migrating When a group of people, animals or birds travel between different habitats to settle in other regions either permanently or at specific times of the year.

missionaries Religious people who went to North America to change the North American Indians' religion from their own traditional beliefs to Christianity, which was the prominent religion in Europe.

moccasins Soft leather, slip-on shoes often decorated with beads.

myth An old tale or legend that describes gods, spirits or fantastic creatures.

N

nation Group of people who live in one territory and usually share the same language or history.

nomadic People who move from one area to another to find food, better land or to follow herds.

O

obsidian Dark, glassy volcanic rock found in the earth.

Oglala Sioux A band of the Western or Teton Sioux.

P

parka Hooded, warm overcoat usually made of caribou or other animal skin and worn by Inuit people in the Arctic.

pelts Skin or fur of a furry animal such as a beaver.

pemmican Food mixture made from ground bison meat, berries and animal fat.

pictographs Picture writing.

Pueblo People from the Southwest who lived in villages built of mud and stone.

Q

quahog Edible round clam found in North America.

R

reservation An area of land chosen by the United States government and set aside for a tribe(s) in the 1800s. Sometimes early reservation land was seized again later by the US and tribes were moved on again to another reservation further away.

rites Solemn procedure normally carried out for a religious purpose or part of a ceremony.

rituals An often repeated set of actions carried out during a religious or other ceremony.

S

sauna Bath of hot steam.

scalps Chunks of skin and long hair which warriors shaved off the heads of their enemy in battle.

settlers People who came from other countries to settle or stay in North America.

shaman The medicine man or woman of the tribe. These people were spiritual and ceremonial leaders and doctors.

shrine A holy place used for worship, often built beside graves.

T

tepee Conical tent with a frame of poles, covered with animal skins, used by Plains Indians.

tomahawk War ax. Its head was of stone, metal or bone.

totem A good luck charm.

totem pole A tall post carved with totems.

trading post General store where people from a wide area traded or swapped goods.

tradition Habits, beliefs or practices handed down from one generation to the next.

trappers People who trap animals, especially for their skin.

travois A V-shaped frame for carrying possessions dragged by dogs and later by horses.

treaty Peace agreement.

tribe Group of people who shared a common language and way of life.

W

wigwam Dwelling made of bark, rushes or skins spread over arched poles lashed together.

wampum Shells, or beads made from shells, strung together and used as currency or to record a historical event.

ARCTIC PEOPLES

The Arctic peoples live in the vast regions of the extreme north. In prehistoric times, hunter-gatherers from Europe and Asia followed migrating herds of animals into these areas. They used knowledge of the natural world to survive in one of the wildest, harshest places on Earth.

JEN GREEN

CONSULTANT: CHERRY ALEXANDER

An Ancient History

THE ARCTIC is one of the wildest, harshest places on Earth. Arctic winters are long, dark and bitterly cold. A thick layer of ice and snow blankets the region for much of the year. Today, people from developed countries can survive in the Arctic with the help of the latest technologies, such as modern homes, snowmobiles and clothes made from warm manmade fibers. Yet the original Arctic inhabitants thrived in this icy world for thousands of years. They did not have any of these modern aids to help them.

Arctic peoples used the natural world around them to survive. Slain animals provided food, skins for clothes and shelter and bones for tools and weapons. Although early Arctic peoples left no written records behind them, archaeologists can piece together the history of these people from finds such as tools and the remains of old buildings. The modern descendants of these early residents continue to carry on some of the traditional ways of Arctic living.

EARLY PORTRAIT
This portrait of three Arctic hunters was painted in the 1800s by one of the first European explorers to visit the Arctic. Drawings made by early European explorers, along with other records they collected, are a good source of information about the history of the region.

TRADITIONAL SKILLS
A girl from Arctic Russia learns to soften reindeer skins, using a method that has been used by her ancestors for thousands of years. Ancient Arctic peoples developed a way of life that was so successful that it has changed very little over the generations.

TIMELINE 10,000 B.C.–A.D. 1600

Humans have lived in the Arctic region for thousands of years. The huge periods of time involved, and the lack of written records, mean that the dates given for some of the earlier events are only approximate.

10,000 B.C. and earlier Groups of people in Arctic Russia and Scandinavia live nomadic lives, following huge herds of reindeer that they hunt for food.

10,000 B.C. During the last Ice Age, nomadic peoples move into North America from Siberia, traveling across a bridge of dry land that linked the two landmasses.

Small Tool People harpoon used to hunt sea mammals

3000–1000 B.C. The Small Tool People live on the shores of the Bering Strait. Later they move east into Arctic Canada and Greenland. They use tools, such as needles, to make clothes, and harpoons to hunt food.

1000 B.C.–A.D. 1000 The Dorset People dominate the North American Arctic. They use sea *kayaks* to hunt sea mammals, such as seals and walruses. The Dorset People live a nomadic life during the summer months, traveling in small groups and living in skin-covered tents.

Dorset culture hunter in his kayak

10,000 B.C.

5000 B.C.

1000 B.C.

ANCIENT SITES

Archaeologists unearth the remains of a prehistoric house in the Canadian Arctic. Excavations of these early settlements reveal tools, weapons and other important objects. This information can tell archaeologists a lot about the lives of early Arctic people.

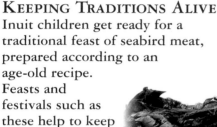

TOOLS AND WEAPONS

This harpoon point was carved from a walrus tusk. In ancient times, Arctic people were skilled at many crafts. Numerous tools and weapons were shaped from the bones of slain animals.

KEEPING TRADITIONS ALIVE

Inuit children get ready for a traditional feast of seabird meat, prepared according to an age-old recipe. Feasts and festivals such as these help to keep ancient Arctic traditions alive, preserving them for future generations of Inuit to enjoy.

FROZEN WORLD

The Arctic region lies at the far north of our planet. Its limit is the Arctic Circle, an imaginary line encircling the Earth at a latitude of 66 degrees north. Much of the Arctic region is a vast, frozen ocean, surrounded by the northernmost parts of Asia, Europe, North America and Greenland. All areas inside the Arctic Circle experience at least one day each year when the sun shines all day and night, and at least one day when the sun never rises.

---

knife of Dorset origin

A.D. 1–A.D. 1000 In winter, the Dorset people live in snow-house communities and use knives and clubs to kill seals at their breathing holes on the sea ice. During the later Dorset period, they develop artistic abilities. Many of the objects they make are used for magic, such as wooden masks. Around A.D. 1000 the climate becomes warmer, which leads to the extinction of many of the Dorset people.

A.D. 983 Viking warrior Erik the Red establishes a colony in Greenland.

Viking colony established in Greenland

A.D. 1000–1600 The Thule People gradually replace the Dorset People. They live in stone and turf huts. They use *kayaks* and *umiaks* to hunt bowhead whales, and kill land animals, such as reindeer and musk oxen.

A.D. 1570 onward European sailors begin to explore the coast of Arctic Canada and also the seas north of Siberia. They come in search of whale oil, furs and wealth, and to find new sea routes to Asia.

Thule People continue to prosper until 1600.

A.D. 1000   A.D. 1500   A.D. 1600

The Arctic World

THE ICY WORLD of the Arctic holds traces of some very ancient civilizations. Indeed, archaeologists have found tools and weapons dating back to around 20,000 B.C. In prehistoric times, Arctic Russia and Scandinavia were inhabited by nomadic (wandering) peoples. They followed huge herds of reindeer, hunting the animals for their meat and fur. During the last Ice Age, more than 12,000 years ago, some of these nomads traveled from Asia to North America, crossing a bridge of land that once linked the two continents. Some settled in Arctic North America, while others moved to the warmer climate of the south.

Around 3000 B.C., a group called the Small Tool People lived on the coast of Alaska. These people carved beautiful tools and weapons from bones and teeth. They made spears to hunt game and needles to sew animal skins into warm clothing. By 1000 B.C., another group called the Dorset People dominated Arctic North America. They roamed the coastal waters in sea canoes, hunting seals and walruses. Two thousand years later, a third group, the Thule People, had replaced the Dorsets. The Thule lived in houses built of turf and stone, used sleds pulled by dogs to travel over the ice and hunted huge bowhead whales.

The first Europeans to contact the Arctic peoples were the Vikings in A.D. 983. From the late 1500s, Europeans came to the Arctic in increasing numbers. Until about 1800, life in the Arctic had changed very little for thousands of years. After that time, it began to change much more quickly.

Extent of summer

Nenet camp

Saami with Reindeer

EUROPE

TIMELINE A.D. 1600–A.D. 1900

A.D. 1600–A.D. 1800 European whaling ships visit the Arctic to hunt whales in the spring. The whaling industry booms until the 1800s.

whale hunting in the Arctic

trading furs with the Inuits

A.D. 1720 Russian explorers map Siberia and cross from Asia to Alaska.

A.D. 1720s onward Russian merchants begin to trade with Arctic groups in Alaska. European merchants begin to trade for furs in northern Canada.

A.D. 1720s Greenland is colonized by Denmark.

A.D. 1750s onward Christian missionaries arrive in North America and build schools and churches. They work to convert the local people to their religion. They discourage the work of shamans and undermine local peoples' faith in the spirit world. Many local people convert to Christianity.

wooden cross

A.D. 1600   A.D. 1700   A.D. 1750   A.D. 1800

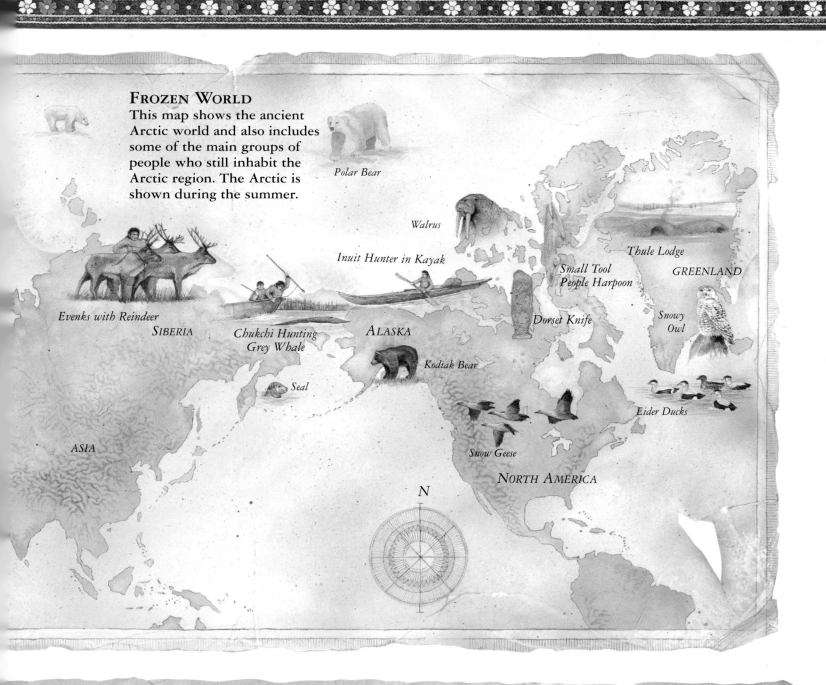

FROZEN WORLD

This map shows the ancient Arctic world and also includes some of the main groups of people who still inhabit the Arctic region. The Arctic is shown during the summer.

Polar Bear

Walrus

Inuit Hunter in Kayak

Thule Lodge

Small Tool People Harpoon

GREENLAND

Evenks with Reindeer

SIBERIA

Chukchi Hunting Grey Whale

ALASKA

Dorset Knife

Snowy Owl

Kodiak Bear

Seal

Eider Ducks

ASIA

Snow Geese

NORTH AMERICA

N

Hudson Bay trading certificate

A.D. 1820 The Hudson Bay Trading Company, a British business, is set up in the Canadian Arctic.

It soon controls the fur trade and a vast area of northern Canada. Native people trade skins for European items, such as rifles.

A.D. 1867 Russia sells Alaska to the United States.

A.D. 1870s Whaling declines in the Arctic, due to overhunting by European whalers.

A.D. 1880–A.D. 1890s A gold rush starts at the Yukon River and Klondike in Alaska. Many new settlers also move to the American Arctic. Gold is discovered in Siberia, and soon coal is mined there as well.

Alaska becomes part of the United States.

A.D. 1900s onward European missionaries convert increasing numbers of Arctic peoples to Christianity. As the influence of southern nations increases, life in the Arctic changes more quickly. The people of Arctic America, Europe and Asia are made subject to their nations' laws.

The lure of gold was the main reason for the mass settlement of Arctic America and Russia.

A.D. 1850

A.D. 1900

Peoples of the North

THE ARCTIC IS HOME to many different groups of people. These groups are the descendants of ancient races who have lived in these frozen lands for thousands of years. Each group has its own distinctive way of life, culture and language.

The Inuit are the most northerly group in the Arctic, living on the coasts of North America from Alaska through Canada to Greenland, and on the tip of eastern Asia. Many Inuit still follow the traditions of their ancestors, harpooning seals, walruses and other sea creatures. The peoples of Arctic Europe and Asia live farther south. The Saami, also called the Lapps, come from Scandinavia. Many Saami continue to herd reindeer for food. Northern Russia is home to more than 20 Arctic peoples. Groups such as the Chukchi, Evenks, Nenets and Yakut herd reindeer and also hunt game, just as their ancestors did before them.

CHUKCHI

A Chukchi man rests on one ski, which is covered in moose hide. The Chukchi came from northeastern Siberia, the part of Russia closest to North America. Traditionally, they have closer links with the Inuit than with any other group from Arctic Asia.

SAAMI

A Saami, or Lapp, man from Norway cuddles his son. The Saami were well-known for their colorful, traditional clothing, decorated with bright bands of red, yellow and blue woven ribbon. The Saami still live in Scandinavia, but many have adopted a modern lifestyle.

TIMELINE A.D. 1900–A.D. 2000

A.D. 1909 American explorer Robert Peary is the first to reach the North Pole, with the help of Inuit teams.

A.D. 1917 After the Russian Revolution, the Soviets take power in Russia. The communist system is imposed in Siberia and throughout the new Soviet Union.

Robert Peary at the North Pole

a radar station in the middle of the Arctic

A.D. 1939–1945 During World War II, army bases are set up throughout the Arctic.

A.D. 1945–1980s As World War II ends, the Cold War begins between the Soviet Union and the West. Radar stations are set up across the Arctic to warn of missile attacks. Gradually, new communities grow up around these bases.

A.D. 1968 Rich fields of oil and gas are discovered at Prudhoe Bay in Alaska. Mining increases in the Arctic, leading to pollution and the loss of some traditional hunting and herding grounds.

oil power station

A.D. 1900   A.D. 1930   A.D. 1960   A.D. 1970

EVENK

An Evenk man and woman show off their tame reindeer. These are draft animals, which means they are used for pulling sleds. In the frozen lands of northern Siberia in Russia, Evenks depend on reindeer for meat and for their hides, which are used to make warm clothing.

INUIT

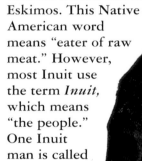

This modern Inuit hunter's breath has frozen onto his beard. The Inuit used to be called Eskimos. This Native American word means "eater of raw meat." However, most Inuit use the term *Inuit,* which means "the people." One Inuit man is called an Inuk.

NENET

This Nenet girl is dressed in a warm coat made from reindeer skins. Nenets live in many parts of Russia. Traditionally, these people live as nomads, traveling with the reindeer herds as they move across the frozen Arctic wastes.

A.D. 1977 Inuit and other Arctic peoples hold the first Inuit Circumpolar Conference. Arctic groups begin to organize, claiming traditional lands and demanding a say in their own affairs.

A.D. 1979 Greenland wins self-government from Denmark.

the national flag of Greenland

seabird killed by an oil spill

A.D. 1986 A fire at the nuclear power plant at Chernobyl in the Ukraine spreads radiation across the Arctic, polluting the reindeer pastures of the Saami and other Arctic herders.

A.D. 1989 The wreck of the oil tanker *Exxon Valdez* pollutes the coast of Alaska and kills thousands of seabirds, otters and other creatures.

A.D. 1990 Nunavut, a large territory in northern Canada, is awarded to the Inuit.

A.D. 1999 The homeland of Nunavut is finally handed over to the Inuit.

modern day Inuit on a motorized snowmobile

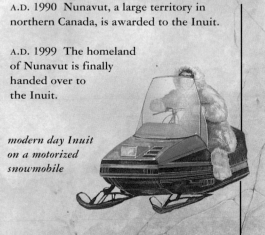

A.D. 1980   A.D. 1990   A.D. 2000

A Frozen Land

SUMMER VISITORS
In spring, birds, such as these guillemots, migrate to the Arctic in huge numbers. The guillemots nest on crowded cliff edges, to lay eggs and raise their young. Other birds nest in open tundra. As the harsh winter weather sets in, the birds move south again. Many Arctic peoples hunted summer visitors such as these.

THE ARCTIC is one of the coldest places on our planet. Freezing winter weather lasts for eight or nine months of the year. Summers provide a brief break from these harsh conditions. The polar regions—the Arctic in the north and the Antarctic in the far south—are so cold because the sun never shines directly over them. Instead, it hangs low in the sky. The ice and snow also help to keep the temperature low because they reflect sunlight back into space.

Most of the Arctic region is actually an ocean, topped by drifting sheets of ice. In winter, most of the ocean surface freezes over. Temperatures on land are almost always colder than in the water. Greenland, the landmass nearest to the North Pole, is covered by a thick ice cap all year round. Further south, the areas of Asia, Europe and North America that lie within the Arctic Circle are mainly tundra—vast areas of barren, treeless lowlands. South of the tundra, a belt of dense, evergreen forests called the taiga dominates.

ICY LANDSCAPE
The Inuit village of Moriussaq in northern Greenland is covered by ice and snow for much of the year. In summer, temperatures rarely rise above 50°F. In winter, they often drop to −40°F. Throughout the Arctic region, the winter cold is so intense that the ground remains permanently frozen. This permanently frozen ground is known as permafrost. It may reach as deep as 1,960 ft in northernmost areas of the Arctic, such as Greenland and Siberia.

USEFUL PLANTS

Arctic peoples used the plants found in the region in many different ways. Some were eaten. For example, the leaves of the Arctic sorrel and the bark of the Arctic willow are rich in vitamins. Purple saxifrage yields a sweet nectar.

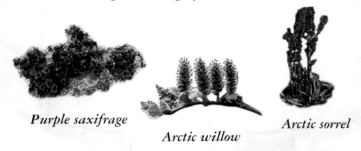

Purple saxifrage

Arctic willow

Arctic sorrel

WATERLOGGED SOIL

In the short Arctic summer, lakes, ponds and streams litter the surface of the Siberian tundra. In winter, the ground is permanently frozen. As summer approaches, however, the top layer of soil thaws. Water cannot penetrate the frozen layer below, so pools of water collect at the surface.

SPRING BLOOMS

In spring, Arctic plants, such as this yellow marsh saxifrage, quickly blossom. Flowering plants are found even in the far north of the Arctic. Many have special features that help them to cope with the bitterly cold conditions.

MIDNIGHT SUN

The midnight sun lights up the pack ice covering the Arctic Ocean. The sun never sets in the Arctic during summer. In winter, it never rises, and the Arctic is a dark place. This is because Earth tilts at an angle as it revolves around the sun. In summer, the Arctic region leans toward the sun, but in winter it tilts away.

NORTHERN LIGHTS

The northern lights or aurora borealis fill the skies over the Northwest Territories of Canada. The northern lights are an amazing display of red, yellow and green lights often seen in Arctic regions. They are caused by particles from the sun striking Earth's atmosphere at the North Pole, releasing energy in the form of light.

Traveling with Reindeer

SOME ARCTIC PEOPLES have long depended on the reindeer. This large mammal is found throughout the frozen Arctic region. In North America, where reindeer are known as caribou, wild herds roam the land in search of food. In Europe and Siberia, they have been domesticated (tamed) for hundreds of years. In ancient times, the Saami, Nenets, Chukchi and other Arctic groups depended on the reindeer as a source of food. These people used reindeer skins to make tents and warm clothes. They also shaped the bones and antlers into tools and weapons.

Many Arctic animals are migratory creatures, which means they travel with the changing seasons. Reindeer are no exception. In spring, huge herds move north toward the shores of the Arctic Ocean. They spend the summer grazing the tundra pastures. In autumn, they journey south again to spend the winter in the sheltered forests of the taiga. In the past, the Saami and Nenets traveled with the reindeer, moving the animals on so they did not graze the pastures bare. Some of their descendants still live the same nomadic life.

TENDING YOUNG DEER
A Saami herdsman lifts a newborn calf. Reindeer calves are born in May and June, following the herd's migration to northern tundra pastures in the spring. Just a few hours after birth, most newborn calves are strong enough to stand up and walk.

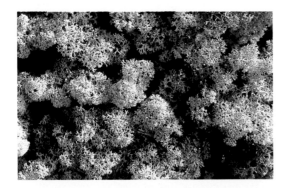

REINDEER FOOD
Reindeer moss carpets the forest floor in Labrador, Canada. Reindeer moss is the main source of food for reindeer, since it is found beneath the snow in winter. In summer, a wider variety of plants is available for the reindeer to eat.

ROPING REINDEER
A Saami herder uses a modern rope lasso to catch a reindeer from the herd. In the past, Saami herdspeople used reindeer hide to make their lassos. Saami families owned herds of between 200 and 1,000 animals. The size of the herd was an indication of the family's wealth.

ARCTIC ADAPTATIONS

A Chukchi herdsman checks his reindeer during a light snowstorm. Reindeer are well adapted to life in the harsh environment of the Arctic. They are warm-blooded mammals, and they must keep their bodies at a constant temperature to survive. A thick layer of insulating fur helps to keep each animal warm. Reindeer also have "heat exchangers" in their muzzles to warm the air they breathe in. Reindeer have broad hooves that help prevent the animals from sinking into the deep snow and becoming stranded.

FENCED IN

A Saami herder uses a long, billowing cloth to drive his animals into a fenced corral. Reindeer herds were driven into corrals to check their health and to decide which animals were the best to kill. The herder could also see if he had another herder's reindeer.

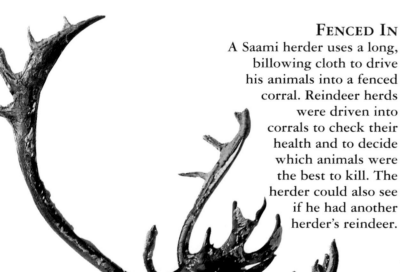

VALUED ANIMAL

Reindeer were extremely useful animals. They provided meat, and their blood and milk were drunk. Reindeer hides were used to make clothes, bedding and rough shelters. Bones and antlers were shaped into harpoons, needles and other tools and weapons. Even the animal's sinews (tendons) were used as sewing thread.

PACK LEADER

Traditionally, reindeer herds were led by tame deer wearing bells. Many Arctic Siberians kept male and female animals in separate groups.

milk

antler

hide

Settlements and Homes

MOST ANCIENT ARCTIC GROUPS lived in small villages containing a few families at most. The villages were spread out over a wide area, so each group had a large territory in which to hunt. In winter, the Inuit, Saami and other groups lived in sturdy houses built partly underground to protect them from the freezing conditions above. In summer, or when traveling from place to place, they lived in tents or temporary shelters.

In Siberia and parts of Scandinavia, groups such as the Nenets did not settle in one place. Their homes were lightweight tents, called chums in Siberia, made up of a framework of wooden poles and covered with animal skins. These chums could withstand severe Arctic blizzards and kept everyone warm inside when temperatures were low.

TENT LIFE
A Nenet herder loads up a sled outside his family's chum in preparation for another day's travel across Siberia. Chums were convenient, light and easy to assemble and dismantle. Some Nenets still live in chums, as their ancestors have done for generations.

BUILDING MATERIALS
A deserted building made from stone and whale bone stands on a cliff in Siberia. Building materials were scarce in the Arctic. In coastal regions, people built houses with whale bones and driftwood gathered from the beach. Inland, houses were mainly built with rocks and turf.

ARCTIC DWELLING
This illustration shows a house in the Alaskan subarctic with a portion cut out to show how it is made. Houses such as this one were buried under the ground. People entered by ladder through the roof.

MAKE A NENET TENT
You will need: 3 blankets (two at 6½ x 5 ft and one at 4 x 4 ft), tape measure, string, scissors, 10 bamboo sticks (nine 72 in. long and one 12 in. long), black marker, black thread, a log or stone.

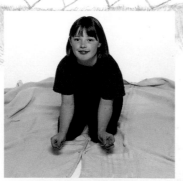

1 Cut small holes 4 in. apart along the shorter sides of the two large blankets. Thread a piece of string through the holes and tie the string together.

2 Cut a 24-in. length of string. Tie the 12-in.-long stick and a black marker 22 in. apart. Use the marker to draw a circle on the smaller blanket.

3 Tie four bamboo sticks together at one end. Open out the sticks onto the base blanket. Place the sticks on the edge of the circle so they stand up.

BONY BUNKER

Whale bone rafters arch over the remains of a home in Siberia. Part of the house was often built underground. First, the builders dug a pit to make the floor. Then they built low walls of rocks and turf. Long bones or driftwood laid on top of the walls formed sturdy rafters that supported a roof made from turf and stones.

MAKING WINDOWS

An old stone and turf house stands in Arctic Greenland. Ancient peoples made windows by stretching dried seal bladders over holes in the wall. The bladder was thin enough to allow light through.

A tent covered with several layers of animal skins made an extremely warm Arctic home, even in the bitterly cold winter. The wooden poles were lashed together with rope.

4 Lean the five extra bamboo sticks against the main frame, placing the ends around the base circle. Leave a gap at the front for the entrance.

5 Tie the middle-of-the-edge of the two larger blankets to the back of the frame, at the top. Make two tight knots to secure the blankets.

6 Bring each blanket around to the entrance. Tie them at the top with string. Roll the blankets down to the base so they lie flat on the frame.

7 Tie 5 3-ft lengths of thread along the front edge of the blanket. Pull these tight and tie to a log or stone to weigh down the base of the tent.

Seasonal Camps

CHEERFUL GLOW

An igloo near Thule in Greenland is lit up by the glow of a primus stove. The light inside reveals the spiraling shape of the blocks of ice used to make the igloo. Snow crystals in the walls scatter the light so the whole room is bathed in the glow. In the Inuit language, *iglu* was actually a word to describe any type of house. A shelter such as this one was called an *igluigaq*.

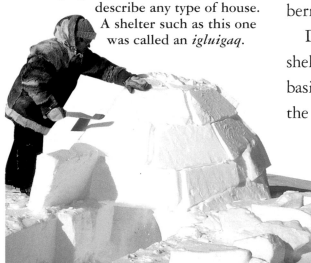

SUMMER is a busy time for Arctic animals and plants. The rising temperature melts the sea ice, and the oceans teem with tiny organisms called plankton. On land, the tundra bursts into flower. Insects hatch, and burrowing creatures, such as lemmings, leave their tunnels in search of food. Wild reindeer, whales and many types of birds migrate to the Arctic to feast on the plentiful supply of food.

The lives of Arctic peoples changed with the seasons too. In Canada, Alaska and Greenland, the Inuit left their winter villages and traveled to the summer hunting grounds. They hunted fish and sea mammals and gathered fruits and berries, taking advantage of the long, bright summer days.

During winter hunting trips, the Inuit built temporary shelters made of snow blocks, commonly called igloos. The basic igloo design was developed hundreds of years ago. It kept the hunters warm even in the harshest Arctic storm.

BUILDING AN IGLOO

An Inuk builds an igloo, using a long ice knife to cut large blocks of tightly packed snow. First, he lays a ring of ice blocks to make a circle up to 10 ft in diameter. Then, some of the blocks are cut to make them slope. As new blocks are added, the walls of the igloo begin to lean inward, forming the familiar dome-shaped igloo. This method is exactly the same as the one used by his ancestors centuries ago.

MAKE A MODEL IGLOO

You will need: self-drying clay, rolling pin, cutting board, ruler, modeling tool, scissors, thick card stock (8 x 8 in.), pencil, water bowl, white paint, paintbrush.

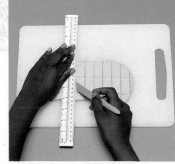

1 Roll out the self-drying clay. It should be around ½ in. thick. Cut out 30 blocks of clay; 24 must be ¾ x 1½ in. and the other 6 blocks must be ½ x ¾ in.

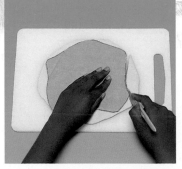

2 Cut out some card stock to make an irregular shape. Roll out more clay (½ in. thick). Put the template on the clay and cut around it to make the base of the igloo.

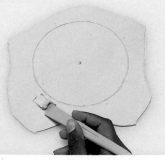

3 Mark out a circle with a diameter of 4¾ in. Cut out a small rectangle on the edge of the circle (¾ x 1½ in.) to make the entrance to the igloo.

IGLOO VILLAGE

This engraving, made in 1871, shows a large Inuit village in the Canadian Arctic. Most Inuit igloos were simple, dome-like structures. The Inuit built these temporary shelters during the winter hunting trips.

THE FINAL BLOCK

An Inuit hunter carefully places the final block of ice onto the roof of his igloo. Ancient hunters used sharp ice knives to shape the blocks so that they fitted together exactly. Any gaps were sealed with snow to prevent the icy winds from entering the shelter.

A SNUG HOME

An Inuit hunter shelters inside his igloo. A small entrance tunnel prevents cold winds from entering the shelter and traps warm air inside. Outside, the temperature may be as low as −90°F. Inside, heat from the stove, candles and the warmth of the hunter's body keeps the air at around 40°F.

Inuit hunters built temporary shelters by fitting ice blocks together to form a spiraling dome structure called an igloo. Only firmly packed snow was used to make the building blocks.

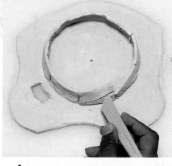

4 Stick nine large blocks around the edge of the circle. Use water to make the clay stick to the base. Cut across two rectangular blocks as shown above.

5 Using your modeling tool, carefully cut a small piece of clay from the corner of each of the remaining blocks as shown above.

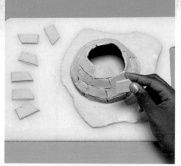

6 Starting from the two blocks cut earlier, build up the walls, slanting each block in as you go. Use the six small blocks at the top. Leave a hole at the top.

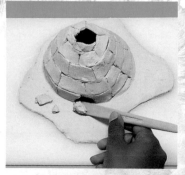

7 Use the modeling tool to form a small entrance to the igloo behind the rectangle already cut into the base. When the clay has dried, paint the igloo white.

Home Comforts

INSIDE ARCTIC SHELTERS, small comforts made life more bearable. From the earliest times, the Inuit and other Arctic groups used the frozen ground for sleeping platforms or made them out of snow. Animal skins were draped across the platforms to make them warm and comfortable. Often, the walls and floor were lined with skins to provide extra insulation from the bitter Arctic winds.

The floor of an ancient Nenet or Saami tent was a meshwork of branches covered with animal skins. In the center of each tent, flat stones made a safe platform for the fire. Arctic peoples started fires with the heat created by the motion of a tool called a bow drill. In Inuit shelters, stone lamps burning seal or whale fat provided heat and lit up the darkness. With lamps or candles burning, the shelters were surprisingly warm, and many people took off the outer layers of their clothing as they entered.

ROCKING THE CRADLE
A Nenet baby sleeps in its cradle. The cradle is usually suspended from the stout wooden struts that hold up the tent. The struts make a frame sturdy enough to support fairly heavy weights.

INSIDE AN IGLOO
This engraving of the inside of an igloo was made by the European traveler Edward Finden in 1824. Inuit women hung all their possessions from strings, poles and even reindeer antlers to warm them in the dry air higher in the igloo.

MAKE AN OIL LAMP

You will need: self-drying clay, rolling pin, cutting board, ruler, compass, sharp pencil, modeling tool, water bowl, dark grey and light gray paint, small paintbrush.

1 Roll out a piece of clay to a thickness of ½ in. Draw a circle with a radius of 2 in., and carefully use the modeling tool to cut the circle out.

2 Using your hands, roll another piece of clay out into a long sausage shape. Make the shape around 12 in. long and ¾ in. thick.

3 Wet the edge of the clay circle and stick the sausage shape around it. Use the rounded end of the modeling tool to blend the edges into the base.

FEEDING THE STOVE

A Nenet woman adds another log to the stove to keep her family's reindeer-skin tent warm. She has hung a pair of wet boots above the stove to dry them out. Stoves such as this one were light enough to be carried on sleds pulled by reindeer when it was time to move on.

IN THE FIRELIGHT

A Saami herder warms his hands in the light of a crackling fire inside his tent. You can see a large stack of wood piled up by the fire. Traditionally, the tent floor was a network of birch branches with skins laid on top. Smoke spiraled upward and escaped through a hole in the roof.

FIRE AND ICE

Two hunters sit on a skin-covered sleeping platform, keeping warm beside the fire. Most fires were balanced on frames made from driftwood or animal bones. That way, the flames did not go out or melt the floor. Wet clothes and animal skins were often dried on a rack set above the fire.

Stone lamps burning seal or whale blubber (fat) have long cast a warm glow in homes throughout the Arctic. A lighted wick of moss or fur was placed in a bowl filled with the fat and left to burn slowly.

4 Use your modeling tool to cut a small triangular notch at the edge of the circle. This will make a small lip for the front of the lamp.

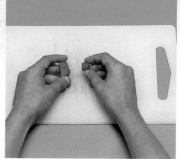

5 Shape a piece of clay into a small head. Use another piece to shape some shoulders. Stick the head to the shoulders by wetting the clay.

6 Stick the small figure just off the center of the base of the lamp. Then use the modeling tool to make a small groove on the base to hold the oil.

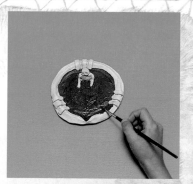

7 You can add extra pieces of clay around the edge of the lamp for decoration. Once the clay has dried, you can paint the lamp different colors.

Family Life

ARCTIC PEOPLES lived in closely knit families. Most family groups were made up not just of a mother, father and their children, but often grandparents, uncles, aunts and cousins, too. These family units often consisted of a dozen people or more, all living in extremely close quarters.

Within the family, men and women had different jobs to do. In Inuit society, men were responsible for hunting. They also maintained the hunting equipment and looked after the dogs that pulled their sleds. Women were responsible for most other chores around the home. Their work included tending the fire, cooking, fetching ice to make drinking water, preparing animal hides and taking care of their children. Sewing was another important job for women. They had to find time to make and repair all the family's clothes and bedding. Surviving in the Arctic was hard, and both men and women often worked long hours to keep everyone warm, clothed and fed.

DIVIDING THE WORKLOAD
A Nenet woman pours tea for her husband inside the family tent. In Nenet families, work was divided among members of the family. Traditionally, men herded reindeer. Women did most other tasks. As well as cooking, women pitched and dismantled the tents, chopped wood, prepared animal hides and sewed all the family's clothing.

ALL-PURPOSE KNIFE
This knife, called an *ulu*, was the traditional tool of Inuit women. It was used for many tasks, including cutting meat and preparing animal hides. The *ulu* had a round blade, made from polished slate or metal. The handle was made from bone or wood.

DRAWSTRING PURSE
You will need: chamois leather (8½ x 14 in.), white glue, glue brush, pencil, ruler, scissors, shoelace (20 in. long), red, dark blue and light blue felt, 2 blue beads.

1 Fold over the piece of chamois leather to make a square shape. Glue down two opposite edges, leaving one end open. Let the glue dry.

2 Across the open end of the purse, pencil in marks ½ in. apart on both sides of the leather. Use your scissors to make small holes at these points.

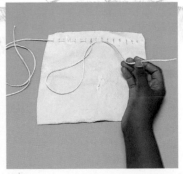

3 Thread a shoelace through the holes on both sides, as shown above. Tie the ends of the shoelace together and leave an excess piece of lace hanging.

CHOPPING ICE

Ice splinters fly as an Inuit hunter chops at a frozen block near a river in the Northwest Territories of Canada. Fetching ice to make drinking water was often a job for women. Once collected, the ice was taken back to the camp and melted over lamps that burned whale or seal blubber (fat).

USING FEATHERS

Arctic women often used the feathers of eider ducks, called eiderdown, to make bedding and warm clothes. Female ducks pluck these feathers from their breasts to help keep their chicks warm in the nest. Women collected the down from the nests or used bird skins complete with feathers. Eiderdown is still used today to make warm quilts.

Eider duck

DRYING SEALSKIN

An Inuit woman stretches a sealskin on a wooden frame to prevent the skin from shrinking as it dries. Preparing animal skins was a woman's job. Using her *ulu,* she would clean the skin by scraping off all the flesh and fat. Then the skin was stretched and dried. Finally, she would soften the hide by chewing it with her front teeth.

FEEDING TIME

An Inuit hunter feeds seal meat to each of his huskies. The Inuits used huskies as draft animals, and they were well looked after by their owners. In winter, they were fed extra meat to provide them with enough energy to pull a heavy sled in the cold climate.

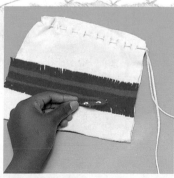

Arctic women often made bags, baskets and other useful containers. Drawstring purses such as this one were made of soft deer hide.

4 Carefully cut two strips of red felt 8 in. long and 2 in. wide. Then, cut a narrow fringe about ½ in. deep along both edges of the felt, as shown above.

5 Glue the strips of red felt to either side of the purse. You can add extra decoration by gluing ½-in. strips of blue felt on other parts of the purse.

6 Tie the two blue beads firmly to each end of the excess shoelace. Close the purse by pulling the shoelace and tying a knot in it.

Arctic Children

MODEL IGLOO

An Inuit toddler plays with a model igloo at a nursery in the Canadian Arctic. The blocks of wood spiral upward in the same way as the blocks of ice do in a real igloo, so the toy helps modern children learn the ancient art of building igloos.

CHILDREN were at the center of most Arctic societies. Inuit babies and younger children spent most of their time riding on their mother's back, nestled in a snug pouch called an *amaut*. The babies of many Arctic groups were named for respected members of the community, and their birth was celebrated with a huge feast. As children grew older, other members of the family helped the mothers bring up the children.

Today, most Arctic children go to school when they are young. However, the children of past generations traveled with their parents as the group moved to fresh reindeer pastures or new hunting grounds. Very young boys and girls were treated equally. As they grew up, however, children helped with different tasks and learned the skills that they would need later on in life. Boys learned how to hunt and look after animals. Girls learned to sew and cook and to work with animal skins.

BIRTHDAY FEAST

Traditional food is prepared at the birthday celebration of the young boy sitting at the table. Parents often named their newborn babies after people who had been respected in the community, such as a great hunter. The baby was thought to inherit that person's skills and personality.

FEEDING BIRDS TOY

You will need: self-drying clay, rolling pin, ruler, modeling tool, board, two toothpicks, white and brown paint, water bowl, paintbrush.

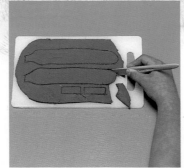

1 Roll out some of the clay into a 9 x 5½ in.-rectangle with a thickness of around ½ in. Cut out two large paddles (7 x 1 in.) and two sticks (1½ x ¾ in.).

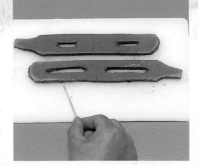

2 Cut two slots on paddle 1 (2 x ½ in.) and two on paddle 2 (1 x ½ in.). Use a toothpick to pierce a hole in the side of paddle 1 through these slots.

3 Roll out two egg shapes, each about 2 x 1½ in., in the palm of your hands. Make two bird heads and stick them to the egg-shaped bodies.

RIDING HIGH

One of the children in this old illustration is being carried in a special hood, called an *amaut,* high on the back of his mother's jacket. The second child is tucked inside her mother's sealskin boots. However, it was less common for a child to be carried in this way.

LENDING A HAND

A Nenet boy and his younger brother help to feed a reindeer calf that has lost its mother. Fathers taught their sons to handle animals from a very early age. Children were encouraged to take care of the family's tame deer and dogs.

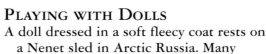

PLAYING WITH DOLLS

A doll dressed in a soft fleecy coat rests on a Nenet sled in Arctic Russia. Many Arctic girls like to play with dolls, as children do around the world. Traditionally, their dolls' heads were carved from ivory. The doll in the picture, however, is made of modern plastic.

Some Arctic children had toys with moving parts, such as this model of two birds. Traditionally, the animals would have been carved from bone or ivory. The child pulled the paddles to make the birds bob up and down.

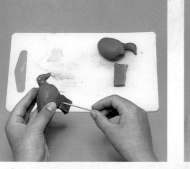

4 Place the sticks you made earlier into the base of each bird's body. Using the toothpick, pierce a small hole through the stick, close to the body.

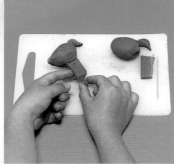

5 Let the clay bird dry on its side. You will need to support the stick with a small piece of clay to hold the bird upright as it dries.

6 Place the stick of each bird in the slots in the paddles. Push a toothpick into the holes in the edge of paddle 1, through the sticks and out the other side.

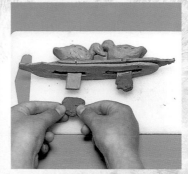

7 Add two small pieces of clay to the bottom of each stick to keep the birds in place. You can paint the toy once the clay has dried.

Fun and Games

THE EARLY YEARS were exciting times for Arctic children, with plenty of time for play and fun. Outdoor games included sliding and sledding on the ice. Indoors, children played traditional games or learned to carve animal bones. In the evenings, everyone gathered around the fire, and adults would tell magical stories featuring brave warriors and terrible monsters. For example, the Saami of Scandinavia told their children tales about *Stallos*—scary monsters that liked to eat people. The hero of the story had to outwit the monster to avoid being eaten.

Ivory, bones, animal hides and sinew (tendons) were all used to make various games and toys. Balls were made from inflated seal bladders. The tiny bones from a seal's flipper were used to make an Inuit version of the game of jacks.

SLEDDING IN THE SNOW
Two children enjoy a toboggan ride in Siberia. Boys and girls who live in the Arctic love to play in the snow. Sledding and playing in the snow help teach children about the different snow conditions that exist in the region.

GOING HUNTING
An Inuit hunter teaches his son how to read tracks in the snow. Boys learned vital hunting skills from an early age. A boy's first kill was very important and a day he would remember for the rest of his life. To mark the occasion, the boy's parents might hold a feast for the whole family to attend. At about the age of twelve, boys were allowed to go on more dangerous hunting trips with their fathers, such as walrus- or whale-hunting expeditions.

HOLE AND PIN GAME
You will need: thin card stock, ruler, pencil, white glue, glue brush, masking tape, scissors, compass, 16-in. length of black thread, thick card stock, cream paint, paintbrush, water bowl, chopstick.

1 Using the thin card stock, mark out a triangle with a base 5 in. long and a height of 6 in. Roll the triangular piece of card stock around a pencil to soften it.

2 Shape the softened card stock into a cone and glue it into position. You may need to secure the cone with a piece of masking tape.

3 Once you have secured it into position, trim off the excess card stock from the base of the cone. Make sure you always cut away from your body.

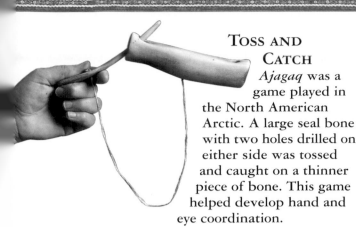

TOSS AND CATCH

Ajagaq was a game played in the North American Arctic. A large seal bone with two holes drilled on either side was tossed and caught on a thinner piece of bone. This game helped develop hand and eye coordination.

LASSOING GAME

A Chukchi boy from Arctic Russia learns to use a lasso by practicing on a reindeer antler. This skill will be essential later on in life. Around the Arctic, various games were played with reindeer antlers. Sometimes children would run around with the antlers on their heads, pretending to be reindeer. The other children would try to lasso or herd them.

STRING PUZZLES

An Inuit woman from Greenland shows a traditional puzzle she has made by winding string around her fingers. The shape depicts two musk oxen—large, fearsome Arctic mammals— charging each other. String puzzles were a common way of passing the time during the long Arctic winter. The strings were made from whale sinew (tendons) or long strips of sealskin.

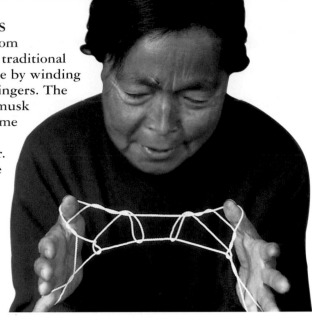

Ajagaq was played with two animal bones strapped together with a thin piece of sealskin. Two small holes were drilled at each end of the larger of the two bones. The thinner bone was used to spear the larger bone through one of the holes.

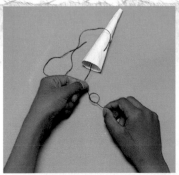

4 Cover the cone in tape. Pierce a hole in the middle of the cone, thread some black thread through, tie a knot on the inside and secure it with tape.

5 Use the base of the cone to draw a circle onto the thicker piece of card stock. Carefully cut around the circle using your pair of scissors.

6 Pierce lots of holes through the thick card stock circle, making sure the chopstick will fit through them. Glue this piece onto the base of the cone.

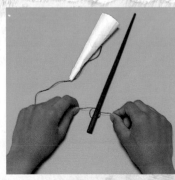

7 Paint the cone carefully, avoiding the holes. Once it has dried, secure the chopstick to the other end of the thread using a tight knot, as shown above.

Over Ice and Snow

DURING THE WINTER, the surface of the Arctic Ocean freezes over, and snow covers the land. In the past, sleds were the most common way of traveling over the ice and snow. They were made from bone or timber lashed together with strips of hide or whale sinew. They glided over the snow on runners made from walrus tusks or wood. Arctic sledges had to be light enough to be pulled by animals, yet strong enough to carry an entire family and its belongings. In North America, the Inuit used huskies to pull their sleds. In Siberia and Scandinavia, however, reindeer were used to pull sleds.

In ancient times, Arctic peoples sometimes used skis and snowshoes to get around. Skis are thought to have been invented by the Saami more than 3,500 years ago. Snowshoes allowed Arctic hunters to stalk prey without sinking into deep snowdrifts.

REINDEER SLEDS
Three reindeer stand by a family and their sled in Siberia. In Arctic Russia and Scandinavia, reindeer were commonly used to pull sleds. Small, narrow sleds carried just one person. Larger, wider models could take much heavier loads.

HITCHING A DOG TEAM
A husky team struggles up a hill in eastern Greenland. Traditionally, the reins, or traces, used by the dogs to pull the sled, were made of walrus hide. Different cultures used one of two arrangements to hitch the dogs together. Some people hitched them in the shape of a fan. Others hitched the dogs as pairs in a long line.

MODEL SLED

You will need: thick card stock, balsa wood, ruler, pencil, scissors, white glue, glue brush, masking tape, compass, wooden skewer, string, chamois leather, brown paint, paintbrush, water bowl.

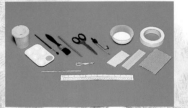

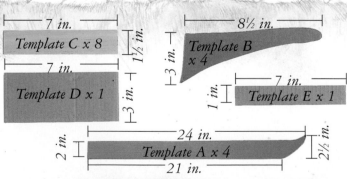

Template C x 8 — 7 in. — 1½ in.

Template D x 1 — 7 in. — 3 in.

Template B x 4 — 8½ in. — 3 in.

Template E x 1 — 7 in. — 1 in.

Template A x 4 — 24 in. — 21 in. — 2 in. — 2½ in.

Using the shapes above for reference, measure out the shapes on the card stock (use balsa wood for template C). Cut the shapes out using your scissors. You will need to make 4 A templates, 4 B templates, 8 C templates (balsa wood), 1 D template and 1 E template. Always remember to cut away from your body when using scissors.

1 Glue 2 A templates together. Repeat this for the other 2 A templates. Repeat this with the 4 B templates. Cover all the edges with masking tape.

SNOWSHOES

Snowshoes are used to walk across deep snowdrifts without sinking into the snow. They spread the person's weight across a large area. To make the snowshoe, thin, flexible birch saplings were steamed to make them supple. The saplings were then bent into the shape of the snowshoe frame. Some shoes were rounded, but others were long and narrow. The netting was woven from long strips of animal hide.

birch sapling

snowshoes

rawhide thongs

MAN'S BEST FRIEND

This picture, painted around 1890, shows an Inuit hunter harnessing one of his huskies. Huskies were vital to Inuit society. Out on the hunt, the dogs helped to find seals hiding in their dens and hauled heavy loads of meat back to camp.

SAAMI SKIS

The Saami have used skis for thousands of years. The skis were made of wood, and the undersides were covered with strips of reindeer skin. The hairs on the skin pointed backward, allowing the skier to climb up hills.

LET SLEEPING DOGS LIE

A husky's thick coat keeps it warm in temperatures as low as −58°F. These hardy animals can sleep peacefully in the fiercest of blizzards. The snow builds up against their fur and insulates them.

Inuit hunters used wooden sleds pulled by huskies to hunt for food over a large area. The wood was lashed together with animal hide or sinew.

2 Using a compass, make small holes along the top edge of the glued A templates. Use the end of a wooden skewer to make the holes a little larger.

3 Glue the balsa wood slats C in position over the holes along the A templates as shown above. You will need to use all 8 balsa wood slats.

4 Carefully glue the B templates and the E and D templates to the end of the sled, as shown above. Let dry, then paint the model.

5 Thread string through the holes to secure the slats on each side. Decorate the sledge with a chamois-covered card stock box and secure it to the sled.

On the Water

IN THE SUMMER, as soon as the sea ice had melted, Arctic people took to the water to hunt. Inuit hunters used one-person canoes called *kayaks* to track their prey. *Kayaks* were powered and steered by a double-bladed paddle. To make the craft more waterproof, the hunter closed up the top of his *kayak,* leaving only a narrow gap to allow him to climb in. The design was so successful that *kayaks* are still in use today.

Kayaks were light, speedy craft, ideal for the solitary hunter to chase seals and small whales. When hunting large bowhead whales, however, Inuit men teamed up into hunting parties of up to ten people and traveled in bigger, open boats called *umiaks*. These craft were also used to transport families across stretches of water and to ferry heavy loads from place to place.

KAYAK TRIP
An engraving made in the 1860s shows an Inuit hunter in a *kayak* chasing a small Arctic whale called a narwhal. The hunter's harpoon is attached to a large float, which is designed to slow down the harpooned whale and prevent its body from sinking when it dies. The hunter's equipment is securely lashed to the *kayak* using thick straps of animal hide.

BUILDING A KAYAK
An Inuit craftsman shapes the final pieces of his *kayak* frame. Traditionally, the wooden frame was covered with sealskins that were sewn together with skillful waterproof seams. All the joints were shaped to fit together exactly or secured with wooden pegs or leather strips.

MODEL UMIAK

You will need: chamois leather, thick card stock, thin card stock, ¼-in. dowel, ruler, pencil, scissors, white glue, glue brush, masking tape, brown paint, paintbrush, water bowl, needle, brown thread.

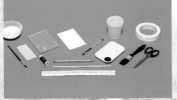

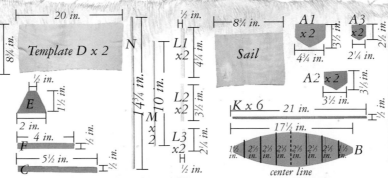

1 Use chamois leather to make the sail and template D. Cut 2 thick card stock templates A1, A2 and A3. Cut 6 thick card templates K. Use thick card stock to cut template B. Cut 10 thick card stock templates C, 4 templates F and 2 templates E. Using the dowel, cut template N and 2 templates M. Templates L1, L2 and L3 should be cut from thin card stock.

2 Mark the center, then mark cutting lines at 2½ in., 4¾ in. and 7¼ in. on either side of the center of template B. Use the scissors to cut along the lines.

UPTURNED *UMIAK*

A photograph taken in Alaska around 1900 shows an Inuit family seeking shelter inside an upturned *umiak*. *Umiaks* were made of seal or walrus skins stretched over a sturdy wooden or bone frame. They were used to transport large hunting parties or heavy loads.

KAYAK PADDLE

An Inuit hunter shapes a new paddle from a wooden plank. Traditional *kayak* paddles were double-bladed, which made it easier to keep the boat steady in rough seas. The twin blades also allowed the hunters to move through the water more quickly as they pursued their prey.

TREACHEROUS WATERS

A large iceberg drifts in the sea off the coast of Greenland. Arctic waters held many dangers for Inuit hunters. Icebergs were a particular problem when they broke up or rolled. In summer, melting ice at the water's edge made it difficult to get in and out of boats. If a hunter slipped and fell into the icy water, he would last only minutes before dying of exposure.

TRAVEL BY *UMIAK*

Three Inuit hunters paddle a small *umiak* though the icy waters off the coast of Alaska. *Umiaks* were more stable than *kayaks* in rough seas and when hunting larger sea mammals. However, they were much heavier to haul over the ice to the water's edge.

3 Glue the middle section of A onto the sections of template B, as shown above. Use the smallest A templates at the end. Use the largest A template at the center.

4 Glue 2 strips of template K to both sides of the structure, as shown above. Glue the K templates together at each end of the structure.

5 Weave templates C through templates K and over templates A, as shown. Attach with glue. Leave ¾-in. excess card stock at the top of the boat.

6 Stick the ends of C together with masking tape. Repeat the last two stages with F for the smaller ends of the structure.
Continued on next page...

Tools and Weapons

ARCTIC HUNTERS used many different weapons, hand-crafted from materials such as animal hide, bone and ivory. Weapons were kept in the best possible condition, and the hunter would inspect his weapons carefully before setting off each day.

Traditional Arctic weapons included bows and arrows and slingshots, used to bring down game birds, reindeer and other prey. Long three-pronged spears, called *kakivaks,* were used to catch fish. Seals, whales and other sea creatures were hunted with harpoons. Many weapons had barbed tips that lodged in the wounded animal's flesh. Other hunting tools included nets, fish hooks and snow goggles. When hunting in *kayaks,* western Inuits of Alaska or Asia, called Yupiks, wore wooden helmets to protect their eyes from the glare of the sun.

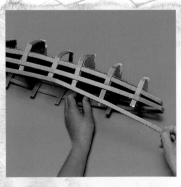

BOW AND ARROW
A Nenet boy hunts birds using a bow and arrow. Bows were made of bone or wood, with a string of twisted sinew. The arrow tips were made from ivory or copper.

SNOW GOGGLES
These Inuit snow goggles are made from the antlers of a reindeer. The hunter peered through the narrow slits. Snow goggles protected hunters' eyes from the reflection of the sun on the snow, which could cause temporary "snow blindness."

FISH SPEAR
An Inuit hunter holds a traditional three-pronged spear called a *kakivak* during a fishing trip in northern Canada. The triple prongs of the spear lodge securely in the flesh of the fish so that it cannot wriggle free and swim away.

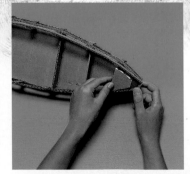

7 Glue the remaining K templates to the sides and ends of the structure as before. Pierce a hole for the mast in the middle of the base of the boat.

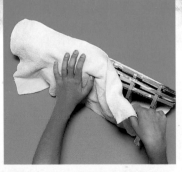

8 Glue in templates E to both ends of the structure, as shown above. Now paint the inside of the boat and let it dry.

9 Cover the sides of the boat with the chamois leather templates D. Stretch and glue the leather in position, as shown above. Leave the base hanging free.

10 Cut two small slits in the base of templates D. Overlap and curve the leather templates around the base of the structure, as shown above.

HARPOON READY

A harpoon rests in the prow of a boat off the coast of Alaska. The harpoon is attached to a float with a length of rope. This ensures that the weapon will not sink and can be retrieved if the hunter misses his target.

HARPOON MAKING

Harpoons were versatile weapons, used to hunt seals, whales and walruses. Each weapon was carefully crafted. Wood and ivory were fitted together to form the shaft, and the ivory point was tipped with metal such as copper. The head detached from the shaft on impact. It was securely fastened to a long hide line, and then the line was attached to a float made of wood or an inflated seal bladder. Today, hunters use a nylon line attached to a float made from an inner tube.

copper

harpoon head

HANDY PICK

This Inuit pick is made of a walrus tusk bound to a wooden handle with thin strips of animal hide. Picks such as this one would have been used to hack away at frozen soil or to smash through thick blocks of ice.

BIRD NET

An Arctic hunter checks his net, called a *lpu*, for damage. In summer, these nets were used to catch birds known as little auks.

Umiaks *were large open boats that were around 30 ft long. They carried up to ten people and were powered by oars or a sail.* Umiaks *were used for transport or for hunting. Women sometimes helped to row the boats.*

11 Glue the base of templates D into position, as shown above. Stretch the ends of the chamois leather tight to make a neat seam.

12 Glue the balsa mast templates M ¾ in. and 6¾ in. down from the top of template N, as shown above. Secure all the pieces with thread.

13 Paint the mast and let it dry. Then, carefully stitch the sail to the mast using large overhead stitches, as shown above.

14 Glue and tape the sail into position using the hole you made before. Glue templates L over section pieces A to make seats, and then paint them.

Going Hunting

A RCTIC PEOPLE were skilled hunters. For most of the year, their diet consisted only of meat. In Russia and Scandinavia, the Saami and other herding peoples ate reindeer meat. In North America and Greenland, the Inuit's main source of food was seals. (In fact, the Inuit word for seal means "giver of life.") Many land animals, such as Arctic hares, musk oxen and nesting birds, were also eaten. Out on the ice or in the water, hunters chased polar bears, fish, walruses and whales.

Only the men went hunting. During the summer, hunters in boats stalked seals and walruses in the water. When the sea froze over in winter, the same creatures were hunted on foot. Arctic hunters worked all year round to provide their families with enough food, even during the long, dark winter days when the sun never rose in the sky.

GOOD FISHING
An Inuk from eastern Greenland sits on his sled, fishing for halibut through a hole in the ice. He has already caught four fish. Arctic hunters used hooks, nets and spears to catch their prey. In summer, fish were usually taken from lakes or from their river spawning grounds.

STALKING SEALS
A drawing from the 1820s shows two Inuit waiting at seals' breathing holes. In summer, seals climb up onto the ice to sleep in the sunlight. Inuit hunters stalked these seals on foot. If the seal awoke, the hunter would lie on the ice, pretending to be another seal. The best hunters could crawl right up to a seal, grab it by the flipper and club it to death.

HUNTING BLIND
You will need: dark green felt (36 x 26 in.), scissors, ruler, string, 6 bamboo sticks (two 32 in. long and four 22 in. long), masking tape, white glue, glue brush, light green felt, pencil, leaves.

1 Fold the dark green felt in half along its length. Using your scissors, cut a small hole in the center of the felt on the fold, as shown above.

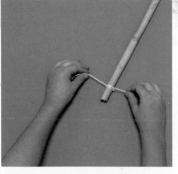

2 Tie a length of string to one end of two 22-in. lengths of bamboo. Use tape to hold the string in position, leaving a 4-in. length of string hanging.

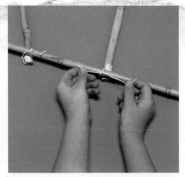

3 Tie the ends of these two 22-in. long bamboo poles to the area around the middle of one of the 32-in. lengths of bamboo, as shown above.

UNDERCOVER

Today, modern Inuit hunters use rifles for hunting prey. The Inuk pictured above is also using a screen called a hunting blind to stalk a seal. The hunting blind conceals the hunter from the watchful eyes of seals. Both the screen and rifle are mounted on a small sled, which allows the hunter to advance slowly toward his target.

IN FOR THE KILL

This engraving shows an Inuit hunter aiming his harpoon at a seal that has come to the surface of the water to breathe. Silent and motionless, hunters would wait at these breathing holes for hours if necessary. The tiniest noise or vibration at the surface would frighten the animal away. When the seal finally surfaced, the hunter would spear it and drag it from the hole. The hunter would then kill the seal by clubbing it over the head.

NETTING BIRDS

An Inuk nets a little auk on the rocky slopes of Pitufik in northwest Greenland. In spring, millions of birds migrate to the Arctic to lay eggs and rear their young. The Inuit and other groups caught these birds by using nets or by throwing weighted strings, known as *bolas*, at the birds.

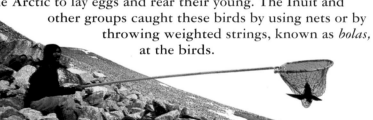

The Inuit and other Arctic peoples used hunting blinds to sneak up on prey, such as seals. Most hunting blinds were white so they blended in with the snow. A green blind would work better in a leafy landscape.

4 Glue the other 22-in. bamboo poles to the two shorter edges of the felt. Glue the last 32-in. pole to one of the longer edges. Tape the bamboo at the corners.

5 Glue the 32-in. bamboo pole from stage three to the fourth edge of the felt. Make sure to glue around the lengths of bamboo that are tied on.

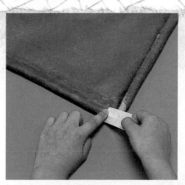

6 Draw some leaf shapes on the light green felt, and use your scissors to cut out the shapes. Always cut away from your body when using scissors.

7 Decorate the hunting blind by sticking the leaves to the front of the screen. You can glue some real leaves for a more dramatic effect.

Big Game Hunters

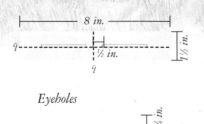

A S WELL AS SMALLER PREY, such as seals and fish, Arctic people also hunted large and dangerous creatures, such as musk oxen, whales and polar bears. Hunting these animals was risky business. A huge whale could easily capsize an *umiak*. Stranded in the icy water, the hunters would die of exposure in a matter of minutes. A cornered polar bear is a very dangerous creature. One swipe of its enormous paws is enough to kill any hunter. This fierce predator is also one of the few animals in the world that hunts humans.

Musk oxen were also able to defend themselves. These large, hairy mammals had long, sharp horns that could impale an unfortunate hunter, inflicting a fatal wound. Hunting dangerous beasts such as these required a team of men and careful planning. If the hunters were successful, one kill could provide enough meat to feed their families for many days.

FEROCIOUS HUNTER
A polar bear stands over a seal it has caught in Arctic Norway. The polar bear is a fearsome creature, with its mighty claws and razor-sharp teeth. This did not deter Inuit hunters, however. They would set their dogs on a bear to keep it at bay, and spear it when they got close enough.

FAIR SHARES
When a white whale was killed, the animal was divided between the hunters so that everyone had a share of the meat. Whales were split up in a particular way. The man who threw the first harpoon got the whale's head and part of the underside (shares 1, 2, 3 and 10). Other hunters and the boat owner got other shares.

SNOW GOGGLES
You will need: a piece of thin card stock, ruler, pencil, scissors, chamois leather (8¾ x 2½ in.), black pen, white glue, glue brush, compass, elastic string.

8 in.

½ in.

1½ in.

Eyeholes

2½ in.

¼ in.

1 Cut the piece of card stock to 8 x 1½ in. Find the center of the piece of card stock, and mark eyeholes ½ in. from the center. The holes should be 2½ x ¼ in.

2 Carefully cut out the eyeholes using the ends of your scissors to pierce the card stock. Always cut away from your body when using scissors.

3 Place the card stock onto the piece of chamois leather. Use the card stock as a template and draw around the goggles shape. Remember to draw in the eyeholes.

A USEFUL CREATURE

Whales were valuable Arctic animals. Every part of a whale's body was used. The flesh, fat and internal organs were divided between all the hunters. Some of the meat was given to the dogs. The whale's skin, called *muktuk,* was eaten as a delicacy. The blubber was burned in lamps to provide light and heat. Finally, the huge bones were used to build shelters or carved into weapons and tools.

muktuk

whale bone

MUSK OX CIRCLE

A circle of musk oxen surround their young to protect them against predators. Musk oxen are peaceful tundra animals unless threatened. Then, the adults lower their heads and ward off attackers with their curving horns. Arctic hunters were wary of musk oxen but still hunted them for food.

WHALE HUNT

Teams of Inuit hunters used *umiaks* to hunt large whales, such as bowheads. The oarsmen kept the boat steady so that skilled marksmen could launch their harpoons at the whale. A wounded whale would attempt to dive or swim away, but floats attached to the harpoons would pull the whale back to the surface. Gradually, the animal would become exhausted. Finally, hunters lanced the animal to death and hauled it to the shore.

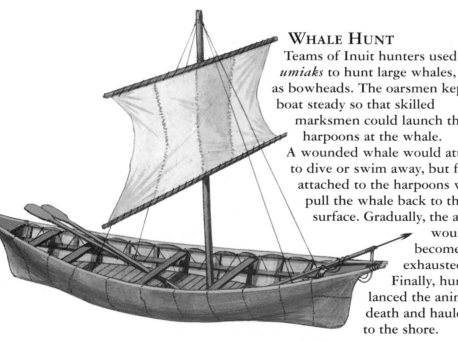

Arctic hunters used snow goggles when hunting both land and sea creatures. The narrow slits cut down the glare caused by sunlight reflecting on the snow and ice, so the hunter could see his prey more clearly.

4 Cut around the goggles shape, leaving a small trim around the edge. Cut down the center of the eyeholes you have drawn on the chamois leather.

5 Glue the card stock onto the chamois leather, making sure that you carefully match up the eyeholes on the leather and the card stock.

6 Fold back the leather trim and glue it to the back of the card stock. Open up the eyeholes, fold those edges back and glue them to the card stock.

7 Pierce a small hole at each end of the goggles and thread elastic string through the holes. Tie a knot at the end. Make sure the elastic string fits around your head.

Hunting Magic

Arctic societies had great respect for nature and the animals they hunted. They believed that all creatures, like people, had spirits. When they killed an animal, they performed rituals that helped to appease (calm) the creature's spirit. The Inuit, for example, beheaded a slain beast to help the animal's spirit leave its body. They made offerings of food and drink in the hope that the animal's spirit would be reborn to be hunted again. Other Arctic hunters put parts of creatures they had killed back into the sea. Hunters took only what they needed to survive. They wasted nothing.

Arctic groups had many taboos, which were rules linked with spiritual practices. Hunting, in particular, was surrounded by many taboos. If a hunter broke a taboo, his action would anger the spirits and he might never hunt successfully again. Shamans were respected members of the community who talked to spirits. They provided a link between ordinary Arctic people and these powerful spirits. Shamans conducted ceremonies to bring good luck to hunting parties.

Sacred Pillar
Inuksuk, pictured above, are stone columns built by Inuit groups in ancient times. Some are very old. They are linked with hunting taboos and some have a religious meaning. The pillars were built to resemble a person with his or her arms outstretched. (The Inuit word *inuksuk* means "like a person.") They marked routes and channeled migrating reindeer into places where hunters could ambush and kill them.

A Respected Beast
This ivory carving of a polar bear comes from Greenland. Many taboos surrounded the hunting of these highly respected creatures. The Inuit held polar bears in high esteem because they were thought to look and act in the same way as humans, particularly when they reared up on their hind legs.

Whale Box
This wooden box is carved in the shape of a whale. It held the lance points used to harpoon whales. The Inuit and other Arctic groups believed that prey animals, such as whales, were more likely to accept being killed by weapons carved in their image. The lance points would also experience being inside a "whale" and would therefore be more likely to hit their target.

MAGIC SCRATCHER

This "Nunivak tusk" was made as a souvenir in the 1920s. When hunting seals, the Inuit sometimes made screeching noises by scraping ivory scratchers such as this one over the ice. The noise attracted seals to within striking distance of their harpoons. Scratchers were often carved into the shape of the seal's head. Arctic hunters thought this would bring them good luck in future hunting trips.

SPRING CEREMONY

The Chukchi people offer sea spirits food at the edge of the water. The Chukchi took to the seashore early in the spring. They offered food to appease the spirits of the sea. This ritual helped to ensure that the year's hunting would be successful. Elsewhere, when a mighty whale was killed, the hunters held a festival to thank the sea spirits for their generosity.

SYMPATHETIC MAGIC

Drag handles were tools that helped hunters haul animals over the ice after they had been killed. The one shown here is decorated with the heads of three polar bears. Hunters' weapons were often carved to resemble the animals they hunted. This was sympathetic magic, which would help to appease the animal's spirit and bring the hunter good luck in future hunting expeditions.

Food and Feasts

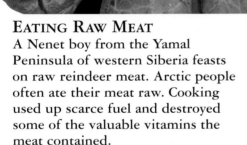

FOR MOST OF THE YEAR, Arctic people lived on a diet of fish and game known as "land food." The fat, flesh, organs and skin of seals, whales, reindeer and other animals contained all the proteins, minerals and vitamins needed for a healthy diet. Vegetables and grain crops, such as wheat, were difficult to grow in most parts of the Arctic region. Few plants could thrive in the frozen soil.

In winter, food was scarce and animals were the main source of food. In the summer, however, food was more varied. People feasted on berries, hunted seabirds and gathered eggs. Siberian and Saami women collected fungi that grew taller than Arctic plants, which were smaller. In autumn, when the reindeer were slaughtered, a great feast was held. Everyone kept very busy, gathering and storing food for the winter months ahead.

EATING RAW MEAT
A Nenet boy from the Yamal Peninsula of western Siberia feasts on raw reindeer meat. Arctic people often ate their meat raw. Cooking used up scarce fuel and destroyed some of the valuable vitamins the meat contained.

DRYING MEAT
An Inuit hunter from northwest Greenland lays strips of narwhal meat on the rocks to dry them. Drying meat in this way was an excellent way of preserving food in the summer. The intestines were washed clean and also dried in this way. Meat was also hidden under the rocks to prevent foxes, wolverines and other carnivorous animals from stealing it. If the meat was left for many months, it developed a strong smell and flavor, but it was unlikely to make anyone ill. In winter, the icy temperatures prevented meat from going bad, so preserving food was not a problem. The bodies of slain animals could be buried under rocks in the snow near the house and dug up when needed.

FILLETS OF FISH

Inuit hunters arrive back at the shore with a catch of fish known as char. Traditionally, women cleaned and filleted the fish, then hung them up on racks to dry and preserve them. They scored the fishes' flesh into squares to speed up the drying process.

BERRIES

Many types of berries grow wild on the Arctic tundra. They include bilberries, cranberries and cloudberries. Ripe berries contain valuable vitamins. Autumn was the time for picking berries, when they were eaten fresh, and could also be frozen.

bilberries   *cranberries*   *cloudberries*

BIRD'S EGGS

This picture shows three eggs in an eider duck's nest. In the spring, many nesting birds came to the Arctic to rear their young. Their eggs were a valuable source of food and protein for Arctic people and helped to vary the basic diet of meat.

TASTY MEAL

A Nenet woman cooks a meal for her family. In all Arctic societies it was the woman who did the cooking, making meat stews and other traditional dishes. Children often clustered around the fire to steal a taste from the pot.

SAAMI FARMERS

A Saami reindeer herder erects a tent by his summer pastures. In Scandinavia, the Saami are able to farm along the shores of narrow coastal inlets called fjords. On these jagged coasts the land is sheltered from icy winds, so cattle and sheep can graze. Some meadows are mown to make hay to feed the animals in winter.

ARCTIC ATTACKERS

This early illustration shows a group of Inuit in conflict with English explorers led by a sea captain named Martin Frobisher. Frobisher led one of the first expeditions to Baffin Island in northeast Canada, where his sailors met with strong opposition from the local people.

VIKING RAIDERS

This early drawing shows Viking warriors attacking an Inuit settlement in Greenland. Vikings were the first Europeans to reach the Arctic. In A.D. 983, a group of Vikings led by Erik the Red established two colonies on Greenland. These Viking settlements survived until about 1500.

The Coming of Europeans

BEFORE 1600, only a tiny handful of Europeans had ever visited the Arctic. After this time, however, travelers began to arrive in larger numbers. Explorers from Britain, France, Holland and Russia searched for a short cut to China and the Pacific Ocean through the seas north of Canada and Siberia. The sea route north of Canada was known as the Northwest Passage; the route north of Siberia was called the Northeast Passage. From the late 1500s, the British explored the northern coast of Canada. In the 1700s, the Russians mapped Siberia and traveled to Alaska, crossing a sea we now call the Bering Strait.

In the end, European explorers failed to find clear sea routes to the Pacific through the ice-laden waters of the Arctic Ocean. However, they did return with tales of waters teeming with whales and other sea creatures. Whaling ships and other hunters soon followed. Every spring, European ships would cross the northern Atlantic Ocean to slaughter whales. Arctic whale oil was used as a source of fuel for European lamps. These giant creatures were also killed for their valuable "whalebone," or baleen.

ROSS EXPEDITION

This picture shows British explorers John Ross and William Parry meeting with the Inuit of northwest Greenland in August 1818. A powerful female shaman had predicted the arrival of strange men in huge boats with "white wings"—actually sailing ships.

WHALE PRODUCTS

European countries found many uses for the whales they killed. Oil from whale blubber was burned to provide light and heat and also made into soap. Whale oil was used in many foods, including ice cream and margarine. Tough, springy baleen was made into many different products, including brushes, umbrellas, corsets and fishing rods.

soap

margarine

LEARNING FROM THE ARCTIC PEOPLES

In 1909, American explorer Robert Peary became the first man to reach the North Pole, helped by teams of Inuit. Peary wore snowshoes and Inuit-style clothing and used huskies to pull sleds in the same way as the Inuit. Many early European explorers died in the Arctic because they did not use the survival techniques developed by Arctic dwellers. Later expeditions drew on local peoples' experience and were more successful.

WHALEBONE CORSET

This picture is taken from a catalog dating back to the early 1900s. It shows a woman wearing a fashionable corset. Women wore these tight undergarments to look thinner and shapely. Corsets were strengthened with bony plates called baleen, which came from the mouths of whales. Baleen was also known as whalebone.

HUNTING THE WHALE

The illustration in the center of this picture shows an early European whale hunt. Small open hunting boats were launched from a larger ship. Around the main picture, some of the ways in which the whales were used are shown. Europeans saw the whale as an extremely valuable resource.

Trappers and Traders

THE WHALING INDUSTRY boomed during the 1700s. By 1800, however, the Europeans had slaughtered so many whales that these great creatures faced extinction, and some Arctic groups lost a valuable source of food. As the whaling industry declined, so the European settlers looked for new ways to profit from the region. Merchants soon realized that the soft, warm fur of Arctic mammals, such as sea otters and Arctic foxes, would fetch a high price in Europe. They began to trade with local hunters for these skins, setting up trading posts across the Arctic. In every region, the fur trade was controlled by the nation that had explored there first. Russia controlled all trade rights in Alaska. A British business called the Hudson Bay Trading Company controlled business in Canada.

Arctic people came to rely on the Europeans for metal tools and weapons. Soon, many Arctic people abandoned their traditional life of hunting. Instead, they trapped mammals for their skins and sold them to the merchants. Arctic people entered troubled times. Diseases previously unknown in the region, such as measles and tuberculosis, killed thousands of men, women and children.

SKINS FOR SALE
The skins of seals and Arctic foxes hang in a store in northwest Greenland. During the 1800s and early 1900s, otter, fox and mink fur became extremely popular in Europe. European merchants made huge profits from the trade but paid Arctic hunters low rates for trapping these valuable animals.

CONVENIENCE FOOD
In 1823 this can of veal was prepared for Sir William Parry's expedition to the Arctic. European explorers, whalers and traders introduced many foods to the native Arctic peoples. Local trappers exchanged furs for food and other goods. However, the result was that some Arctic people began to rely on the food provided by the traders rather than hunting for their own food.

TRADING POST
This engraving, made around 1900, shows an Inuk hunter loading his sled with European goods at a trading post in the far north of Canada. By the mid-1800s, fortified posts such as this had sprung up all over Arctic North America. The British Hudson Bay Trading Company, set up in the 1820s, became very wealthy exploiting Canada's natural resources.

ADDICTED TO ALCOHOL

Whiskey was traded throughout the Arctic in the 1800s and 1900s. As well as goods made from metal, merchants introduced European foods and stimulants, such as tea, coffee, sugar, alcohol and tobacco, to the Arctic. Many Arctic hunters became addicted to alcohol, such as whiskey.

SCRIMSHAW

During the long Arctic nights or lengthy voyages across the ocean, European explorers, sailors and traders occupied their time carving pictures and patterns on whale bones and walrus tusks. This work was called scrimshaw. First, he scratched a design in the bone or tusk using a knife or needle. Then the artist made the picture visible by rubbing soot into the scratches.

soot

scrimshaw

walrus tusk

POWERFUL WEAPON

This engraving shows a number of British rifles from the 1840s. During the 1800s and 1900s, European guns and rifles transformed traditional hunting methods in the Arctic. Rifles were much more accurate than the old Arctic weapons, bows and arrows, and could target prey from a much greater distance.

GOODS FOR TRADE

Local hunters trade with Europeans in a local store in this engraving. Hundreds of metal tools and weapons were traded by Europeans in the Arctic, most often for animal skins. European merchants also bartered rifles, saws, knives, drills, axes and needles. The Inuit and other Arctic groups soon came to depend on these valuable tools and weapons.

Cold-Weather Clothing

In the bitterly cold winds and snowstorms, Arctic people needed warm, waterproof clothing to survive. They used animal skins to insulate them from the harsh conditions. Two layers of skins were worn—a tough outer layer with the fur facing outward and soft, warm underclothes with the fur facing inward. The fur of the underclothes trapped a layer of warm air next to the person's skin, thus maintaining a constant body temperature. Only a tiny part of a person's body was left exposed to the freezing air.

Outer garments included hooded coats made from reindeer skin, trousers made from the hide of polar bears, and deer- or sealskin boots. When hunting in *kayaks,* Inuit men often wore waterproof *anoraks* (an Inuit word) made from thin strips of seal intestine sewn together. Underclothes included seabird-skin undershirts and socks made from the skins of reindeer calves.

FUR COAT
This girl is wearing a *yagushka*, the traditional jacket worn by Nenet women. The girl's mother has used dark strips of reindeer skin to decorate the jacket. Mittens and a fur-trimmed hood provide extra protection against the icy winds.

GRASS-LINED BOOTS
A Saami herder lines his reindeer-skin boots with dried grass. Hay provided soft padding and also trapped a layer of air inside the boots to protect the herder's feet against the bitter cold.

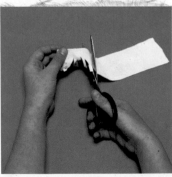

MAKE SOME MITTENS
You will need: 4 pieces of chamois leather, black marker, scissors, white glue, glue brush, ruler, light blue and red felt, black pen.

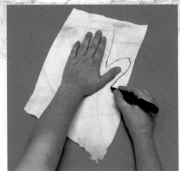

1 Draw around your hand on a piece of chamois leather, leaving a ½-in. gap around your hand shape. You will need two pieces of leather per hand.

2 Glue around the edge of the right-hand glove and glue a left-hand glove into position. Repeat this with the other two glove shapes. Let them dry.

3 Cut out two pieces of chamois leather, each approximately 8 x 2 in. Cut a ¾-in. fringe on the edge of each piece of chamois leather.

PREPARING SKINS

This Inuit woman is chewing a piece of sealskin to soften it. She uses her front teeth so the skin does not get too wet. In the past, the teeth of old women were worn right down by years of chewing skins. The skin of a bearded seal was used to make the soles of sealskin boots, because it was waterproof and gripped the ice well.

SEWING MATERIALS

Arctic women made all their family's clothes by hand. Bone or antler needles were shaved to a fine point, then rubbed smooth on stones so they did not snag or tear the animal skins. Whale or reindeer sinew was used as thread. When wet, the sinew swelled slightly to make the seams waterproof. Today, Arctic women sew with fine steel needles and use dental floss as thread. Cotton is now used to line boots instead of grass.

cotton wool   *dental floss*   *grasses*

DRESSED IN SKINS

Inuit hunters wore warm jackets, such as this parka, as well as leggings made from reindeer hide and *kamik*, or sealskin, boots. The warm hood of the jacket helped to preserve body heat. Hoods were often trimmed with wolf or wolverine hair, because these furs shed the ice that formed as the person breathed.

NEEDLE CASE

This needle case is made from reindeer bone and hide. It would have been worn on the belt of a Saami woman. The needles it held were made from slivers of bone, walrus tusk or antler. Needles were very important to Arctic people. Hand-sewn clothes and bedding took many hours to make and often needed repairs to keep the items warm and waterproof.

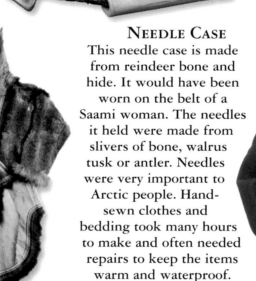

Rather than gloves, people of the Arctic wore fingerless mittens to keep their hands warm. Children's mittens were sometimes sewn into the sleeves of their parka to stop them from getting lost. Some mittens were embroidered with decorative patterns.

4 Glue along the edge of the fringe chamois and position it around the wrist area of one of the mittens. Make sure the fringe faces forward.

5 Use a black marker to draw six blue flower shapes (about 2 in. in diameter) and six red circles (about ¾ in. in diameter). Cut these shapes out.

6 Glue the red dots you have made to the center of each blue flower. Repeat this procedure for all six blue flowers and wait for the glue to dry.

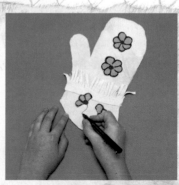

7 Decorate the back of the mittens with the flowers. Cut two flowers in half for the wrists and draw in the leaves and stems with a black pen.

Costumes and Ornaments

ARCTIC CLOTHES were often beautiful as well as practical. Strips or patches of different furs were used to form designs and geometric patterns on outer clothes. Fur trimmings, toggles and other decorative fastenings added the final touches to many clothes. Jewelry included pendants, bracelets, necklaces and brooches. These ornaments were traditionally made of natural materials, such as bone and walrus ivory.

In North America, Inuit women often decorated clothes with birds' beaks, tiny feathers and even porcupine quills. In Greenland, lace and glass beads were popular decorations. Saami clothes were the most colorful in the Arctic. Saami men, women and children wore blue outfits with a bright red and yellow trim. Men's costumes included a tall hat and a short flared tunic. Women's clothes included flared skirts with embroidered hems and colorful hats, shawls and scarves.

SAAMI COSTUME
A Saami man wears the traditional costume of his region, including a flared tunic trimmed with bright woven ribbon at the neck, shoulders, cuffs and hem. Outfits such as the one above were worn all year round. In winter, Saami people wore thick fur parkas, called *peskes,* over the bright tunics.

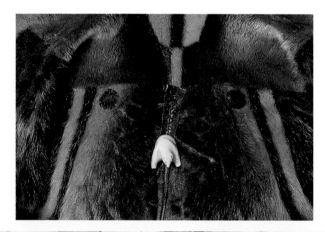

BEAR TOGGLE
An ivory toggle carved into the shape of a polar bear completes this traditional sealskin jacket. Arctic people took great pride in their appearance and loved to decorate their clothes in this way. In ancient times, the Inuit, for example, decorated their garments with hundreds of tiny feathers or the claws of mammals, such as foxes or hares. Women often decorated all the family's clothes.

MAKE A SAAMI HAT
You will need: red felt (23 x 12 in.), white glue, glue brush, black ribbon (23 x ¾ in.), colored ribbon, white felt, ruler, pencil, compass, red card stock, scissors, red, green and white ribbon (3 at 17½ x 1½ in.), red ribbon (23 x 1½ in.).

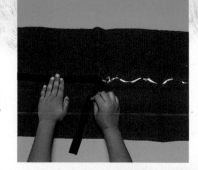

1 Mark the center of the red felt along its length. Carefully glue the length of black ribbon along the center line, as shown above.

2 Continue to decorate the felt with different kinds of colored ribbon and white felt, making a series of strips along the red felt, as shown above.

3 Cut out a circle of red card stock with a diameter of 7 in. Draw a circle inside with a diameter of 6 in. Cut into the larger circle to the 6-in. line.

CURVED BOOT

This picture shows a curved boot worn by the Saami people from Arctic Scandinavia. These boots are designed for use with skis and are decorated with traditional yarn pompoms. The curved boot tips stop the skier from slipping out of the skis when traveling uphill.

WEDDING FINERY

The bride, bridegroom and a guest at a Saami wedding in north Norway all wear traditional outfits. Notice that the style of the man's wedding hat differs from the one shown in the picture on the opposite page. Both men and women wear brooches encrusted with metal disks. Saami women's wedding outfits include tall hats, tasseled shawls and ribbons.

BEADS AND LACE

A woman from western Greenland wears the traditional beaded costume of her nation, which includes a top with a wide black collar and cuffs and high sealskin boots. After European settlers arrived in Greenland, glass beads and lace became traditional decorations on clothing. Hundreds of beads were sewn onto jackets to make intricate patterns.

The style of Saami hats varied from region to region. In southern Norway, men's hats were tall and rounded. Further north, their hats had four points.

4 Glue the ends of the decorated red felt together, as shown above. You will need to find the right size to fit around your head.

5 Fold down the tabs cut into the red card stock circle. Glue the tabs, then stick the card stock circle to the felt inside one end of the hat.

6 While the hat is drying, glue the colored ribbon strips together. Glue these strips 6 in. from the end of the 25-in. long red ribbon band.

7 Glue the 23-in. band of red ribbon onto the base of the hat, making sure the shorter strips of red, green and white ribbons go over the top of the band.

Arts and Crafts

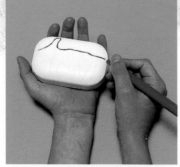

Arctic people were accomplished artists. Tools, weapons and ornaments were all made by hand. Across the Arctic, men and women were skilled at carving, sewing, leatherwork, basketmaking, beadwork and, in some areas, metalworking. In ancient times, objects were always made to be as useful as possible and were not seen as works of art. Today, however, tools and ornaments made by Arctic craftspeople are prized as works of art and fetch high prices when they are sold around the world.

Carving was one of the most important arts in the Arctic, but carving materials were always scarce. Artists engraved designs on bone and ivory, and they carved stone, bone, ivory and reindeer antlers into tools and sculptures. Carving tools included knives, needles and bow drills. Some carvings were polished using natural abrasives, such as sand, stone and rough animal skins.

FINE CARVING
This Inuit soapstone carving shows a hunter with his harpoon ready. Arctic carvings traditionally featured animals and birds of the region, scenes from everyday life and figures from myths and legends. They were made using knives, needles and bow drills.

MALE AND FEMALE ARTISTS
This early photograph, taken in 1900, shows an Inuit hunter using a bow drill to carve a piece of ivory. His wife makes a pair of *mukluks,* or deerskin boots. Today, Inuit sculptors use electrical power tools as well as knives and hand-drills for carving.

INUIT CARVING
You will need: a bar of soap (about 4 x 3 in.), dark colored felt-tip pen, a metal nail file.

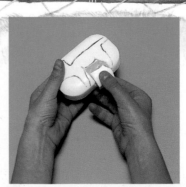

1 First, wash your hands so that the bar of soap does not get dirty. Draw the basic shape of a dog on the bar of soap using your felt-tip pen.

2 Begin the carving by cutting off the areas of soap around the shape you have drawn. Always make sure you cut away from your hand.

3 Carefully cut off the largest areas of the soap first, as shown above. Make sure the soap does not crumble as you break the pieces off.

SOAPSTONE POTS

Pots and other containers were sometimes made from soapstone (steatite) in the Arctic. This stone is soft enough to carve and hollow out. Knives and bow drills were used as carving tools. People often made long trips by dogsled to collect the stone from the places in which it was found.

soapstone

HAND-CRAFTED TOOLS

This cup and knife were crafted by Saami artists. The cover of the long knife is made from the antler of a reindeer and has been engraved with a decorative pattern. The handle is covered with leather. The drinking cup is carved from a piece of wood. You can just see the small piece of reindeer antler set into the handle of the cup.

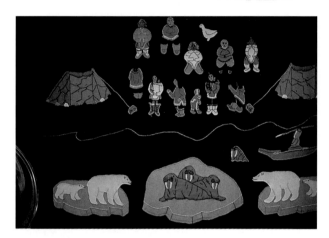

SKILLFUL STITCHERS

This picture shows a wall hanging from an Inuit church in Canada. Arctic women were skilled sewers. Many clothes and items such as blankets are now considered works of art.

PRINT-MAKING

An artist from Holman Island in the Canadian Arctic works on her print, dabbing paint through a stencil using a short, stubby brush. Print-making is a relatively new craft in the Arctic, but many of the subjects chosen are traditional.

In the Arctic, carving is a skill that dates back thousands of years. Weapons, tools and various ornaments were carved from natural materials, such as bone, ivory, stone or driftwood.

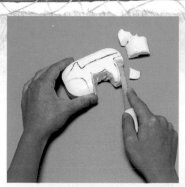

4 Carve out the smaller areas to make the shape more detailed. You should see the basic shape of the dog appear. Continue to carve the soap slowly.

5 Once you have cut out the basic shape of the dog, gradually and gently smooth the rough edges. The legs and tail will be particularly fragile.

6 Continue to shape the smaller areas to give the dog carving more detail around the ears, legs, tail, stomach, neck and snout.

7 Finally, carefully carve out the smaller features of the head, such as the mouth and the eyes. Flatten the feet so the dog can stand on its legs.

Beliefs and Rituals

Long before Christian missionaries arrived in the Arctic, local people had developed their own beliefs. Arctic people thought that all living creatures possessed a spirit, or *inua*. When an animal died, its spirit lived on and was reborn in another creature. Powerful spirits were thought to control the natural world, and these invisible forces influenced people's everyday lives. Some spirits were believed to be friendly toward humans. Others were malevolent or harmful. People showed their respect for the spirits by obeying taboos—rules that surrounded every aspect of life. If a taboo was broken the spirits would be angered. People called shamans could communicate with the spirit world. Shamans had many different roles in the community. They performed rituals to bring good luck in hunting, predicted the weather and the movements of the reindeer herds and helped to heal the sick. They worked as doctors, priests and prophets, all rolled into one.

SHAMAN AND DRUM
An engraving from the early 1800s shows a female shaman from Siberia. Most, but not all, shamans were male. Shamans often sang and beat on special drums, such as the one shown above, to enter a trance. Some drums had symbols drawn on them and helped the shamans to predict the future.

TUPILAK CARVING
This little ivory carving from Greenland shows a monster called a *tupilak. Tupilaks* were evil spirits. If someone wished an enemy harm, he might secretly make a little carving similar to this, which would bring a real *tupilak* to life. It would destroy the enemy unless the person possessed even more powerful magic to ward it off.

SHAMAN'S DRUM

You will need: ruler, scissors, thick card stock, white glue, glue brush, masking tape, compass, pencil, chamois leather, brown paint, paintbrush, water bowl, brown thread or string

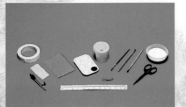

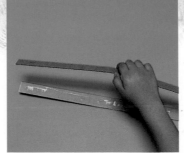

1 Cut out two strips of thick card stock, each strip measuring 31 in. long and 1 in. wide. Glue the two strips together to give the card stock extra thickness.

2 Once the glue has dried, use masking tape to cover the edges of the double-thick card stock. Try to make the edges as neat as possible.

3 Using a compass, draw a circle with a 9½-in. diameter on a piece of chamois leather. Cut it out, leaving a ¾-in. strip around the edge of the circle.

HERBAL MEDICINES

An Innu woman collects pitcher plants that she will use to make herbal medicines. In ancient times, shamans acted as community doctors. They made medicines from plants and gave them to sick people to heal them. They also entered trances to soothe angry spirits, which helped the sick to recover from their illness.

SEA SPIRIT

This beautiful Inuit sculpture shows a powerful spirit called Sedna. The Inuit believed that Sedna controlled storms and all sea creatures. If anyone offended Sedna, she withheld her blessing, and hunting was poor. Here Sedna is portrayed with a mermaid's tail and accompanied by a narwhal and two seals. This very delicate carving has been made from a piece of reindeer antler.

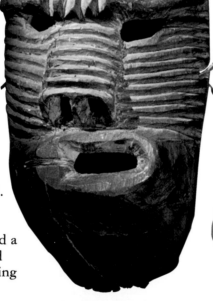

MAGIC MASK

This mask is from Arctic North America. It was worn by Inuit shamans during a special ritual to communicate with the spirit world. Shamans wore wooden masks similar to this one. They also wore headdresses. Each mask represented a powerful spirit. The shaman would call on the spirit by chanting, dancing and beating on a special drum.

Shamans' drums were made of deerskin stretched over a round wooden frame. The shaman sometimes drew pictures of people, animals and stars on the side of the drum.

4 Using your fingers, curve the strip of card stock, as shown above. Make sure you curve the card stock slowly so that it does not crease.

5 Glue the card stock onto the circle. Ask someone to help keep the chamois leather stretched as you go. Tape the ends of the card stock together.

6 Make cuts 1 in. apart along the edge of the excess chamois leather toward the card stock, as shown above. Glue the edges to the card stock ring.

7 Paint the card stock with dark brown paint and let it dry. Decorate the drum with thick brown thread or string by tying it around the edges.

The Long Polar Night

WINTER LASTS FOR MANY MONTHS IN THE ARCTIC. Communities living in the far north experience nearly three months of darkness in winter, because the sun never rises above the horizon. During the long, dark days and nights, ancient peoples gathered around the fire to keep warm. The men still went out hunting so their families could eat, but there were many days when bad weather kept them in the camp. During this time, the family came together and listened to stories, sang, laughed and swapped jokes. The older people told myths and legends that had been passed down for generations. These stories explained the existence of the heavens or told how people and animals came to live in the Arctic. Adults practiced crafts and taught their children new skills. Men carved tools and fixed their hunting equipment, while women repaired the family's clothes and bedding. Winter was also a time for making ornaments, such as bracelets and brooches. Children practiced with string puzzles and played traditional games such as *ajagaq*.

SAAMI SONG

This Saami man is singing a traditional song called a *joik* (pronounced yoik). These light-hearted songs were made up on the spot, and there were no instruments to accompany the singer. These songs told the story of the day's events but used nonsense words and puns. Often, they poked fun at friends and family.

SINGING AND DRUMMING

Four young men perform a traditional drum-song in the Northwest Territories of Canada. Music provided entertainment during long Arctic evenings. Families sang and beat on skin drums with sticks of bone or reindeer antler.

MAKE A BROOCH

You will need: ruler, compass, pencil, thin card stock, scissors, white glue, glue brush, large button, aluminum foil, small roll of tape, small nail polish bottle, masking tape, safety pin.

1 Using the ruler, set your compass to draw a circle with a diameter of 3 in. on the thin card stock. Mark the circle lightly in pencil.

2 Cut the 3-in. circle out with your pair of scissors. When using scissors, always make sure that you cut away from your body.

3 Carefully glue the large button to the center of the card stock circle. The compass point will have marked out the center of the circle for you.

MYTHS AND LEGENDS

In the story illustrated at right, a young Inuk named Taligvak uses magic to catch a seal at a time when other hunters in his village are finding it impossible to catch food. During the long Arctic winter, young children listened to stories like these told by their parents and grandparents. In this way, traditional legends passed down through the generations.

A TIME FOR CRAFTS

Beadwork is a traditional craft in Siberia. The Arctic winter was a good time to practice all kinds of crafts and to repair equipment. Men mended fishing nets and harpoons, while the women stitched new clothes and bedding and repaired garments that were torn.

The Saami of Lapland used beautiful brooches to fasten their jackets and shawls.

4 Cover the front of the card stock and the button with aluminum foil. Fold the edge over onto the back of the card stock circle and secure it with glue.

5 Draw around the inside of a small roll of tape on a piece of foil. Repeat this 24 times. Cut out the silver foil circles with your scissors.

6 Place each foil circle over the lid of the nail polish bottle, and carefully mold the edges over the lid to make 24 small disks.

7 Glue the disks onto the brooch, starting from the middle and working out. Tape a safety pin to the back of the brooch to make a fastening.

Development of the Arctic

DURING THE LATE 1800s, gold was discovered in the Yukon and at Klondike in the North American subarctic. A gold rush began, and thousands of prospectors flooded into the region to make their fortunes. Many new settlements were founded on the tundra. In the wake of the new settlers, Christian missionaries arrived. They built schools and churches and worked to convert the local people to Christianity. Traditional ways of life in the Arctic began to vanish forever.

By 1900, all of the Arctic was owned by countries such as the United States, Canada and Russia, whose capitals lay much farther to the south. Greenland became part of Denmark, and Lapland was divided between Norway, Sweden, Finland and Russia. The governments of these nations cared little about local peoples. They were mainly interested in exploiting the minerals and other riches of the Arctic. Police posts were set up, and southern laws and traditions were imposed. Around the time of World War II (1939–1945), southern governments became interested in the Arctic for military purposes. Army radar bases sprang up throughout the region. Gradually, some of these bases became new towns.

PANNING FOR GOLD

An early photograph shows a prospector panning for gold in a stream in the Klondike region of Alaska. Russia sold Alaska to the United States in 1867. In the late 1800s, gold was discovered there, and many new settlers rushed to the region to get rich quick.

GOLD MINING IN SIBERIA

This picture shows a modern gold mine near the town of Bilibino in the mountains of eastern Siberia. Gold was discovered in Siberia around the same time as the famous gold rush in North America. Soon diamonds, platinum, coal and other valuable minerals and metals were also mined in Arctic Russia. The exploitation of Siberia's natural resources had a devastating effect on the local people. The new mines scarred the countryside and took over lands where Siberian herders had lived for centuries.

COMMUNIST RUSSIA

This picture shows a Nenet work brigade during the spring migration of the reindeer. Following the Russian Revolution in 1917, the Soviet Union took power in Russia, and the communist system was imposed in Siberia. Nenet, Chukchi and other herders were divided into Soviet brigades and sent to work on state farms and in industry. Traditional reindeer pastures were taken over by oil companies and other state businesses.

MILITARY BASES

This photograph shows a Distance Early Warning (DEW) radar station in Alaska. After World War II ended in 1945, a time of hostility between the United States and Russia known as the Cold War began. The Americans set up a line of DEW radar stations across the Arctic to warn of an impending Soviet attack, and the Soviets set up similar bases in Siberia. New towns grew up around some stations as the threat of war receded.

MINING TOWN

An early photograph taken in 1898 shows hundreds of people flocking to a newly opened drug store in Dawson City in the Klondike. As more and more gold prospectors arrived in the Arctic, the early ramshackle communities of miners' huts grew into major towns, such as Dawson City, each with southern laws and traditions.

CHRISTIANITY IN THE ARCTIC

The dean of north Greenland stands outside Zion's Church in Illulissat. In the 1800s and early 1900s, Christian missionaries arrived in the Arctic in increasing numbers. They discouraged the work of the shamans and undermined local peoples' faith in the spirit world. Although Christianity helped to destroy traditional Arctic beliefs and customs, many Arctic people converted to Christianity, and it remains the most popular religion in the Arctic today.

Learning and Change

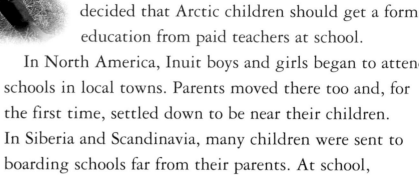

B Y THE MID-1900s, the lives of some Arctic people had been affected by mining and other activities in the region. However, the issue of children's education brought about the biggest changes of all. In the past, Arctic children had learned traditional skills from their parents at home or as they traveled from place to place. Now, governments in the south decided that Arctic children should get a formal education from paid teachers at school.

In North America, Inuit boys and girls began to attend schools in local towns. Parents moved there too and, for the first time, settled down to be near their children. In Siberia and Scandinavia, many children were sent to boarding schools far from their parents. At school, children learned new subjects and grew up with very different values than those of their parents. They turned away from the old life of hunting and herding, and many of the old Arctic skills and customs were lost.

SOUTHERN VALUES
Two Inuit boys play cowboys using "guns" made from the jawbones of reindeer. For most of the 20th century, Arctic children learned more about the history and culture of nations such as the United States and Russia than they did about their own culture. As a result, the traditional customs of Arctic people were undermined and, in many cases, lost.

KAYAK BUILDING
Inuit women teach the young wife of a hunter to sew sealskin onto a *kayak* frame, using a method that has been used for hundreds of years. Nowadays, many young Arctic people want to learn more about their ancestors. All over the Arctic, people are now being encouraged to take an interest in reviving the traditional skills of their predecessors.

SYLLABIC SYSTEM

This illustration shows the syllabic language system used by the Inuit in the Arctic. It was invented by Christian missionaries. Traditionally, Arctic languages were never written down. Each symbol represents a sound rather than a single letter. This makes it more difficult to use than alphabetic script.

LANGUAGE AND TEACHING

Inuit children work at a computer in a school in northern Canada. The words on the screen are written in syllabics. For most of the 20th century, children learned their lessons in languages such as English, Swedish and Russian. By the time they returned home, they had forgotten much of their own language and could hardly talk to their parents.

HUNTING TRIP

A young Inuit boy and his father skin a reindeer they have killed on a hunting expedition. For much of the 20th century, traditional skills, such as hunting, skinning and herding, were no longer considered important. Recently, however, they have been revived. The school system has been improved, and in many schools boys are now given time off to go on hunting trips.

TRADITIONAL SKILLS

Two Inuit boys learn to build a sled at school in northwest Greenland. For many years, the old skills of Arctic groups were not taught in schools. Recently, however, Arctic people have taken a new pride in their culture. Sled-building and sewing lessons are now part of the curriculum at many schools.

The Arctic Today

D URING THE SECOND HALF of the 20th century, mining continued to accelerate in the Arctic. In 1968, vast deposits of oil and gas were found at Prudhoe Bay in Alaska. Mining caused pollution and disturbed traditional ways of life. In the 1980s, there were several major disasters. The giant oil spill from the supertanker *Exxon Valdez* polluted a huge area of the Alaskan coastline, killing many plants and animals. In 1986, the Chernobyl nuclear power station in the Ukraine caught fire and released a cloud of radioactive gas. The radiation poisoned the feeding grounds of the reindeer in Lapland—a disaster for the Saami herders.

From the 1970s, Arctic groups began to organize their own response to development in the region. They laid claim to land where their ancestors had hunted and herded for centuries. In recent years, Arctic groups have won many major land claims. In 1990, the Inuit gained a large homeland in northern Canada, which they named Nunavut. It was handed over in 1999. Today, Arctic groups take new pride in their heritage, and lost skills are being revived.

OLD AND NEW
A Saami rides a modern snowmobile across a frozen lake in Finland. In the past, Saami herders used reindeer to pull sleds across the frozen Arctic landscape. For most Arctic people, however, life today is a mix of ancient and modern ways. The Inuit, Saami and many other Arctic groups use the new technologies of the developed world while holding onto the traditions and culture of their ancestors.

OIL MINING IN ALASKA
The Trans-Alaskan pipeline snakes for thousands of miles across the Arctic tundra, carrying oil mined at Prudhoe Bay in northern Alaska south to the ice-free port of Valdez. From there, the oil is shipped all over the world in giant supertankers. Unfortunately, the Trans-Alaskan pipeline cuts across traditional Inuit hunting grounds and caribou migration routes that have been used by the deer for thousands of years. The Trans-Alaskan pipeline is just one example of how development and industry in the Arctic has disturbed the traditional way of life in the region.

OIL SPILL

A cormorant whose feathers are clogged with oil from the *Exxon Valdez* disaster lies dead on the coast of Alaska. In 1989, the oil tanker *Exxon Valdez* struck a reef in Alaskan waters. Thousands of tons of oil were spilled into the sea. Alaskan coasts were polluted with the oil as it washed ashore, and thousands of sea otters, seabirds and other creatures died.

OUR LAND

In 1999, Inuit and other Arctic groups celebrated as the large homeland of Nunavut in northern Canada was handed over to them. The name *Nunavut* means "our land" in the Inuit language. The territory is the size of Norway. Nunavut is just one of a number of land claims that have been settled in recent years. Arctic groups have also won a share in profits from mining and industrial operations conducted on their lands.

PROTEST GROUPS

Bulldozers clear the site of a new dam in 1979 while protesters look on in horror. Between 1979 and 1981, the Saami organized a major protest against plans to build a dam on the River Alta in Norway. Unfortunately, the protest was unsuccessful—the campaigners lost the battle to prevent construction in the courts. Peaceful protest is an essential part of a democratic society. People can get their views heard through campaigns such as these. They may even be able to influence the outcome of controversial plans.

POWER OF THE PEOPLE

Young people who live in the Arctic have much to look forward to in the future. Computers and communications allow them to overcome the problems of distance and be in touch with people around the world. They can share their pride in their culture and their unique environment with visitors and also via the Internet. By the time this boy has grown up, he will be a citizen of the world, not just of the Arctic.

Glossary

A

Ajagaq An ancient spear game played by children in the Arctic.

Amaut Pouch used to carry Inuit babies and young children.

Anorak An Inuit word meaning "outer jacket."

Archaeologist A scientist who studies the past.

Arctic The region in the far north of our planet, surrounding the North Pole.

Arctic Circle An imaginary line circling the earth at a latitude of 66° 33' North that marks the limit of the Arctic. All areas inside the Arctic Circle experience at least one day a year when the sun never sets, and one day on which it never rises.

B

Baleen The horny plates that hang down inside the mouths of some whales and are used to filter small sea creatures, the whale's food, from the water.

Beluga A small, white-skinned Arctic whale.

Blizzard A strong wind that blows at the same time as a heavy snowfall.

Blubber A layer of fat found under the skin of seals, whales and walruses, which helps them keep warm in icy water.

Bow drill Ancient tool used to start a fire by creating heat.

C

Cache To hide food, or the hidden food itself.

Caribou A wild reindeer native to the Arctic.

Chukchi A reindeer-herding people of northeastern Siberia.

Cold War A time of hostility between the West and the Soviet Union. It followed World War II and lasted until the 1980s.

Continent Name for the large areas of land that cover Earth. The continents are Antarctica, North and South America, Asia, Africa, Australia and Europe.

D

Distance Early Warning (DEW) A line of radar stations that were built across the American Arctic.

Drag handle Tool that is used to haul animal carcasses across the ice and snow.

Evenk A once-nomadic people of eastern Siberia.

F

Floe A floating sheet of sea ice.

Fiord Narrow coastal inlet found in Scandinavia, where the land falls steeply to the sea.

H

Harpoon A spear-like weapon attached to a long line that is used to catch whales and seals.

I

Ice Age One of a number of times in Earth's history when large parts of the planet's surface became covered with ice.

Iceberg An enormous chunk of ice that floats in the sea.

Ice cap A mass of ice that permanently covers land in the polar regions. Greenland has the largest ice cap in the Arctic.

Igloo An Inuit word meaning house, often used to refer to Inuit shelters built of ice blocks.

Inua An Inuit word that means spirit.

Inuit An ancient people of the American Arctic. The name simply means "the people."

Inukshuk A stone column made by Inuit hunters, used to herd caribou into an ambush.

Ivory The hard, smooth, cream-colored part of the tusks of elephants and walruses.

J

Joik Traditional Saami improvised songs that tell the story of the day's events.

K

Kakivak A three-pronged Inuit spear used to catch fish.

Kamik Sealskin boots.

Kapp *see* Saami

Kayak A one-person Inuit canoe powered by a double-bladed paddle. The boat's wooden or bone frame is covered with sealskin.

L

Land bridge An area of dry land joining two land masses. In prehistoric times, a land bridge linked the continents of Asia and North America.

Latitude Imaginary lines that run parallel to the equator, going north and south. The equator, running around the center of Earth, is 0°. The North Pole is 90°N and the South Pole is 90°S. Latitude is used by geographers to calculate the positions of places.

Lichen A living organism that grows on rocks in the Arctic and is eaten by caribou.

M

Mammal A type of warm-blooded animal, such as human beings, whales, cats and bats.

Migration A seasonal journey made by people or animals to find food or avoid extreme cold.

Missionary Someone who is sent by a religious organization to a foreign country to do religious and social work.

Mukluk Deerskin boots.

Muktuk A gristly layer found just below a whale's skin, eaten as a delicacy in the Arctic.

N

Narwhal A species of small Arctic whale.

Nenet A reindeer-herding people of western Siberia.

Nomad A person who continually moves from place to place to find food and water.

North Pole The most northerly point on Earth.

Nunavut A large Inuit territory in northern Canada, established in 1999.

P

Pack ice Floating sea-ice.

Permafrost Permanently frozen ground. Permafrost can reach depths of over 1,900 feet in some areas.

Peske Thick fur parka worn by Saami people over their tunics.

Plankton Tiny plants and animals that drift around the surface of a sea or lake.

Prospector A person who searches for valuable minerals, such as gold.

Pulkka A boat-shaped sleigh used in Siberia and Scandinavia.

S

Saami The ancient people of Lapland in Scandinavia.

Shaman A kind of priest thought to be able to contact spirits and heal the sick.

Sinew The tissue that connects an animal's bones and muscles.

Slingshot Another name for a catapult.

Stallos People-eating monsters in Saami legends.

T

Taboo A rule or custom linked with religious beliefs that shows respect to the spirits.

Taiga A belt of forests found in the far north, south of the tundra.

Toboggan A wooden frame on runners used for sliding over snow and ice.

Tundra The barren, treeless lowlands of the far north.

U

Ulu A rounded knife used mostly by Inuit women to skin and cut meat.

Umiak An open boat, powered by oars and sometimes sails, used by the Inuit to hunt whales.

W

Whalebone *see* baleen

Wolverine A furry mammal that looks like a small bear, found in many of the northern forests of Europe, Asia and North America.

Y

Yagushka Traditional jacket worn by Nenet women.

Yakut A reindeer-herding people of northern Siberia.

Index

A

Adena 134, 136
adobe 91-3, 151
Ajagaq 215, 242
akllakuna 80, 84, 113, 130
Alaska 196, 197, 198, 206
alcohol, 26, 36, 233
Algonquin 144, 160, 162, 175
alpacas 74, 98, 102-3, 116, 130
Anasazi 134, 135, 164
Andes Mountains 74, 86
animals 136, 141, 142, 146, 156, 174
ankle bells 178-9
antlers 208, 215, 238, 239
Apache 135, 136, 138, 154, 168, 186
aqueducts 88, 130
Arapaho 140, 160
Arawak 136, 168
archaeology 89, 90, 105, 112, 124, 125, 130, 194, 195, 196
Arctic animals 194, 195, 206, 219, 232
Arctic history, 194-9
army 83, 86, 87, 104, 126
arts 195, 238-9
Asia 195, 196, 197, 198
astronomy 17, 18, 22, 56, 66-7, 120-1, 130
Aurora Borealis 201
ayllu 82, 92, 130
Aymara people 75, 117

B

baleen 230, 231
ball game 64-5, 66
barter 45
baskets 154, 164, 174

beads 146, 148-9, 165, 186, 189, 237, 243
bean stew 100-1
beer 94, 97, 100, 123
Bering Strait 134, 194, 230
berries 206, 228, 229
Big Foot 139
Bingham, Dr. Hiram 75, 83
bison see buffalo
Black Hawk 138
Black Hills 139
Blackfoot 141, 145, 152, 159, 160, 172, 173, 176
blankets 146, 164, 165, 173, 174
blood offerings 49, 60
blubber 209, 210, 225, 231
boats 46, 47, 87, 96-7, 129, 141, 142-3, 155, 194, 195, 218-21, 246
bolas 223
Bonampak 13, 40
bones 194, 195, 196, 213, 214, 215, 216, 219, 220, 238, 239
boots 209, 213, 234, 235, 237, 238
bow drills 208, 238, 239
bridges 87
buffalo 136, 139, 140, 150, 152, 156-9
buildings 13, 16, 20, 21, 28-9, 54, 83, 88-9, 90-1, 92-3, 94
burial 13, 16, 18, 28, 42, 51, 60, 124-5, 186-7

C

cactus plants 21, 26, 36, 38, 39, 40, 60
calendars 14, 56-7, 64, 67, 120
Calusa 135, 136, 154
Canadian Arctic 194, 195, 196, 197, 198, 206, 230
canals 30, 47
candles 207, 208, 209

Caracol 56
carving, 238, 238-9, 242
Catlin, George 138, 162
Cayuse 172
ceremonies 145, 158, 182, 184
Chan Chan 76, 90, 91, 108
Chancay people 105, 125
Chavin 74, 75
Chernobyl 199, 248
Cherokee 144, 160, 169, 178, 188
Cheyenne 139, 140, 176, 184, 186
Chichen-Itza 13, 14-15, 50, 58, 65
Chichimec 15
Chickasaw 144, 178
children 22-5, 40, 85, 148, 152-3, 166, 182-3, 208, 212-15, 246-7
chile peppers 22, 24, 36, 39, 53
Chimor 77, 80, 91
Chim 74, 76, 85, 90-4, 97, 99, 100, 103-4, 108-9, 112, 125
chinampas 15, 32-3, 47
Chinook 138
Chipewya 143
Chippewa 160
Choctaw 134, 166, 178
Christianity 113, 115, 128, 129, 196, 244, 245, 247
Chukchi 198, 202-3, 215, 245
Chumash 137
cities 50-1, 70-1, 114, 126, 127
Classic era 12, 14
climate 196, 200-11
clothes 18, 19, 24-5, 26, 40-1, 42, 48-9, 102-3, 104, 122, 143, 144-9, 152, 156-7, 164-5, 184, 194, 196, 208, 209, 210, 234-5, 236-7, 242
cochineal beetles 25, 34
cocoa 33, 35, 37, 45
codex books 12, 13, 54-5
Columbus, Christopher 17, 68, 136, 168
Comanche 172, 173, 177, 187

Copan 13, 15, 20, 26, 28, 32, 51, 54, 66
copper 108, 109, 124, 220, 221
Coricancha 88, 111, 113
corn 19, 23, 24, 27, 32, 36-7, 44, 58, 61, 98, 99, 100, 101, 108, 110, 111, 112, 114, 120
Cornplanter 138
Cortes, Hernan 17, 68
cradleboards 142, 153
crafts 42-3, 44, 74, 84, 91, 103, 104, 106-9, 238-9, 242, 243
Cree 142, 153, 160, 186
Creek 134, 178, 184
Crow 172, 173, 189
Custer, General 139, 179
Cuzco 76, 77, 79, 81, 82, 89, 90, 97, 102, 108, 111, 113-17, 120, 121, 123, 127, 129

D

dance 115, 116, 122
death 124-5, 186-7
Denmark 196, 199
deserts 86, 98
disease 232
dogs 37, 46-7, 69, 196, 216-17, 225
dolls 118, 124-5, 213
Dorset People 194, 195, 196
drag handles 227
driftwood 204, 205, 209, 239
drugs 104, 112, 118, 119
drums 115, 117, 167, 240-1, 242
dyes 25, 34, 35, 103, 146, 148-9, 184

E

earth lodges 150-1
education 22, 54-5
emperors 77-9, 80-1, 85, 95,
  98-9, 104, 113-15, 123,
  124, 128
empresses 78, 80, 105, 123
Eskimos 199
Europe 195, 197, 202
Europeans 135, 136-9, 159,
  168-171, 174-5, 178-9,
  194, 195, 196, 197, 230-1,
  232-3, 237
Evenk 198, 199
Exxon Valdez 9, 60

F

family life 22-5
fans 20-1, 27, 42
farming 12, 15, 19, 27, 32-3,
  36, 44, 56, 58, 59, 62, 74,
  75, 85, 98-9, 123, 134,
  136, 154-5
feasts 195, 212, 218-19
feathers 20-1, 27, 34, 35, 41,
  42, 45, 48, 49, 80-1, 104,
  105, 106
festivals 56, 62-3, 64,
  80, 85, 94, 101, 103,
  104, 111, 114-16, 116,
  124, 129, 195, 227

fields 98, 99, 123
fire 208-9
fire ceremony 67
fish 206, 222, 224, 229
fishing 34-5, 36, 75, 96-7,
  154-5
food 19, 22, 23, 24, 26, 27, 32-
  3, 44, 45, 61, 94, 99, 100-1,
  134, 154-7, 164, 194, 195,
  196, 228, 229
fortresses 88, 89, 126, 127
fuel 95, 107
funerals 124-5
furniture 208-9
furs 34, 35, 45, 48, 49, 195,
  196, 197, 232-3

G

games 64-5, 214-15, 242
gas 198, 248
glyphs 51, 54-5
gods and goddesses 58-61, 62,
  66-7, 80, 99, 101, 108, 110-
  13, 115, 119, 120
gold 14, 40-1, 43, 48, 74, 85,
  99, 102, 104-5, 108, 109,
  124, 125, 128
gold rush 197, 244-5
granaries 98-9
Greenland 194, 195, 196, 198,
  199, 200, 206, 222, 236,
  237, 244, 247
guanaco 96, 97, 130

H

haida 137, 150, 162, 186, 187
hairstyles 41, 48, 58, 146, 148
harpoons 194, 195, 221,
  224, 225
hats 236-7
heat 206, 207, 208, 209, 225
helmets 126-7
herding 74, 198, 199, 212, 244,
  245, 248
Hidatsa, 130, 184
Hohokam 134, 136, 186
hole and pin game 214-15
Hopewell 134, 135, 136
Hopi 135, 146, 153, 163, 165,
  168, 181, 188

horses 136, 137, 140, 142, 150,
  172-3, 176, 186
houses 28-9, 38, 90, 91, 92-5,
  123, 134, 135, 136, 194,
  195, 196, 204-5
huacas 112, 119, 130
Huastec 41
Hudson Bay Trading Company
  197, 232
Huitzilopochtli 30, 31, 58, 59

hunting 27, 34-5, 36, 96, 136,
  140-3, 146, 152, 154, 156-9,
  187, 198, 212, 214, 218,
  219, 222-7, 246, 247
Huron 187
huskies 211, 216-17

I

ice picks 221
icebergs 219
igloos 206-7
Inuit 134, 136, 140, 141, 142-
  3, 146, 149, 150, 154-5, 150,
  163, 164, 166, 180, 187,
  189, 196, 198, 204, 206,
  209, 210, 211, 212, 214,
  216, 218, 222, 223, 230,
  231, 234, 238-9, 241, 243,
  246, 247, 248, 249
Inuit Circumpolar Conference
  199
Iroquois 135, 137, 138, 144,
  145, 151, 155, 162-3, 173,
  174-5, 176, 178
irrigation 12, 88, 98, 114,
  123, 130
ivory 213, 214, 220, 238, 239

J

jade 12, 43, 45, 51
jaguars 106-7, 110, 112
jewelry 40-1, 42-3, 50,
  53, 85, 90, 102, 104-5,
  108, 148-9, 165, 189, 236,
  237, 242-3
Joseph, Chief 139

K

Kabah 13, 16
karakas 82, 84, 130
kachina dolls 152-3, 163, 181
kayaks 194, 195, 218, 246
Kinich Ahau 59
kivas 135, 152
Klondike 197, 244, 245
knives 108-9, 195, 207, 210,
  238, 239

L

lacrosse 166-7
lamps 208-9
languages 76, 160-1, 247
Lapowinsa 139
Lapps see Saami
laws 18, 20,1, 22, 33, 44
League of Five Nations 136,
  137, 144, 174, 178
Lenape 138
Lèon, Ponce de 136, 168
lip-plugs 40
Little Bighorn 139, 179
llamas 74, 80, 86, 87, 95, 98,
  103, 104, 108, 112, 120, 131
Long Walk 139

M

Machu Picchu
  75, 77, 89,
  90, 91-2,
  94, 18, 120-
  1, 123, 126
magic 195,
  226-7,
  240-1
Malintzin 17
mamakuna 80,
  94, 122, 131

Mandan 148, 150, 151, 158, 167, 182, 186
markets 44-5, 47
marriage 122-3, 145, 146, 152, 181
masks 12, 13, 15, 42-3, 51, 110-11, 115, 124, 125, 135, 162-3, 173, 184, 195, 241
mathematics 120
medicine 22, 34, 38-9, 118-19, 241
medicine men see shamans
men 210-11, 236-7, 242, 243
Menominee 181
merchants 44-5, 55
Mesa Verde 135
Mesoamerica 12-15
messengers 86, 97, 117
metalwork 14, 40-1, 43, 108-9
Midnight Sun 195, 201
mining 109, 128, 129, 198, 244, 245, 246, 248-9
mit'a 83, 84, 87, 88, 90, 123, 126, 131
mittens 234-5
Mixtec 14, 15, 40, 60
Moche 74, 76, 97, 104-6, 108, 110-12, 117, 118, 122, 124, 126
Moctezuma II 17, 20, 66, 67, 68
Mogollon 136
Mohawk 136
Monte Alban 15
mosaics 42-3
Mound Builders 134, 135, 136
mummies 74, 81, 124-5, 131
music 62-3, 115, 116-17, 122, 124, 167
musk oxen 195, 215, 222, 224
myths and legends 162-3, 241, 242-3

N
Navajo 139, 146, 149, 162, 180, 186, 188, 189
Nazca 74, 75, 96, 101, 106, 107, 111, 119, 124, 125
needles 194, 196, 235, 238
Nenet 198, 199, 202, 208, 209, 210, 213, 229, 234, 245
Nez Perce 139, 172, 183
nomads 140-1, 172-3
Nootka 141, 147, 164
North America 194, 195, 196, 198, 202, 216, 222, 236, 244, 246
North Pole 198, 200, 201
Northern Lights 201
numbers 54-5
Nunavut 199, 248, 249

O
obsidian 23, 43, 49, 60
Ocelotl 49
oil 198, 248-9
Ojibwa 141, 160, 180
Oklahoma 159
Ollantaytambo 83, 89
Olmec 12, 14, 64
Opechancanough 138
Osage 149
Oscelo 139
Ottawa 138
otters 199, 249

P
Pacal, Lord 13, 16, 51
Pachacamac 113
paint 146, 148-9, 184
Paiute 139, 164
palaces 20-1, 80, 81, 88, 89, 91
Palenque 13, 14, 15, 16, 51
Palouse 139, 172
paper 45, 54
Paracas 74, 75, 76
Parry, William 231
patolli 64-5
Pawnee 140, 148, 168

Peary, Robert 198, 231
pilgrims 50
pima 140, 182
pipes 145, 182
Pizarro, Francisco 78, 79, 128
Plains 140-3, 147, 150, 156-9, 169, 170-3, 176, 180
plants 201, 202, 228, 241
Pocahontas 138
polar bears 222, 224, 226, 227
pollution 198, 248, 249
Pontiac 138, 139
Popol Vuh 66-7
Postclassic era 14
potlatch 145
pottery 12, 18, 24, 35, 36, 42-3, 44-5, 54, 74, 75, 84, 85, 90, 93, 94, 96, 100, 106-7, 110, 134, 136, 164-5, 186
Powhatan 137, 138, 144
powwows 134, 188
Preclassic era 12, 14
priests 58, 60-1, 62, 84, 85, 98, 103, 112, 113, 114, 118, 120, 128
print-making 239
Prudhoe Bay 198, 248
Pueblo 134, 135, 137, 150-1, 154, 163, 165, 186
punishment 21, 22
purse, drawstring, making 210-11
Putun 13, 14, 50
pyramids 112, 113, 130

Q
Quechua language 76
Quechua people 87, 114, 117, 129
Quetzalcoatl 14, 66, 67
quills 147, 165
Quinault 162
quinua 98, 100, 131
quipu 82, 120-1, 131

R
radar bases 198, 244, 245
rafts 87, 96, 97
railways 139, 159, 171
Raleigh, Sir Walter 136

rattles 167, 180-1, 183
rawhide 159, 181
record-keeping 160-1, 163, 174-5, 187
Red Cloud 139
reeds 87, 92, 95-7, 106
reindeer 194, 195, 199, 202-3, 206, 213, 216, 226, 228, 245, 246, 248
religion 13, 14, 17, 18-21, 22, 26, 30-1, 32, 38, 50, 58-63, 85, 99, 103-6, 110-15, 118, 122, 124, 127, 129, 162-3, 180-3, 186-7
reservations 136, 178, 188-9
rifles 197, 223, 232, 233
Rivera, Diego 32, 38, 43, 69
roads 77, 86, 87, 90, 117, 123
Ross, John 231
Russian Arctic 194, 196, 198, 199, 215, 216, 222, 230, 245, 246

S
Saami 198, 199, 202-3, 204, 214, 216, 222, 229, 235, 236, 237, 242, 243, 248, 249
Sacawagea 138, 170
sacred pillars 226
sacrifice 14, 17, 30-1, 48, 49, 50, 52-3, 58-61, 62, 64, 67, 80, 112, 113, 131
Sacsahuaman 89, 102, 114, 127
Salish 174, 180
scalplocks 147
Scandinavian Arctic 194, 196, 198, 204, 214, 216, 222, 229, 246

scratchers 227

scribes 18, 52, 54-5

scrimshaw 233

seabirds 195, 199, 200, 206, 211, 221, 222, 223, 228, 229, 249

seals 194, 195, 196, 198, 205,

214, 218, 222, 224

Secotan 136, 154, 155

Seminole 139, 144, 178, 188

Seneca 136

sewing 203, 210, 218, 235, 238, 239, 247

shamans 149, 158, 163, 179, 180-1, 185, 196, 226, 240-1, 245

Shawnee 138, 139, 187

shells 134, 136, 174-5

shields 176-7, 179

Shoshone 137, 170, 180

Siberia 194, 195, 196, 197, 198, 200, 202, 204, 228, 230, 246

Sican civilization 108

sign language 160

silver 102, 104, 108, 109, 124, 128-9

sinew 214, 215, 216, 217, 220

Sioux 139, 144, 147, 148, 153, 158, 160-1, 162-3, 176, 179, 180, 182, 185

Sipan 74, 124

Sitting Bull 139

skins 194, 196, 197, 211, 214, 215, 216, 217, 218, 221, 234-5, 246

skis 216, 217

skull racks 61

slash and burn 32, 33

sleds 166, 196, 204, 214, 216-17, 247, 248

Small Tool People 194, 196

smoke signals 161

Snohomish 162

snow goggles 220, 224-5

snowmobiles 194, 199, 248

snowshoes 216, 217

soapstone 238, 239

Spanish 12, 17, 31, 42, 46, 49, 55, 68-9, 76, 78, 79, 83, 90, 96, 104, 105, 108, 113, 115, 117, 119, 126, 127, 128-9

spears 196, 220

spirit world 196, 226-7, 240-1, 245

steam baths 39

stelae 20, 51

stonework 78-9, 92, 93, 110, 111

stories 214, 241, 242, 243

string puzzles 215

summer 206, 219, 228

Sun stone 56-7

sweat lodges 182-3

T

taboos 226, 240

taiga 200, 202

tanning 159, 189

tattoos 148, 149

taxes 83, 122, 123

Tecumseh 138, 139

temples 74, 75, 88, 91, 104, 108, 109, 111, 112-13, 114

Tenochtitlan 15, 16, 17, 29, 30-1, 32, 43, 48, 52, 53, 59, 60, 61, 68

tents 194, 204-5, 209, 210

tepees 130-1, 150, 152, 156, 159

Teotihuacan 12, 13, 14, 15, 26

terraces 86, 98, 99, 127

Texcoco, Lake 15, 30-1, 32-3, 47

textiles 102-3, 131

Thule People 195, 196

Thunderbird 162, 179, 181

Tikal 13, 15, 26, 43, 50

Titicaca, Lake 75, 76, 87, 90, 92, 95, 97, 106, 109, 113

Tiwanaku 74-7, 90, 106, 110-12

Tlingit 164, 165

toboggans see sleds

Toltec 12, 14, 15, 48, 66

tomahawks 176

tools 194, 195, 196, 221, 223, 227, 232-3, 238, 240-1

toss and catch 215

totem poles 150, 160, 186-7

towns 86, 90-1, 126

toys 118, 212-13

trade 14, 16, 35, 43, 44-5, 47, 48, 50, 135, 138, 142-3, 156, 174-5

traditions and skills, preserving 195, 246-7, 248

Trail of Tears 178

Trans-Alaskan pipeline 248

travel 86-7

travois 140, 142-3

tribute 20, 19, 22, 24, 33, 35, 43, 44, 48, 52, 53

Triple Alliance 20, 52

Tula 14, 15, 48

tundra 200, 201, 202, 206, 225, 244

turquoise 15, 42, 43, 53

U

umiaks 195, 218-21, 225

Uru people 87, 92, 95

V

vicunas 103, 131

Vikings 135, 136, 168, 195, 196, 230

villages 74, 86, 90, 114, 204, 207

W

walruses 194, 196, 198, 218, 221, 233

wampum 136, 174-5

warfare 176-9

Wari 74, 76, 112

warriors 18, 19, 30, 38, 41, 43, 48-9, 52-3, 60, 64, 83, 114, 126-7

water 30, 51, 59, 84-5, 88, 90, 98, 107, 114

weapons 108, 126, 167, 176, 177, 195, 196, 220-1, 232-3

weaving 15, 24-5, 102, 103, 122, 123, 146, 165

weddings see marriage

whales 195, 196, 204, 205, 206, 218, 233

whaling 196, 197, 224-5, 230-1

Wichita 168

wigwams 141, 150

Winnemucca, Sarah 139

winter 216, 222, 228, 242-3

Winter Count 160-1

women 18-19, 20, 22-5, 36-7, 38, 40-1, 44, 45, 54, 145, 146, 152-3, 180, 210-11, 236-7, 242, 243

wood, 87, 92, 93, 106, 209, 210, 217, 218, 219

Wounded Knee 139

writing 12, 13, 16, 18, 19, 22, 51, 54-5, 57

Y

Yakut 198, 199

Yukon River 197, 244

Z

Zapotec 12

Zuni 135, 136, 163, 164, 181, 186, 189

Acknowledgments

ANNESS PUBLISHING would like to thank the following children for modeling for this book:

Josie Aiscough, Laurence Aiscough, Jamal Ali, Jake Lewis Courtney Andrews, Nathanael Arnott-Davies, Hazel Askew, Rhiannon Atkins, Anthony Bainbridge, Sabirah Bari, Harriet Bartholomew, Sarah Bone, Trung Chu Vinh, Rory Clarke, Patrick Clifford, Molly Cooper, Carissa Cork, Daniel Djanan, Ricky Garrett, Louan Harrison, Stephanie Harvey, Daniel Haston, Sasha Haworth, Kane Ives, John Jlitakryan, Eka Karumidze, Jodie King, Muhammed Laher, Alex Lindblom-Smith, Bianca Loucaides, Monilola Majekodunmi, Salem Miah, Lucy Nightingale, Ifi Obi, Graham Oppong, Daniel A. Otalvora, Joshua Adam Laidlaw Parkin, Mai-Anh Peterson, Sarah Louise Phillips, Adrianne S. Punzalan, Charlie Ray, Ben Rodden, Carl Simpson, Katie Louise Stevens, Samantha Street, Simon Paul Anthony Thexton, Shahema Uddowlla-Tafader, Isemfon Udoh, Reece Warman, Joseph Williams.

PICTURE CREDITS

b=bottom, t-top, c=centre, l=left, r=right
AKG: 79cl, 79r, 81tl, 82t, 85c, 111bl, 130b; 139r, 140l, 142l, 145br, 147tr, 149tc, 149bl, 250bl, 256bl, 257cl, 361cl, 165l, 169r, 170bl, 171tl, 171b, 172bl, 172br, 178tl, 179tr, 184tr, 185t; Bryan & Cherry Alexander: 194cl; 195c, cl & tl; 198c & tl; 199tl, cl & cr; 200bl & tl; 201tl, tr, cl & cr; 202 tl, bl & br; 203cr, bl & br; 204 tl & cl; 205tr & cl; 206bl; 207c; 208tl; 209tl & tr; 210c & tl; 211cl & cr; 212cl & cr; 213tr & cl; 214c; 215tl & tr; 217ct & cr; 218cr; 219cl; 220tl, cl & cr; 221tr; 222cl; 223cl; 225tl; 226tl; 228tl & bl; 229tl, cr, bl, & br; 231tl; 232tr; 233tl; 234tl; 235c & tl; 236c & tl; 237tl, cl & tr; 238tl; 239tr, cl & cr; 240cr; 241tl & tr; 242tl; 244bl; 245tl, tr & br; 246tl; 247tl, bl & br; 248tl & bl; 249 tr & br; The Ancient Art and Architecture Collection: 74l, 80l, 81cl, 91t, 121tr, 124tl; Andes Press Agency: 85t, 90t, 110tr, 115b, 123bl; The Art Archive: 230tl; GDR Barnett Images: 28tl; 29bl, 50bl; BBC Natural History Unit /Jose Schell: 211tr; The Bodleian Library: 21cl, 22b, 23br, 25c; The Bridgeman Art Library: 17tl, 53bl, 110cl, 208cr; 227t; 230b; 231cl; Camera Press: 242tl; Jean-Loup Charmet: 123t, 123br; Bruce Coleman: 35c; 19cl, 42br, 49br; Corbis: 134, 135br, 140tr, 145tr, 147tl, 150br, 150c, 153tl, 153c, 156tr, 159c, 169br, 170tl, 172tr, 182tl, 183tl, 183c, 183bl, 183br, 186bl, 187bl, 188tl, 189cr, 189c, 189bc, 189bl; Corbis Bettman: 141cl, 143tr, 144tr, 146tl, 148bl, 152c, 154b, 155bl, 157bl, 158bl, 160cl, 164br, 166bl, 168tl, 168b, 169bl, 170br, 173t, 173cl, 175t, 177tr, 178bl, 179bl, 182b, 188bl, 188br; Corbis Images: 207tl; 217cl; 219cr & tl; 226br; 227b; 233b; 234cr; 235cl; 241c; Sue Cunningham Photographic: 75tr, 86t, 88l, 89tl, 93tl, 93tr, 94t, 101bl, 116t, 120c, 124tr, 124cl, 126tr, 128cr; Dagli Orti: 67tl; James Davis: 10, 16br, 26tl, 47bl, 58c, 60tl, 67br; C M Dixon: 18tl, 22tl, 24r, 35bl, 135tl, 135tc, 135tr, 141tl, 141cl, 145bl, 147bl, 152l, 152tr, 153tl, 154tl, 159tr, 161tl, 162l, 163tl, 163bl, 163c, 163tr, 164l, 165tr, 173bl, 174tl, 176tr, 176c, 176bl, 179tl, 179c, 180tl, 181tr, 181cl, 181bl, 185c, 186tl, 186r, 187tr; E T Archive: 17br, 18br, 19bl, 19tr, 21tl, 23bl, 29tr, 30tl, 31br, 32tl, 32bl, 33br, 34tl, 35tl, 36c, 38, 39, 40b, 41, 43tl, 44bl, 47r, 49tl, 49tr, 49bl, 50tl, 55tl, 59l, 59tr, 60c, 61c, 62, 63, 64cr, 64tl, 66t, 68br, 73tl, 78r, 96t, 96cr, 97bl, 105c, 107tl, 107cl, 109c, 112cl, 126tl, 128tl; Mary Evans Picture Library: 30br, 47bl, 68tl, 79tl, 79c, 129b, 194tl; 213tl; 217tr; 218tl; 223tr; 231bl; 232b; 233tl; 238cr; Werner Forman Archive: 12tl, 23tr, 24tl, 36tl, 44tl, 63tl, 72t, 72br, 73br, 74cr, 80r, 84l, 84t, 87t, 97tl, 101tl, 102t, 103cl, 103tr, 104cl, 105tr, 106cr, 108l, 116c, 117c, 118t, 121bl, 122t, 122br, 127cl; Robert Harding / W. Herbert: 221cl; Michael Holford:

13c, 19br, 20br, 42tl, 51tr, 58tl, 59r, 69, 99b, 104t, 108cr, 125tr; The Hutchison Library: 45c, 90bl, 90r, 98t, 117t; Chris Kapolka: 114bl; Peter Newark's Pictures: 132, 138tl, 138tr, 139tl, 139tc, 141tl, 142tr, 144l, 145tl, 145tr, 147tc, 148tr, 149tr, 150tr, 151tl, 153bl, 153tr, 155c, 157cl, 158tr, 158br, 159tl, 159bl, 162tr, 164tr, 166tr, 167tl, 167bl, 171tr, 173br, 174tr, 174b, 175b, 176bl, 180br, 184br, 187bc; NHPA: 35c; Oxford Scientific Films / Doug Allen:221tl; / Richard & Julia Kemp: 214tr & 216tl; / Malcolm Penny: 249tl; Panos: 86r; Planet Earth Pictures: 33c, 92b, 219tr; 246tl; / Bryan & Cherry Alexander: 206tl; / John Eastcott: 211tl & 228tl; / F. Jack Jackson: 216cl, 222tl & 223tl; / Tom Walker: 224tl & 225tr; Popperfoto: 113tr; Ann Ronan: 233cl; N.J. Saunders: 83b; Scanpix Norge: 249cl; Science & Society: 232cr; Science Photo Library: 105tl, 109 cl, 119l, 119cl; Scott Polar Research Institute: 240tl; 243cl; 244tl; 245cl; South American Photo Library: 12br, 13tl, 16tl, 17tl, 20tl, 21tr, 25tl, 26tr, 27tr, 28b, 30tl, 31bl, 32br, 34bl, 37tr, 38bl, 41br, 43bl, 45, 51br, 52tl, 54c, 56c, 61b, 65tl, 65c, 66b, 69; South American Pictures: 72, 75cr, 78l, 81tr, 83t, 83c, 85bl, 86bl, 87bl, 87r, 88r, 89r, 91br, 92t, 94l, 94b, 95t, 96c, 98bl, 98br, 99t, 100l, 100r, 102l, 106l, 111tl, 111tr, 112tr, 113tl, 113bl, 114t, 114br, 115t, 115c, 118bl, 118br, 119tr, 120t, 122bl, 125cl, 126c, 127t, 129cl, 129tr; Still Pictures: 75tl, 82b, 109tr, 110cr, 121tl; Tony Stone Images / James Balog 207tr; / P H Cornutt: 209cl; / Natalie Fobes: 203tl; / Derke-O'Hara: 215cl; / George Lepp: 211br. Visual Arts Library: 18br, 27t, 27b, 35tl, 36tc, 36tl, 40tl, 41tl, 46cr, 48c, 48tl, 51bl, 53t, 54tl, 55tr, 63tl, 64tr, 64cl, 67tr, 68bl; Wilderness Photo Library: 74tr; Zefa: 51tr.

This edition is published by Southwater

Southwater is an imprint of
Anness Publishing Limited
Hermes House, 88-89 Blackfriars Road
London, SE1 8HA
tel. 020 7401 2077
fax 020 7633 9499

Distributed in the UK by
The Manning Partnership
251-253 London Road East
Batheaston, Bath BA1 7RL
tel. 01225 852 727
fax 01225 852 852

Distributed in the USA by
Anness Publishing Inc.
27 West 20th Street
Suite 504, New York
NY 10011
tel. 212 807 6739
fax 212 807 6813

Distributed in Australia by
Sandstone Publishing
Unit 1, 360 Norton Street
Leichhardt
New South Wales 2040
tel. 02 9560 7888
fax 02 9560 7488

Publisher: Joanna Lorenz
Managing Editor, Children's Books: Gilly Cameron Cooper
Editor: Joy Wotton
Birth of Ancient American Cultures: Dr David Jones
Senior Editor: Nicole Pearson
Project Editors: Joy Wotton, Joanna Hanks
Editors: Nicola Baxter, Leon Gray, Jayne Miller
Designer: Joyce Mason, Caroline Reeves, Margaret Sadler
Illustration: Rob Ashby, Julian Baker, Vanessa Card, Stuart Carter, Stephen Gyapay, Shane Marsh, Clive Spong, Shane Watson
Special Photography: John Freeman
Stylists: Konika Shakar, Melanie Williams
Production Controller: Steve Lang

Previously published as four separate volumes, *Step Into the Aztec and Maya Worlds*, *Step Into the Inca World*, *Step Into the World of North American Indians* and *Step Into the Arctic World*.